"'What is it I really need?' is a ke
sacrifice in *Serving Well,* a must read ~~ ~~ ~~ ... .... .... .... ... .... ....~~
who love them. This is a book you really need if you are 'called to go, or
called to let go.'

In *Serving Well* we read both the spiritual and practical, simple and profound, funny and compelling in chapters written by Elizabeth and then
Jonathan Trotter; hearing from each their voices and their hearts, the
struggles and the victories, 'the bad days and the good days' of preparing
to go and serving well overseas.

Their down-to-earth yet godly insights were born from living overseas
and from authentically wrestling with the 'yays and yucks' of missionary
life. They draw wisdom from both Scripture and sci-fi authors, Psalms
and funny YouTube videos, encounters with Jesus and encounters with
cops looking for a bribe.

Take two books with you to the mission field: the Bible, and *Serving Well.*"

—**MARK R. AVERS**
Barnabas International

"*Serving Well* is deep and rich, covering all aspects of an international
life of service from multiple angles. It is full of comfort, challenge, and
good advice for anyone who serves abroad, or has ever thought about it,
no matter where they find themselves in their journeys. It is also really
helpful reading for anyone who has loved ones, friends or family, serving
abroad—or returning, to visit or repatriate. Jonathan and Elizabeth Trotter are both insightful and empathetic writers, full of humility and quick
to extend grace—both to themselves and to others. Their writing covers
sorrow and joy, hope and crisis, weariness and determination. Best of all,
from my perspective as someone who has worked with TCKs for over 13
years, it contains an excellent collection of important advice on the topic
of raising missionary kids. Choose particular topics, or slowly meander
through the entire volume piece by piece, but whatever you do—read this
book!"

—**TANYA CROSSMAN**
cross cultural consultant and author of *Misunderstood: The Impact of Growing Up*
*Overseas in the 21st Century*

"Overseas workers face a barrage of junk when they arrive on their field location: identity issues, fear/anxiety issues, and faith issues. I have worked with missionaries for well over a decade now and see how these common themes cry out for a grace-filled approach to truth and authenticity. The Trotters live this out loud, intentionally seeking a way to minister out of their own pain, striving, humor, and failure. Keep this reference close at hand!"

—JEANNIE HARTSFIELD
Clinical Counselor, Global Member Care Coordinator, World Team

"This book is the definitive guide to thriving in cross-cultural ministry. The Trotters have distilled years of experience into pithy chapters filled with helpful tips and wise insights. Put it on your must-read list."

—CRAIG GREENFIELD
Founder, Alongsiders International, author of *Subversive Jesus*

"*Serving Well* is more than a book to sit down and read once. It is a tool box to return to over and over, a companion for dark and confusing days, and a guide for effective and long-lasting service. Elizabeth and Jonathan are the real deal and *Serving Well*, like the Trotters, is wise, compassionate, vulnerable, and honest. This needs to be on the shelves of everyone involved in international, faith-based ministry."

—RACHEL PIEH JONES
author of *Finding Home: Third Culture Kids in the World*, and *Stronger Than Death: How Annalena Tonelli Defied Terror and Tuberculosis in the Horn of Africa*

"In this must-read missions book, Jonathan and Elizabeth unearth the underlying motivations of the cross-cultural call. Penned with copious compassion and startling transparency, *Serving Well* is sure to make you laugh, cry, and, in the end, rejoice as you partner with God in his global missions mandate."

—DAVID JOANNES
author of *The Mind of a Missionary*

# Serving Well

# Serving Well

*Help for the Wannabe, Newbie, or Weary*
*Cross-cultural Christian Worker*

JONATHAN AND ELIZABETH
TROTTER

Foreword by Marilyn R. Gardner

RESOURCE *Publications* · Eugene, Oregon

SERVING WELL
Help for the Wannabe, Newbie, or Weary Cross-cultural Christian Worker

Resource Publications
An Imprint of Wipf and Stock Publishers
199 W. 8th Ave., Suite 3
Eugene, OR 97401

www.wipfandstock.com

PAPERBACK ISBN: 978-1-5326-5854-9
HARDCOVER ISBN: 978-1-5326-5855-6
EBOOK ISBN: 978-1-5326-5856-3

Manufactured in the U.S.A.                                    02/21/19

# Contents

## Recalculating Well (When Things Don't Go as Planned)

## Communicating Well

## Returning Well

# Permissions

# Foreword

WHEN IT COMES TO missions, missionaries, and the missions conversations, we live in a cynical and skeptical age. Those who are serving or want to serve overseas are assaulted with everything from failed missionary blogs and podcasts to heated debates on colonialism and white saviors.

Despite the cynicism, God is still moving people to places around the world where they are putting down roots in unfamiliar soil and seeking to write their names in the lands where God has directed them. They seek to live out God's story in a cross-cultural context.

Where do those who are intent on pressing forward in a life of cross-cultural service turn? How can they live well in places where they don't belong?

Jonathan and Elizabeth's book, *Serving Well*, emerges as a bright light and resource for those who are intent on pressing forward. Transcending place, this book is a wellspring of wisdom, perspective, truth, and encouragement for cross-cultural workers. Beginning with preparation, the book covers everything from preparation to returning, with sections on grieving, marriage, children, communicating, and more. It can be read consecutively or, depending on the reader's needs, by section.

I am a missionary kid, a failed missionary, and someone who continues to serve cross-culturally. I met Jonathan and Elizabeth as all those identities merged, and I read their words and heard their hearts with incredible gratitude. Here was the real deal. My cynical heart found solace and foundational wisdom and understanding through their writing. This couple is living out God's big story, and they are living it out in a cross-cultural setting. Their writing reflects their lives—the good, the hard, the awful, and the fun. We are not only invited into their words, we are invited into their lives. In Elizabeth, readers will find a friend and wise confidante; in Jonathan, they will find a counselor and brother; and in both they will find a couple who exemplify cultural humility, godly leadership, and deep joy in the journey of serving.

In the New Testament, the apostle Paul writes to people in Thessaloniki, Greece, and says this: "Because we loved you so much, we were delighted to share with you not only the gospel of God but our lives as well" (1 Thess 2:8). In the library of missions literature you can find many things, but to be invited into a life through a book is something rare and precious. *Serving Well* is not just a book; it is a shared life.

Marilyn R. Gardner
Author of *Between Worlds* and *Worlds Apart*

# Introduction

WE WERE SUPPOSED TO be church-planting missionaries. We were supposed to save the world, or at least our little corner of it. We were *not* supposed to be writers.

In January 2012, we showed up in Phnom Penh, Cambodia with our two selves, our four children, and a call. We started riding in tuk-tuks, driving motorcycles, and speaking Khmer. And we fell in love.

We tried to be faithful with the next thing, seldom seeing around the next bend. But we knew, come what may, God would be there—ahead of us and behind us—and so we kept driving. Trying to do the next thing faithfully, and with love.

He was faithful, and he was loving.

He *is* faithful, and he *is* loving.

And now, our deepest hope is that these words, these ink blots from Asia, will encourage you no matter what part of the road you're on. Maybe you're moving next month. Godspeed! Maybe you've been working cross-culturally for decades. Strong work! Maybe you're disenfranchised and you're preparing to return to a country you once called home. Grace to you.

Or maybe you just picked this up because somewhere in the distant future there is a sliver of a possibility that you might perhaps move abroad and/or minister across cultures. Awesome. And hello!

For all of you, our hearts are with you. And our prayers too.

It's not always an easy road, but it can be a good one.

~~~~~~~~~~

We've had the privilege and joy of living and ministering overseas because people have sent us. They've prayed for us, they've prayed with us, and they've financially supported us. To those people, we say THANK

YOU! Whatever victories this book represents, be assured that they are yours too.

And of course, we're so grateful for the leaders and readers at A Life Overseas, Velvet Ashes, and trotters41.com.

It was with you that we discovered our voices.

All for ONE,
Jonathan & Elizabeth Trotter
Phnom Penh, Cambodia

# PREPARING WELL

# Why Are We Here? An Important Question We Must Ask and Keep Asking

*BY JONATHAN*

WHY ARE WE HERE? Why have we chosen lives that cause us to engage suffering in very raw ways? Visible ways? Why do we expose our hearts to people in pain? Why are you preparing for cross-cultural work? Why do we use our passports for more than an occasional vacation? Why do we live in places where we sweat more than we thought possible? Places where we get diseases we can't even spell?

We say goodbyes. Our kids say goodbyes. And sometimes we say goodbye to our kids. Why?

- To give someone clean water?
- Access to healthcare?
- A chance at democracy?
- Education?
- Sustainable agriculture?
- Counseling?
- Economic viability?
- The Bible?

Yes, of course.

But there's more, isn't there? Those things, by themselves are good and right and worth doing, out of common decency and love for humanity. But on top of all that, and indeed overarching all those good things, is Jesus. He takes those good things and infuses them with something else entirely. Something holy, eternal, and altogether lovely.

The gospel compels us to love as we've been loved, and that's something worth remembering. If our work gets separated from the Word, we're in trouble. We must let our "roots grow down into him, and let [our] lives be built on him." Then we'll overflow with thankfulness, strong in truth (Col 2:7).

We must remain in him, refusing to forget the story of his immense love and our surprising salvation (John 15:5–8; Rom 5:8).

~~~~~~~~~~~

*Through our actions, our preachings, our service, we announce the news that God is not absent. We show and tell the redemption of all things.*

~~~~~~~~~~~

Why are we here? Because the story is bigger than suffering and pain and death. Because there is a glorious, mysterious hope that's code-named Jesus. Why are we here? Because we are in awe of the love of God. The magnificent, sky-shattering love of God that tears time and dimensions to deliver a Son. Because there's a Savior who was willing to bleed his heart out for the "bad guys."

Like me.

And you.

The gospel is a time capsule from the future, announcing what will be; not what might be, or could be, but what will be, and in part is already.

It's a saving which is available to all because of One. It's redemption. It's a Father who loves unendingly and perfectly, fully and wholeheartedly. It's justice that won't blow up in our faces (although that's what we deserve) because it's been disarmed, defused, and fully satisfied by a Lamb. The gospel is peace with God.

We echo a messenger from another time and place who said, "He is not here; he has risen, just as he said" (Matt 28:6 NIV). We say he lived, and he lives still: "But God released him from the horrors of death and raised him back to life, for death could not keep him in its grip" (Acts 2:24).

The gospel travels to "the land where death casts its shadow" and does what light does, revealing reality, removing fear: "[T]he people who sat in darkness have seen a great light. And for those who lived in the land where death casts its shadow, a light has shined. (Matt 4:16)

May we never forget the gospel.

Through our medicine and our activism, our education and our micro-finance, our preaching and our translation, our counseling and our parenting, may we preach his death and resurrection until he comes again.

May we preach the gospel of a poor man who purchased the world: "Who gave himself for us to redeem us from all wickedness and to purify for himself a people that are his very own, eager to do what is good" (Titus 2:14 NIV).

May we preach the gospel of a day-laborer who's coming back for his bride. May we preach Jesus, the One who steals death's sting: "And the last enemy to be destroyed is death" (1 Cor 15:26).

May we remember the truths penned by John Donne:

> *Death, be not proud, though some have called thee*
> *Mighty and dreadful, for thou art not so;*
> *For those whom thou think'st thou dost overthrow*
> *die not, poor Death, nor yet canst thou kill me.*
> *From rest and sleep, which but thy pictures be,*
> *Much pleasure; then from thee much more must flow,*
> *And soonest our best men with thee do go,*
> *Rest of their bones, and soul's delivery.*
> *Thou art slave to fate, chance, kings, and desperate men,*
> *And dost with poison, war, and sickness dwell,*
> *And poppy or charms can make us sleep as well*
> *And better than thy stroke; why swell'st thou then?*
> *One short sleep past, we wake eternally*
> *And death shall be no more; Death, thou shalt die.*[1]

Death does not win; Jesus does, and "everyone who belongs to Christ will be given new life" (1 Cor 15:22).

So why are we here?

Because Jesus is here, proclaiming "that captives will be released, that the blind will see, that the oppressed will be set free, and that the time of the LORD's favor has come" (Luke 4:18–19).

And that, my friends, is good news indeed.

---

1. Donne, "Death, Be Not Proud," lines 1–14.

# How to Transition to the Foreign Field and Not Croak

*BY ELIZABETH*

I BELIEVE IF A missionary family is happy and healthy, they will be more sustainable in the long-term. I also believe that the key to happy and healthy missionaries is preparation. One of the things I learned my first two years is that there is a lot of heartache among cross-cultural workers. After a while, I noticed that often, people's heartache shared common characteristics, and *could have been addressed before arriving on the field.*

These are practical steps you can take before you leave your home country. They will make your on-field life more smooth, more stable, and more productive. I'm incredibly grateful to our sending church and sending agency, who helped us take these steps prior to arriving in Cambodia. We simply followed their instructions. At the time, we didn't realize the immense wisdom of their requirements, or how much our years of preparation would help us in settling well in Cambodia. We could not have transitioned well without their guidance.

*You should be aware that none of this preparation will prevent difficult things from happening to you on the field.* Dealing with the following issues simply eases the strain of regular life, as the pain they cause is largely preventable. In no particular order, those issues are:

1) Being underfunded

2) One spouse doesn't feel called into missions

3) Marriage/personal problems

4) Pornography/sexual sin

5) Team stress

6) Not getting enough pre-field training

## Not Having Enough Financial Support

Financial troubles are stressful in America, but they become even more stressful in a cross-cultural setting. When all of life is consumed in getting the best price at the market or saving just a little more money, you have no time margin. Your mind never rests.

Please don't try to move overseas without sufficient funding, assuming you will be able to pinch pennies once you get there. Missionaries are known to lose financial support over the years—which means it's difficult to prevent underfunding completely. However, it also means that starting underfunded will only lead to more underfunding. It is for this reason that our agency won't even clear workers to move overseas until they've raised 100% of their proposed budget.

We modeled our budget off the budget of a missionary who was already in this field, but we also added some financial margin (about 10%). Although our overall projected budget was accurate, we had to seriously shift items once we got here. Some bills were much lower than expected, while others were much higher. And we are so thankful we planned for some financial margin so that when we got ripped off in the beginning (which will inevitably happen before you know the language well and intuitively know what a fair price is), we weren't worried.

## One Spouse Doesn't Feel Called Into Missions (a "Trailing Spouse")

I can really relate to this one because I *was* a trailing spouse for a while. Being a missionary has been my husband's dream since he was ten years old. I think I knew this on a subconscious level when we got married, but I was so blissfully in love that any missionary living seemed very far away. When he "suddenly" wanted to apply with a sending agency several years ago, I was shocked. Most of my concerns were about safety and health, as I'm a recovering germophobe/hypochondriac.

We pursued the application process in spite of my reservations. At times I was less supportive, and at times I was more supportive. I thought

I could survive missionary life by imitating the way Sarah followed God's leading through her husband Abraham. In the end, though, when it came to setting a departure date, I just couldn't leave home. I needed to hear directly from God myself.

I was able to hear my own "call" only after we set aside special time to hear from God individually. During this time we didn't talk about the subject as a couple, but I did listen to a veteran missionary's story about fear and faith on the mission field. Then my husband and I went to our elders for advice. It was after this time of individual thinking and praying that I was able to drop the "trailing spouse" label.

I have my own call now, so I don't have doubts about why I'm here, nor do I want to move back to America. I've made Cambodia my home, and I've made peace with missionary life. But I've seen other women who are still trailing spouses. Their husbands' desires to be here and do mission work are stronger than theirs, and they are unhappy. They constantly want to go home. Please, trailing spouses, take time to verify your call to missions *before* leaving home. Taking the time to do that now will be worth it later on.

## Not Having Marital Intimacy

My husband has always been my best friend, and he remained my best friend even as I started forming close female friendships here. Because of my relationship with my husband, I am not emotionally dependent on anyone back home (although I still keep in close contact with my best friend in America). In general, my husband and I communicate easily and well, but if you have difficulty communicating, be aware that your difficulties will be magnified on the field.

Our elders required that we attend a week-long intensive counseling session. I initially resisted this, as I did not think we had any glaring problems. We'd been happy for ten years! Why did we need counseling?? Once we were in the counselor's office, though, we quickly realized we needed to deal with some areas in our life that we had not yet dealt with. (These issues were separate from the trailing spouse issue, which had been resolved by that time.) The experience was a major breakthrough for us and has helped us to be more understanding and supportive of each other.

If you are planning on long-term overseas missions, make your relationship with your spouse your strongest earthly relationship. A happy marriage makes those unavoidable annoyances of daily life much less noticeable. To that end, I highly recommend counseling.

(As a side note, you really do need a good friend on the field, whether you are married or not. Pray for one before you get there, and trust God to provide one. He will!)

## Pornography/Sexual Sin

Unaddressed sin problems are going to show up on the mission field. There are a lot of unique stressors to living cross-culturally, and that stress can be a trigger for issues like pornography, which absolutely destroys intimacy, trust, and happiness (yes, even among missionaries).

And I hate to be the one to tell you the ugly truth, but in contexts like Southeast Asia, porn problems can easily slip into prostitution problems.

So please, if you have a pornography problem or some other serious struggle, either address it before you go to the field, or just don't go. Seek counseling and find freedom first, because that deep, dark, buried secret will bubble to the surface a lot when you live within the stress of a new culture. (By the way: Although my husband did not have a pornography problem either before or after coming to Cambodia, our particular organization seeks to address porn problems through addiction counseling, *before* they will clear you to leave.)

## Poor Team Dynamics

I love the vision that is born when people collaborate on a team. As wonderful as working on a team can be, teams also provide an opportunity for conflict and interpersonal stress. Conversely, sometimes missionaries have no team, either because they arrived without a team, or their team broke apart at some point. Neither a stressful team nor lack of a team is ideal.

In addition to taking conflict-resolution training (which is part of the training I discuss in the next point), you need to accept that your team situation may change over the years. Teams lose members, and they gain members. For varying reasons, you might need to choose teammates again after you get to the field, and you need to know that is okay. Your commitment to serving God needs to be deeper than your commitment to your team.

## Not Getting Enough Pre-field Training

Sometimes people simply don't get enough training. Our required training was very thorough, and each step along the way we learned something more about cross-cultural work or about ourselves. The two most life-changing trainings we took were Mission Training International's (MTI) pre-field course and the Kairos worldview course. I consider MTI to be essential preparation for cross-cultural service, and it should be attended *in addition to any Bible school or seminary training* you may already have.

Before becoming missionaries-in-training, we had been involved in paid or volunteer ministry for several years. That ministry experience has been very helpful to us in setting boundaries between family time and ministry time (something that especially affects a wife's happiness). It's also easy for missionaries to become frustrated with nationals who change slowly or not at all, but I remember times in the States when we worked with people stuck in harmful behavior patterns who didn't seem to be showing evidence of positive change. So we've concluded that some of the stresses of missionary life are just ministry stresses, located in another country. It would be useful to get some ministry experience before leaving.

## Conclusion: Practical Steps to Take

1) Build margin into your budget, and raise it fully.

2) Ensure both partners have a strong missionary call.

3) Make your marriage your strongest relationship; possibly seek counseling.

4) Tackle big problems like pornography before leaving.

5) Be prepared for the possibility of team issues.

6) Get ministry experience in addition to specific pre-field missions training.

~~~~~~~~~~

*For more information on Mission Training International, see www.mti.org. For more information on Kairos, see www.kairosusa.com.*

# Living Well Abroad: Four Areas to Consider

### BY *JONATHAN*

MY DAY JOB IN *Cambodia is serving as a pastoral counselor. In a typical week, I meet with clients from Asia, the Americas, Australia, Europe, and occasionally Africa. And whether these clients are missionaries, NGO workers, or international business people, they're all trying to figure out how to live well here in Cambodia.*

*I was recently asked to share at an international church on the topic of living well abroad. I gave it all I had and presented my compiled thoughts and hopes. This chapter is an extension of that presentation.*

*My hope is that it might help you as you prepare well.*

~~~~~~~~~~

How long will you be in your host country before you cry really hard? You know, one of those famous *ugly* cries that no one sees but which certainly exists? Will it be sometime in your first year? Month? Week? For me, it took about twenty-seven hours.

Our theme verse for those early days was 2 Corinthians 1:8: "We think you ought to know, dear brothers and sisters, about the trouble we went through in the province of Asia. We were crushed and overwhelmed beyond our ability to endure, and we thought we would never live through it."

But we did.

For as Paul Hiebert writes in his seminal work, *Anthropological Insights for Missionaries*, "Culture shock is rarely terminal."[1]

Theory can only get you so far. At some point, you have to get your feet wet and Nike the thing. That's what this chapter's about. It's

1.  Hiebert, *Anthropological Insights for Missionaries*, 80.

an attempt to give some practical, hands-on, nitty-gritty, [insert random epic language here], rubber-meets-the-road, advice.

Much of this comes from my own experience of transitioning a family of six from the suburbs of Midwest America to the concrete vistas of Phnom Penh. The rest comes from observing lives and stories in that enigmatic place we call "the counseling room."

The four specific areas we'll consider include living well abroad:

1. Theologically

2. Spiritually

3. Relationally

4. Psychologically

## 1. Living Well Abroad: Theologically

How we think about God matters. Of course it does. You already know that. But we sometimes forget that our theology also plays a vital role in how well we fare on the field.

First, we must remember that productivity does *not* equal fruitfulness. Indeed, our aim is not even to be fruitful, but to stay attached to the Vine from which all fruit comes. Our aim is to know him and his heart, to remain in him. Staying attached to the Source, hearing his heartbeat, is the only way we will be able to do "the will of him who sent us" (see John 4:34). There is *so* much to do and God does not want you to do it all. Let me repeat: there is *so* much to do and God does *not* want you to do it all. He does not expect you to kill yourself in his service. Now, you might die in his service, of course, but it should not be because you're a workaholic.

If you want to thrive abroad, you can't try to meet your deep insecurities through making someone (a missions boss, a sending church, God) happy. No amount of productivity will heal the wounds in your soul.

In fact, trying to meet your own deep emotional or psychological needs through missions will tear you up. And it won't be good for those close to you either.

## Simple prayers are your friend

For me, after we'd gone through a really rough patch (misdiagnosed typhoid fever, culture stripping,[2] bad news from home, etc.), I clung to one simple cry-prayer: "I will worship the Lord my God; I will serve only him." It's a declaration from Jesus at the peak of his temptation. It's what Jesus fell back on at the very end. So I did too. And honestly, for a while, it was the only prayer I prayed.

That being said, in Matthew 4, when Jesus made that declaration, Satan left him and angels came and ministered to him. I'm not a businessman, but that seems like a pretty good trade.

## Your theology of Satan matters a lot

Don't give Satan more credit than he's due. Don't blame him for everything. Why not? Well, it'll keep you from taking responsibility for your own stuff, and it'll keep you from doing the hard interpersonal and *inner*-personal work that you need to do. Here's my general rule: don't blame Satan for things that are reasonably foreseeable.

If it was reasonably foreseeable that eating that street food would give you giardia, don't blame the devil when you get sick and can't leave the bathroom! I'll be really sorry you're sick, but you don't need to bring the devil into it to garner my compassion and prayers.

If you ignore Sabbath and run yourself ragged, don't blame Satan when you feel depressed and burned out. Don't blame the natural result of your workaholism on "the darkness." (Note: I am NOT saying that depression and burnout always result from a missionary's failure to rest. But if a person has been burning the candle at both ends and then starts to feel the flame, it's not fair to blame the devil.)

Proverbs 7:6–9 provides a noteworthy example of reasonable foreseeability:

> "While I was at the window of my house, looking through the curtain, I saw some naive young men, and one in particular who lacked common sense. He was crossing the street near the house of an immoral woman, strolling down the path by her house. It was at twilight, in the evening, as deep darkness fell."

---

2 See http://www.alifeoverseas.com/beyond-culture-shock-culture-pain-culture-stripping/

The wisdom literature doesn't blame some massive evil scheme for this guy's sin. Its lesson for us? Do the hard work of not being naive. Do the hard work of getting some common sense. And don't open your computer at night or visit the red-light district when you're lonely and it's dark.

## You need a robust theology of heaven

You want to live and thrive abroad long-term? You're going to have to have a pretty good grasp of heaven. I'm not talking about end-times theology, I'm talking about the reality of eternity, for the saved and the lost.

## 2. Living Well Abroad: Spiritually

There are two powerful words we need to understand deeply. Those words are "Yes" and "No," and they are sacred words indeed.

Initially, when you move abroad, you don't know anyone and you're probably in language school, so you can say yes to everyone and pretty much everything. But watch out, because your ratio of yeses to nos will have to change. If you want to stay healthy, you will have to start saying no to more and more things. And if you don't make that transition well, if you don't learn to say no, you will end up saying yes to all the wrong things.

Recently, I heard a preacher boldly state: "Satan is always trying to get your yes." Indeed, from the beginning, the Liar has been getting people to say yes to stuff that will make them say no to the Father. And it continues. Balancing our yeses and nos can get tricky, triggering our fear of missing out or our fear of being completely overwhelmed.

Learning when to say yes and when to say no requires both faith *and* wisdom. After all, it is possible to say yes to too much because of our faith, and it is possible to say no to too much because of our wisdom.

Again, this is precisely why we need to spend time connected to the Vine. We must remind ourselves often of this truth: the most fruitful thing I can do today is connect with the heart of Jesus.

May God give us the grace to serve with both faith *and* wisdom. Not as opposite ideas, fighting for domination, but as buffers and guardrails, keeping us from veering too far to one side or the other.

## 3. Living Well Abroad: Relationally

Life abroad can be bone-jarringly lonely, so connecting with friends is vitally important. Those friendships might surprise you; they might be with expats and nationals and folks you find to be strange at first. But whatever the case, deep connection with other human beings IRL (in real life) is crucial to whether or not you live well abroad.

### Marriage

I've been living with my best friend for nearly seventeen years, and frankly, we'd like to stay friends. If you're married, I'd like for you to stay friends with your spouse too. Here are some ideas that have helped us:

- Google "First date questions" and screen capture the results. Next time you're out on a date or alone together, whip out your phone and get to know each other again.

- Be a tourist for a night. Pretend you don't speak the language and go where the tourists go. (I realize this might not apply to everyone, but I know it'll apply to some.)

- If you have kids, try to get away for twenty-four hours, because even twenty-four hours away can feel like forever. And when you're away, don't talk about work or the kids. (And if you don't have anything to talk about besides work and the kids, take that as a sign that you need to get away more often!)

- Read a book about marriage. I'm continually amazed at how little effort we put into the one relationship that we want to be the deepest and longest and best.

- If a book is too much, check out The Gottman Institute on Facebook. Follow them and read an occasional article.

Dudes, remember this: your wife lives here too. If you're doing great but she's really struggling, you gotta push pause and figure it out. Are you both thriving? And when it comes to arguing, remember the age-old adage our marriage therapist said over and over and over: "If one person wins, the couple loses."

## Parenthood

We moved to Asia when our boys were six and seven and our girls were one and three. And the loss of how I used to parent nearly killed me. Really. Most Saturdays, I'd get depressed and overwhelmed by all the good we had left behind. Here's a snapshot of what helped me:

- Be Creative. Early on in transition, creativity is very hard to come by. You're exhausted and on the edge already, so ask around. Ask other parents, "What do you do for family time here? Where?" Just remember, what works for one family might not work for your family. That's okay. Find the things that work for your family, and then do those things. Boldly. Remember, use other parents and their ideas, but don't judge yourself by other parents and their ideas. Some ideas will work for others that will not work for you. Figure out what'll work for your family, then do those things.

- Be Crazy. The Cambodians think we're crazy, and maybe they're right. We have a badminton court on our roof and a ping pong table in our garage. And we use our moto as a jet ski during rainy season. Maybe I am crazy, but I'm also not depressed.

- Spend Cash. If you need to spend some money to share a fun experience with your family, spend it. And don't feel guilty about it. Now, if you feel like God doesn't want you to spend it, then don't. But if you're afraid of spending money because of what your donors might think, that's a pretty good reason to go ahead and spend it. Don't let your kids grow up thinking that the most important question when discussing a family activity is, "What will our supporters think?" That question destroys kids.

## 4. Living Well Abroad: Psychologically

At various points in our overseas journey, Elizabeth and I have needed debriefing, coaching, and counseling. In fact, so many of the good things in our life and ministry have been directly influenced by specific psychological help.

One area that's so simple (and important) to talk about is meta-emotions. Simply put, meta-emotions are what you feel about feelings. Don't freak out on me just yet. I know this sounds like a Pixar movie.

But honestly, a healthy question that we need to ask much more often is this: How do I feel about what I'm feeling?

For example, if you feel angry at your host country and then feel *guilty* for feeling angry, your feelings of guilt will actually block you from dealing with the root of your anger. Does your anger make you feel like a bad person? A bad Christian? Like you're a failure because you don't even like the people you came to serve?

You see, how you feel about your feelings will make a huge difference with how you handle them. Do you keep talking to God about your feelings? If you're ashamed of your feelings or believe that you shouldn't have them, chances are your praying will cease forthwith. And that's not cool.

An illuminating question in all of this is, "How were emotions handled in my family of origin? Did I grow up in an emotion-coaching home, where emotions were safe and expression was easy? Was I taught how to feel and name and share my feelings?" If so, that's awesome. It's also pretty rare.

Did you grow up in an emotion-dismissing home? Were emotions anything but safe? Did you hear, "Don't be sad/angry/whatever?" In your family, did emotions hurt people? If so, I'm sorry. The first step is to acknowledge that this is the case, and maybe see a counselor.

Why does this matter? Because meta-emotions will massively impact what you do with your feelings, and what you do with your feelings will massively impact how you do with life abroad.

~~~~~~~~~~~

*This material was originally presented at an international church in Phnom Penh. It is now available as a podcast. Just search iTunes for "trotters41" and look for "Living Well Abroad."*

# The Journey to Feel Starts Small

### BY ELIZABETH

BEFORE MY HUSBAND AND I moved overseas, we met with a pastor who specializes in counseling ministers and overseas workers. At the very first session, he launched into ideas like *pain, connection,* and *empathy.* I was both unfamiliar and uncomfortable with much of the emotional language he spoke, but I was too embarrassed to admit I didn't know what in the world he was talking about. So I just sat there, nodding my head silently.

As we continued with the counseling sessions, however, I realized that the reason I didn't understand the language of the heart was because I had shut off my own emotions. I didn't know how to deal with emotional pain, so I simply turned off my ability to feel—thereby avoiding the pain altogether. Our counselor described this phenomenon as an "intellectually locked heart" or a "head-heart-disconnect."

How had I disconnected my head from my heart? For starters, I had grown up in a military family that moved frequently. Each time I was at a new school, the other kids didn't accept me. I often found myself alone and in want of friends. Weary of rejection, I turned instead to academics, burying myself in books and living inside my own head, where pain couldn't touch me. Then in high school, I developed an eating disorder. Addiction to academics and weight control were two of the ways I avoided dealing with my emotions.

I looked good on the outside, though. I was a dedicated student and high-achiever. I was a "good girl" who stayed away from big, obvious sins. But I couldn't relate to others without fear, and I couldn't trust God to love and save me on *his* merit, not mine. My life was all about earning and performing, and there was absolutely no place in that life for emotions.

Well, that's not entirely true. I knew happiness and joy, and was well-versed in emotions like anger, bitterness, and depression. But I had no ability to dip into the feelings *underlying* them: sorrow, sadness, grief, loss. I couldn't feel my own painful emotions, so I couldn't possibly feel the pain of others, which meant I couldn't extend love to them, either.

Meeting with that counselor was the beginning of my journey to *feel*. My heart was locked up so tightly that I needed someone to guide me through the process—I could not have found emotional healing on my own. The counselor led us in prayers to ask God for healing. I asked God to unlock my heart from its lifeless prison, and he did. Then both my husband and I asked Jesus to heal our own separate unresolved grief and loss. And heal he did.

I began to see that Jesus was right there with me, as I moved from home to home, from school to school. Jesus was right there with me, through every bad thing that had ever happened to me. He was with me when other kids made fun of me. He was with me when I was excluded on the playground. He was with me every time I uprooted my life and moved again. He was there all along—I had never been alone.

Jesus knew every teeny, tiny detail of my life, and he began giving me the emotional healing I needed. I could now see Jesus walking beside me through some of my most painful memories. His hand was clasped in mine when I felt lonely and uncared for. His arm was around my shoulder at my most vulnerable point—when a church leader repeatedly took advantage of me in a sexual way. Suddenly my memories didn't seem so painful anymore, because I could feel the tender presence of Immanuel, God with us, in those moments. I had buried my deepest wounds so far below the surface that I had to unearth them during counseling, but after Jesus entered into those experiences, they no longer hurt.

When Jesus unlocked my heart and healed my emotional pain, I started to feel other people's pain—and that hurts. But now I can offer deeper, truer love to people, because it's from the heart. I'm no longer stuck in my head, oblivious to hurting people. I no longer struggle with either restrictive eating *or* binge eating. I no longer suffer from obsessive negativity about my body, either. This is not to say that I never overeat or think negatively about my body, or that I always care lovingly for other people. It just means that these snares don't *control* me anymore.

Our God delights in the work of healing. He created us in his image, emotions and all, and he knows every fiber of our being. He knows we are dust, and that we need him desperately. He longs to bind up our broken hearts and free us from our prison chains. He is Jehovah-Rapha, the God who heals. He alone can mend our hearts; he alone can make bitter water sweet. His love can turn our mourning into dancing, and our sorrow into joy. Our God is a healer of hearts.

# One Question You Should Get Used to Asking

*BY JONATHAN*

IT'S A SIMPLE QUESTION, carrying with it the power to clarify purpose and extend longevity. It's a question that buttresses against the nasty cousins of burnout and bitterness. It's a question we need to ask more often.

It's simply this: "What is it that I really need?"

We've got to start asking our cross-culturally working selves, "In an ideal world, what is it that I really need to make it? To thrive? To be okay? To survive where God's called me? What is it that I really need?" Before you crucify me for turning the gospel inside out and hamstringing it with a message about me and my needs, hear me out.

I'm not at all advocating a life without obedient sacrifice; I am expressly advocating a life of eyes-open sacrifice. You might not get what you need. In fact, I'm pretty sure you won't. There are a lot of things you need that a life of cross-cultural service just won't be able to provide. I'm talking about the full spectrum here, from a Starbucks latte all the way to the absence of gunfire. And that's where this gets real.

When you realize that some legitimate needs won't get met, when you realize that safety and functioning utilities and access to public libraries and date night just aren't as much a thing where you live, you can do two things. You can seek to mitigate, or you can choose to sacrifice. In reality, I actually recommend both.

1. Mitigate it: Consider whether there are any creative workarounds that might meet the need, in whole or in part.

2. Sacrifice it: Obediently, with a full heart and open eyes, sacrifice the thing as a holy act of worship.

## The Importance of Knowing Your Sacrifice

It can appear holy to deny that there even is a sacrifice. Rachel Pieh Jones wrote of this[1] when she responded to some missionary heroes who claimed they never made a sacrifice. She writes: "While I understand the sentiment and the faith-filled valor behind it, I respectfully disagree."

So do I.

Denial and acceptance appear to be identical twins—that is, they look pretty similar—but they're not at all the same. In fact, denial and acceptance have extremely different personalities and life goals.

Denial claims to honor God by minimizing the sacrifice; acceptance actually honors God by embracing the sacrifice and *still considering him to be worth it.* Denial shrinks the story, collapsing grief and trauma and fear and loss into a singularity; acceptance explodes the story, showcasing the magnificent power of God *through* the grief and trauma and fear and loss.

Acceptance leads to deep emotional health, grace, contentment, processed grief, and a willingness to see the long view, both forward and backward. Denial leads to, well, nothing. Denial is a full stop, halting maturation and ongoing discipleship. Acceptance is a grand "to be continued," allowing for what was, while simultaneously looking forward to what will be.

## What Is it that I Really Need?

Before deciding whether to mitigate or sacrifice, we must seek to know our sacrifice. How do we do that? Ask the question, "What is it that I really need?" Many of us never do this. We have a strong aversion to saying "I need," which is ironic because the Jesus we serve often responded really well to folks who led with their needs.

Our needs must be named, if only to be offered up willingly. Abraham's boy who carried wood and fire had a name. Paul sought to mitigate his thorn, and then ended up gloriously sacrificing his need to have it extracted. Jesus saw and comprehended skull-hill, attempted to mitigate it, and then climbed it.

Sometimes the cup doesn't pass.

---

1. Jones, "Why I Will Not Say," line 4.

## Mitigate and Sacrifice

To mitigate is to make something less severe, less painful, less onerous. So, can I please encourage you? If there's something severe, painful, and onerous about life and ministry abroad, and if that hard thing can be lessened, for goodness sake, lessen it.

But if it cannot be lessened (and this will often be the case), then it must be sacrificed with your eyes and hearts open. At those times, we must remember, over and over and over again, why we're here. And when a sacrifice is required, we rest in God's ultimate goodness. We obediently make the sacrifice, casting ourselves on the grace and mercy of our King.

~~~~~~~~~~

*We believe that there are indeed sacrifices to be made.*
> *We believe that those sacrifices do in fact cost something.*
> *AND*
> *We believe that eternity will bear witness:*
> *The cost was not too high,*
> *The cross remains enough,*
> *The Christ, once seen face to face, will make it all imminently worth it,*
> *Forever.*

# The Gaping Hole in Modern Missions

BY *JONATHAN*

I THINK SOMETHING'S MISSING.

It's something that Jesus loved (and studied) a whole lot.

It's missing because it doesn't really fit into our Discovery Bible story sets. It doesn't seem to add value to our NGOs or leadership trainings. It doesn't offer an immediate return on investment or accelerate the planting and growing of churches.

It's the Psalms. We're missing the Psalms, and it's hurting us.

I grew up reading the psalms. Our family did the "read a psalm and then add thirty until you can't go any further" thing. For example, on the 12th of the month we'd read Psalm 12 and Psalm 42 and Psalm 72 and so on. It was boring and predictable, but also transformational.

I began re-reading the Psalms in earnest about a year ago. I bought a commentary. I started reading books and articles. I began teaching them, singing them, and preaching them. And I started noticing their conspicuous absence.

And I've come to believe that my country of origin (America) and my country of destination (Cambodia) desperately need the depth and breadth of the Psalms. We need more psalms in our families and our agencies. We need more psalms in our church plants and Bible schools. We need to steep our discipleship strategies in the Psalms. (Many of our more liturgical siblings never really stopped reading the Psalms, and for this portion of their orthopraxy, I'm very grateful.)

But we don't spend much time in the Psalms. We really don't. The prayer book of the Bible, the book most oft-quoted by Jesus himself, gets relegated to the background with an occasional nod to the pastoral Psalm 23 and a sideways glance at the beautiful Psalm 139. But that's not enough.

Full immersion is needed.

## Making the Case for the Psalms

We need the Psalms; not because they will teach us how to be super Christians, but because they will teach us how to be human Christians. I know that sounds silly, but there are a lot of dissociated folks who are trying to follow the Son of Man divorced from their own earthy humanity.

The Psalms teach us what it means to live, breathe, feel, and follow. Here. Now. What does it look like to follow Jesus and still *feel* all this stuff? Life's a freaking roller coaster. Just like the Psalms.

Author N. T. Wright describes the Psalter Coaster like this:

> "The celebration is wild and uninhibited; the misery is deep and horrible. One moment we are chanting, perhaps clapping our hands in time, even stamping our feet . . . The next moment we have tears running down our cheeks, and we want the earth to open and swallow us."[1]

Sounds a bit like life. Basically, the Psalms identify (and make allowance for) our humanity. In fact, the Psalms allow more raw humanity than many churches. Again, Wright illuminates:

> "The Psalms not only insist that we are called to live at the intersection of God's space and our space, of heaven and earth, to be (in other words) Temple people. They call us to live at the intersection of sacred space, the Temple and the holy land that surrounds it, and the rest of human space, the world where idolatry and injustice still wreak their misery."[2]

How do we live at that intersection, connecting worlds, without being ripped apart? The Psalms will show us.

## The Full Spectrum of Emotions

The Psalms speak to core human needs and feelings without resorting to clichés. There are more than enough platitudes floating around already; we need the Psalms to teach us how to care about people without adding to the detritus.

What emotions are a believer allowed to have? What feelings are against the rules? The Psalms show us, and the answer is shocking:

1. Wright, *Case for the Psalms,* 43.
2. Wright, *Case for the Psalms,* 91.

they're pretty much all allowed. That's not to say that all *actions* are allowed, but pretty much all the feelings are. In fact, the Psalms teach us how *not* to avoid uncomfortable feelings.

Whatever the emotion, keep talking to God. The psalmists sure did. We are to pray with (maybe because of) our uncomfortable emotions. We enter our prayer closets with all of our hearts. There's no need to cut pieces off before initiating a conversation with our Papa. We don't have to make ourselves presentable for God. Jesus did that already.

Many people have a hard time identifying and allowing emotions; some countries and cultures (and denominations) struggle with this more than others. But wherever we're from, the Psalms draw back the curtain and help us to see things as they really are.

The Psalms provide emotional nomenclature.

Furthermore, the Psalms can help people to acknowledge the presence of pain, an important first step towards healing. This is especially crucial in honor/shame cultures; the Psalms give the reader permission to feel negative emotions: "Well hey, he felt this and he's in the Bible! Maybe it's OK if I feel it too."

Once, after watching a young believer read a psalm that discussed "unacceptable" feelings, I simply asked, "Have you ever felt that?" The resulting heart-level conversation would not have happened without the ice-breaking action of the psalm.

## Letting Others Make the Case for the Psalms

Are you tired of listening to me talk about the Psalms? How about these guys?

Dietrich Bonhoeffer wrote: "Whenever the Psalter is abandoned, an incomparable treasure vanishes from the Christian church,"[3] and then went so far as to say that "The Psalter impregnated the life of early Christianity."[4]

Billy Graham once said: "I used to read five Psalms every day–that teaches me how to get along with God. Then I read a chapter of Proverbs every day and that teaches me how to get along with my fellow man."[5]

---

3. Bonhoeffer, *Psalms*, 26.

4. Bonhoeffer, *Psalms*, 26.

5. Graham, in Kroll, "Psalms," lines 26–27.

And Martin Luther even wrote: "The Psalter promises Christ's death and resurrection so clearly–and pictures his kingdom and the condition and nature of all Christendom–that it might well be called a little Bible. In it is comprehended most beautifully and briefly everything that is in the entire Bible."[6]

And yet we hardly ever read or teach or preach them! Could we change that, please?

## Letting Jesus Make the Case for the Psalms

You know, Jesus really loved Psalms. In fact, Jesus quotes it more than any other book in the Old Testament. These are the four Old Testament books that Jesus quoted the most:

#4 Exodus

#3 Isaiah

#2 Deuteronomy

#1 Psalms

Kind of makes me think they're important. But here's the kicker, when Jesus quoted from Psalms, it was almost *always* in a difficult situation. That is to say, when Jesus was in a stressful situation, he fell back on Psalms. Here are some examples:

- Jesus outwits angry, accusing, scheming, educated guys (aka Pharisees) with the Psalms on several occasions (Ps 8:2, 110:1; Matt 21:16, 22:44; Mark 12:36, 14:62; Luke 20:42–43).

- He quotes the Twenty-Second Psalm while dying on the cross (Ps 22:1; Matt 27:46; Mark 15:34).

- Jesus is hated without cause, which he says the Psalms foretold (Ps 35:19, 69:4; John 15:25).

- He quotes Psalms when talking about his betrayal (Ps 41:9; John 13:18).

- When the Jews want to stone him for claiming to be God, he responds with a line from Psalms (Ps 82:6; John 10:34).

---

6. Godfrey, "Why I Love the Psalms," lines 47–52.

- He quotes Psalm 110 when Pilate asks if he is the Son of God (Ps 110:1; Matt 26:64).

- After having his authority challenged, he quotes Psalms to the chief priests and elders, calling himself the chief cornerstone (Ps 118:22–23; Matt 21:42; Mark 12:10; Luke 20:17).

- He references Psalms when foretelling Jerusalem's destruction (Ps 118:26; Matt 23:39; Luke 13:35).

So basically, when Jesus quoted from Psalms, good things *weren't* happening. In stressful situations, when he was under duress or attack, Jesus referred back to Psalms. Maybe that's when we need to remember them too.

And for what it's worth, it's not a great idea to pack for a trip after the trip has started. (Although, with this audience, I'm sure some of you have tried!) You know life's going to be crazy. You know it's not all going to be smooth sailing. Pack your bags now. Read Psalms now. Soak in the Psalms now.

Repeated exposure to the Psalms etches into the hearts of young believers (and old ones too) a biblical response to pain and suffering. The Psalms show the new way.

~~~~~~~~~~

Theologically, we need the Psalms.
Emotionally, we need the Psalms.

~~~~~~~~~~

## Looking for Balance

The Psalms balance Paul's head with David's heart. We tend to idolize Paul, valuing an intellectual (rational) approach that prizes productivity and aims at finishing the task. But if we're not careful, we become automatons on an assembly line to salvation. We show up, clock in, put a rivet here and a prayer there. The Psalms protect us from heartless evangelism and cold workaholism, modeling integration and allowing the mind and heart to be simultaneously present.

The psalmists weren't scaredy cats, but they were sometimes scared. They weren't sobbing piles of emotion, but they sometimes cried. They weren't angry men, but they sometimes demanded sovereign revenge. They got depressed. They sang. They wept. They danced.

And they prayed.

## Closing Argument

We're working in hard places in dangerous times; we need the Psalms. We're working among people who've suffered tremendously and endured courageously; they need the Psalms.

Jesus knew the Psalms and used them. *A lot.* So should we.

How? Read them. Sing them. Pray them.

Especially when you have no words to pray, pray the Psalms. Have you ever been there? Wordless but hurting? Bonhoeffer said, "That can be very painful, to want to speak with God and not to be able to."[7]

We need the Psalms to be deeply planted and carefully cultivated.

~~~~~~~~~~

For more in depth study of the Psalms, check out these books:
*The Songs of Jesus: A Year of Daily Devotions in the Psalms*, Tim Keller
*The Case for the Psalms: Why They are Essential*, N.T. Wright
*Psalms: The Prayer Book of the Bible*, Dietrich Bonhoeffer

7. Bonhoeffer, *Psalms*, 10.

# Develop Deeper Emotional Intelligence

BY *JONATHAN*

I PERSONALLY THINK WE missionaries are a smart bunch. Our textbook education is typically high. We've been to college, perhaps seminary, and we know some stuff. We've figured out how to use our cognition for the King, our intellect for the Incarnated. But while western education is first and foremost intellectual (and that's not necessarily a bad thing), life is lived and people are loved on the street level, not the lecture hall.

The classic quip about people caring how much you know only after they know how much you care is classic for a reason: it's true. When we approach a hurting, lost world with brains first, we risk showing a skewed image of Christ. We need our hearts too.

Hearts can seem to get in the way of missiology, and emotions are inefficient. Emotionally detached workaholics may be great at getting the job done. They might not make wonderful spouses or parents, but disconnected, task-oriented, stoic workers can be low-maintenance, efficient missionaries.

Conversely, we must remember that emotions are Christlike. A missions force with low emotional intelligence is bad for missions, not to mention families, teams, and planted churches. When the DNA of new believers and new churches excludes the sometimes messy reality of the heart, it's not healthy DNA. Furthermore, a disconnected, task-oriented, stoic missions force isn't much like Jesus.

Have you ever met a man or woman who seems bottled up emotionally, but the minute they start talking about the lost or missions, they start crying? I've met many folks like this, and I'm always baffled. When it comes to their families or other interpersonal relationships, they seem distant and cold, but the minute you mention unreached peoples, cue the waterworks. Something is not right about this picture.

It's awesome that they care about the lost, but how is it that all of their emotional capital got put there? Religion should not be the only place in their life where they really feel emotion.

## Building Emotional Intelligence

So, how do we add some heart back in? How do we build emotional intelligence in ourselves and our teams? I believe both the Psalms and the life of Jesus can help us find our hearts. John Calvin, in describing the Psalms, said this: "What various and resplendent riches are contained in this treasury, it were difficult to describe. . .for there is not an emotion of which any one can be conscious that is not here represented as in a mirror."[1]

To grow in emotional intelligence and awareness, we must practice. Read a psalm and the gospels and try to identify as many emotions as you can. Both involve people, and people feel. Ask yourself, "How do the hands of Jesus reveal the heart of the Father?" If Paul helps us to know the mind of Christ (a good thing), the Psalms show us Christ's heart. It is the Psalms that Jesus turned to and quoted more often than any other book in the Hebrew Scriptures.

But even more telling, the context in which Jesus referenced the Psalms was almost always when he was in a difficult situation. Jesus was hated without cause, which the Psalms foretold (Ps 35:19, 69:4; John 15:25). He quoted Psalm 22 while dying on the cross (Ps 22:1; Matt 27:46; Mark 15:34) and when talking about his betrayal (Ps 41:9; John 13:18). These are just a few of many examples. In stressful situations, when he was under duress or attack, Jesus referred to the Psalms. Maybe that's when we need to remember the Psalms too.

In our own lives, and in the lives of the people we live among, bad stuff is common. Corruption, danger, and loss are daily realities, and so we need the psalms. As we watch global instability and fear spread, we need workers with hearts that understand grief and loss. We need workers who know Christ as healer. We need workers who bring their full hearts to the mission field, not just their work ethic or their seminarian intellect, but also their vulnerable, wounded, and healing hearts.

1. Calvin, in Allender and Longman, *Cry of the Soul*, 31–32.

If we connected heart and mind, we'd get kinder, gentler, more sensitive cross-cultural workers. And kinder, gentler, more sensitive disciples.

## Making Room for Warrior Poets

The foreign field appeals to warriors, and we amplify this fighting spirit with our dramatic quotes and motivational epigrams. But the unreached peoples of the world also need poets and artists, those who see and speak in different tones, with different cadence and quality.

Too often we think of the soft qualities as counterproductive in church-planting work, especially among the least-reached. We recruit hard people for hard fields, and we can't even imagine the artist or highly emotive worker surviving, let alone thriving. We need warriors, go-getters.

But this approach is wrong, and for the sake of the gospel, we must change it. Tenderness, creativity, gentleness, and whimsy are not soft, esoteric qualities. These are qualities flowing straight from the heart of Christ.

Yes, we should study the mind of Christ, but there is so much more. Christ's death was not by guillotine, disconnecting head and body. His head was bloodied, his heart was pierced, and all of him was raised.

Let's make sure that all of him is preached. Let's make sure that all of him is shown:

Jesus the advocate and disrupter, the wild one who defied Rome from underneath.

The brilliant intellect who befuddled the learned men.

Let's make sure we preach his heart too:

A heart that felt the sting of death and the tip of the spear.

A heart that felt abandonment and despair and cared about a widow's son.

A heart that laughed and wept and wrote in the dirt.

Let's remember a Christ who loved the psalms, and let's imitate him. Let's connect with the heart of God, and let's show the world a richer, fuller, more complete image of Christ.

# Remember the Ten Reasons You Should Be a Missionary

*BY JONATHAN*

SOMETIMES, WE'RE A PRETTY serious bunch, and sometimes, that's okay. But when I was a teenager and our house had five kids in diapers (long story), my dad used to say, "If we don't laugh, we'll cry." He was right, and we chose to laugh. A lot. (The five in diapers hadn't learned this maxim yet, though, so there was still plenty of crying.)

I'm not opposed to crying. I'm also not opposed to laughing. So, if you will, journey with me through a Top Ten list of why the job of a missionary is just plain awesome.

## 10. You'll get to try new things, like typhoid fever and amoebas

On the bright side, most of the time your illnesses will sound cool. And cool illnesses make people pray more. Note: ulcers aren't cool. If you get an ulcer, don't tell anyone.

Oh, and make sure your kids know how great all these new things are too. I was hanging out at an international high school once and overheard a kid say something about a student who was absent. He nonchalantly said, "Oh, he's not here; he has an amoeba." I wanted to grab the kid by the collar and say, "You know that's not a normal sentence, right?"

## 9. You will have friends from countries you didn't know existed

Faroe Islands? East Timor? Canada? Living abroad tends to add countries to the map. But consider yourself warned, living abroad also confuses things. For example, I'm no longer sure if a boot is a type of shoe or a part of a car. Is paste something with which you build a house or a sandwich? Is a biscuit breakfast food or dessert? And what about this thing called "a barbie?"

Your kids might be confused too. Our little girl loves the story of the "Ten Leopards." You know, the one where Jesus healed ten leopards, but only one came back to say "thank you?" Thank you, you wonderful world of missions, for giving our whole family such a linguistic advantage and wide worldview. A worldview in which Jesus cares so much about jungle animals, he sometimes heals ten at a time.

## 8. Your driving skills will "improve"

Who knew you could survive so well without rearview mirrors, turn signals, or lanes? Who knew driving 20mph (or 32kph for those of you who don't know how to measure stuff correctly) could be so exhilarating? And sometimes, cars on the mission field actually get younger, with fewer miles on them than when they were imported. How cool is that?

## 7. You'll learn to be grateful for the little things, like cheese

Older missionaries in my part of the world remember when cheese came to town. Cheese and stop lights apparently arrived at the same time. So if you're in a part of the world without cheese, extra points for you. And may I recommend you start praying for a stop light? (I was going to include bacon in this section, but then I remembered we were talking about "the little things.")

## 6. Your bargaining skills will improve. . .with the police

The police don't want to write you a ticket, and you don't really want to pay a ticket. And everyone knows you didn't really violate a law anyway.

One time, a pot-bellied officer demanded beer money, so naturally I offered Twizzlers. He pondered for a second, then held up four fingers. I complied and drove off, chuckling as I watched him and three buddies chow down. Apparently, Twizzlers make mouths (and cops) happy.

## 5. You will learn how to complain in multiple languages

The ability to complain, out loud, in front of other people, without them knowing, is the gift of a lifetime. Just be sure to do a quick perimeter check for possible same-language listeners within earshot.

A hotel worker didn't do a proper perimeter check once, and I clearly heard him complaining about some rude tourists, "Sure, why don't they just go sunbathe by the pool. I hope a massive rock falls off the building and smashes their heads." I made a mental note to self: speak extra nice to that employee. And get a cabana with a roof.

## 4. You'll always be able to use the excuse, "I'm not from around here"

When you need to explain why you wear clothes, or why you don't really care much for fried spiders or bony duck embryos, simply state: "I'm not from around here."

Really though, and I think we all know it already, this one's most useful during furlough. Can't figure out the ATM? Or the drive-through? Or Wal-Mart? Just smile, mumble something in another language about massive rocks smashing things, and say "I'm not from around here." But don't forget your perimeter check.

## 3. Fashion rules will no longer apply

You ever seen a missionary? Yeah.

## 2. You'll get to report to hundreds of people, every month, details about your work, your family, and how you spend your money

Who needs Dave Ramsey when you have the entire deacon board of multiple churches analyzing your finances? It's accountability on huge quantities of steroids.

They may ask why you need so much, or why you have to pay for your kids' education, or why you save for retirement, but at the end of the day, they are paying you to do this thing we call missions. It's an honor to serve, even when the reports are due, the power's out, it's hot season, the spreadsheet's rebelling, and you can't figure out how to get that .docx into a .pdf into an html into a mobile-friendly, print-friendly, e-mail-friendly format. But hey, at least you don't have to use envelopes.

## 1. You'll get to experience the raw joy of crossing language barriers, cultural barriers, time zones, and comfort zones, simply to invite someone to follow Jesus

Maybe you preach the gospel straight up, street-corner style. Maybe you serve the sickest and the poorest, touching the folks no one else wants to touch. Maybe you teach English or a vocation, aiming to empower. Maybe you do a thousand things for economies or community health or justice. Whatever you do, there is one love that draws us all together and pushes us out the door. Every day.

His name is Jesus, and at the end of the day, he is worth it all.

# When I Was a Trailing Spouse

## BY *ELIZABETH*

*"The Lord had said to Abram, 'Go from your country, your people and your father's household to the land I will show you.'"* (Gen 12:1 NIV)

WHEN MY HUSBAND FIRST told me, rather excitedly, that he wanted to apply with a mission agency to become a missionary in Cambodia, I did not in any way share his excitement. I had many mistaken ideas about missionary life—mistaken ideas that told me, "No! Never! Don't go!"

## Mistaken Ideas

I thought I was facing a permanent relocation, regardless of how miserable I might become–and I was convinced I would be quite miserable. I believed I would live in a hut somewhere in the jungle and spend my days lugging water for laundry and gathering firewood for cooking. Housework would so consume me that I wouldn't have time to homeschool, and I would never see my husband again. I thought a missionary husband is never at home, but instead serves the needs of his community, twenty-four hours a day, seven days a week, fifty-two weeks a year, for years on end.

I'm also some sort of unstable cross between a germophobe and a hypochondriac. This condition can lead to some rather interesting conversations about deadly infectious possibilities, and is especially virulent during pregnancy and childbirth. As a woman who had recently given birth, but who was also quite sure she wanted another baby, I didn't take my husband's missionary suggestion well.

My situation has a name: trailing spouse. The term can apply to spouses of missionaries, diplomats, members of the armed forces, and international businessmen or women. In my case, it meant that my husband had a strong call to missions, and I did not. I could not manufacture a call. Believe me. I tried.

I thought, however, that in order to be a good wife, I was required to go. I wanted to have the faith of Sarah, who followed her husband Abraham away from her homeland through the desert to a land they didn't even know.

## Trying to Be Sarah

So we did what we had always done for big decisions: we asked God what he wanted us to do. I tried hard to listen to God's voice, but it seemed like my husband's voice was so loud, I couldn't hear God. I felt tremendous internal pressure to say yes, because, after all, God would never tell people not to obey the Great Commission and become missionaries, would he? And God would never tell a husband one thing and a wife another, would he?

I felt guilty for not wanting to apply with our agency, and in my guilt, I agreed to apply. I was not happy about this decision. Each morning when I woke up, I would suddenly remember the path we were trodding, and I wasn't sure I wanted to live anymore. It took a lot of work to get out of bed in the morning to face a life I didn't want to live.

I studied Saint Patrick, the man who brought Christianity to Ireland. I tried conjuring up my high school dreams of being a Peace Corps worker and doing grand things in some developing country. I tried to emulate Sarah, who followed her husband, who was following God. I even dragged my husband to my grief counselor to discuss this issue. Her advice? We needed more information in order to make a reasonable decision.

In an effort to gain more information, and in spite of the fact that I still didn't feel a call, we attended our organization's two-week orientation. Everyone at the home office was excited about missions, and their excitement was contagious. At the time I thought that excitement would be enough for me to overcome my doubts.

After orientation, my husband made a survey trip. He made the trip alone because I was in the first trimester of a new pregnancy and far too scared to visit a third-world country. He explored Phnom Penh, uninhibited by my many fears. He returned home with a love for the Cambodian people and quite convinced that we could survive in the capital city. His research about daily living details, which are of utmost importance to me, was thorough enough that I, too, was convinced of the livability of the city.

However, when we tried to set an actual departure date, I froze in fear. I realized I couldn't go. I had too many fears. There were simply too many unknowns. In my mind, my abundant life in America was filmed in color. I looked ahead into a future in Cambodia, and saw only darkness.

What on earth were we going to do about this?

## Hearing My Own Call

We took a week-long break from discussing Cambodia with each other. (Remember how I had difficulty discerning God's voice from my husband's voice?) For one week, we planned to talk only to God about it. During this time of seeking, a veteran missionary shared her story with me. She spoke of fear and faith, and how she learned to trust God to go with her to new places, even though she was afraid—and she was often afraid. She said her fear problem was really about not having enough faith.

Her faith story helped me see that God was going to go with me wherever I went in this world. I had not thought that God would go with me to new places. I unconsciously thought I would step on a plane and leave him in America—as if God is confined to one place.

She advised us that whatever decision we made, both of us needed to be one hundred percent sure. I couldn't go to Cambodia and make my husband feel responsible for ruining my happy American lifestyle. He couldn't stay in America and make me feel responsible for ruining his missionary dreams.

During that week we also asked our church's elders to meet with us. When we met, they spoke of husbands loving and sacrificing for their wives. They spoke of God's love and esteem for marriage. I absorbed all the wisdom we had received that week, and I began to understand that this needed to be a joint decision—not one person submitting to another person, but a unified decision.

I had been listening to my husband's call for a long time, and had told myself I didn't need a call if he had one. I thought I could simply follow him, like Sarah. In the end, I'm not sure I had enough faith to use my husband's call as my own. I needed one myself, and God graciously provided.

My call wasn't a big epiphany moment or an audible voice, but I had a deep sense of peace about going overseas that I had never had before. I needed to know that God would go with me, and that gave me the courage to say yes to his call. I didn't know how he was going to help with my fears. I didn't know how all the daily living details were going to work out. But I knew God was with me, and that I was safe with God. Suddenly, he didn't feel distant to me anymore.

I knew I could choose to go or stay, and either would be OK. For the first time, I could say "Yes" in my heart without hesitation, but I could no longer say "No" without hesitation.

## GOING INTO THE LAND GOD SHOWED US

I was finally able to lay down that trailing spouse label. I survived hard times in our first year overseas—difficult transitions, illnesses of all kinds, even an attempted break-in—without blaming my husband. I have assurance that I'm supposed to be here, and not just because God called my husband here, but because God called me here. I am glad I followed him.

I have seen my already-happy marriage blossom as a result of following God to Cambodia. Our family has grown closer together. I have watched my children grow in flexibility, maturity, and spiritual sensitivity. I am a different person myself. I'm less rigid. I'm no longer such an extreme hypochondriac and germaphobe. I'm less judgmental of others.

I've experienced God in deeper ways than ever before, and he has helped me see and meet other people's needs more readily. I would never go back to the way I was before. This journey is just beginning, but each day, I'm more thankful that I finally said, "Yes."

# How to Deal with Trailing Spouse Issues

## BY ELIZABETH

"FEELING SO FEARFUL AND *alone since moving as a trailing spouse.*"
Once someone found my blog because they did an internet search
for that phrase, and it reminded me how much pain a trailing spouse
endures. I remember the struggle; I remember the suffering. And while
whoever typed those search terms is actually *not* alone, I can attest to the
fact that it very much *feels* that way. I remember how dark it felt, how
black the future seemed. I remember how much pressure I was placing
on myself not to ruin my husband's dreams. I remember being afraid that
nothing would ever be okay again and that it would all be my fault.

Telling my trailing spouse story has opened up conversations with
women all over the world, both before and after they reach the field. (A
trailing spouse doesn't have to be a woman, but women are the ones who
have reached out to me.) So with that in mind, I'm going to share parts
of emails I've sent to women who have asked for more of my story. I've
deleted identifying details to protect their privacy. These are the things I
would say to any marriage dealing with a trailing spouse issue.

But first I want to clarify what I mean by the "call." It's confusing
when Christians talk about "call"; different people have different definitions for "call," and they tell very different stories. So what I'm generally
referring to when I say "call" is a strong feeling or desire to be where you
are (or where you'll soon be going). It feels like a peace and a settledness
about your current (or future) location.

It was about a year and a half from my husband's initial "Let's move
overseas!!" to hearing a call of my own. I know that might not seem like
long in retrospect, but it felt like *forever* at the time. These times can be
so dark that they seem to stretch out forever and ever, with no bend in
the road, to borrow a phrase from Anne of Avonlea. I know you and your

spouse might be on such different pages regarding your life right now, and it's hard to understand each other's point of view. But it's important to hear each other's hearts in this. You are different, and both of your perspectives are valid, because they are true for each of you.

I'm going to take a deep breath here and say some hard stuff. I hope and pray it comes out right, because I only ever want to point people to God and do for others what my mentor did for me when I was still trailing—provide hope without pressure. In an ideal world, both you and your husband would feel called to your work where you are. But we don't live in an ideal world, and you are *not* the only wife who at this very moment does not feel called to where she is. A call is very important, true, but it's also true that you can't force it.

There are so many moving parts in a marriage. It's hard to predict what one or the other will feel or do many years from now. And so I need to say this: it is not the end of the world if this does not work out. I think it's very important to internalize that. Your vows are to *each other*, not to overseas work. You are both separately committed to following God, but now that you are husband and wife, you are a team and have to make decisions as a team. I know that does not sound like a traditional explanation of marriage where the husband makes the decisions and the wife follows, but in overseas work especially, having unity is essential.

Please don't hear what I'm not saying. I'm not saying this overseas thing will never work out. I don't believe that. I'm also not saying you should just grin and bear it. And I'm not saying you can just pretend to hear a call from God and that acting like you have one will convince your heart you have one. I'm just saying this issue is important and worth investing in. And here's how I would suggest you approach it, based off the advice I received several years ago when I was in your shoes.

Now this is going to sound scary, but I promise, in the end, it's not. What you and your husband have to do—both of you—is open up your future to God. Both of you have to be able to say: if I have to give up this life abroad business, it's not the end of the world. You can't just decide you know what God needs to change in your heart. You even have to give that expectation up. Now that won't sound as scary to you as it will to your husband. When he has a long-standing dream, it's going to be hard to say, "God, can I give this up?"

During all this time that I didn't have a call, it was so stressful for my husband that he developed an ulcer. An ulcer. Major stomach pain. Not going felt like the end of his life, and going felt like the end of my life. But ideally, you would both be able to say those things to God. And then, you would talk to him and ask him where he wants you to be, and what he wants to do in you, and all those things. But first you both have to surrender your preferred futures.

It's trickier to find your call if you're already overseas, because if you don't find it, you feel stuck and unhappy where you are. This is another reason seeking God is so scary. What if he doesn't come through? What if he disappoints me and doesn't talk to me? What if I'm still in the dark? Or worse, what if he actually tells me to stay here? (I think that was part of my fear, that if I really opened up, he would tell me to go, and I did *not* want to go.) But I just don't think you can actually hear from God unless you put it all on the line—living overseas or living back home; you've got to put them both on the table. And your husband has to, too.

Incidentally, when we did this, when both my husband and I put it all on the line and simultaneously opened up our future to God, my husband came back to me saying we didn't have to move overseas. He was willing to stay in America. I say this to explain that it wasn't just me and my problem; my husband was talking to God too, asking him questions and trying to listen for answers. And that openness to change on *both* our parts is very significant for our story.

I remember my mentor telling me some things that really freed me up to hear from God. "If you go, and you really, really hate it, you can always come home." That was brand spanking new to me. I thought it was a lifelong commitment. I thought you went and never came back. Just knowing there was an escape valve allowed me to be able to say yes. I don't think I could have heard a call otherwise.

The other thing my mentor said that really helped was to say to both of us, "No matter what you decide, one person can't ever come back and blame the other person for the decision" (or something to that effect). She meant that if we stayed in the United States, my husband couldn't blame me for ruining his ministry, and if we left, I couldn't ever blame him for ruining my life. Getting rid of potential blame is a *huge* part of being able and free to hear from God. It's hard to hear from him when we put all these pressures on ourselves.

So what I would recommend is seeking God all over again for living overseas, and both of you laying your plans and dreams down and being open to God either taking you back home or keeping you overseas. I really believe he is with you, no matter what you choose. I also do not believe it's a failure either way, whether you stay overseas, or whether you leave (but especially if you leave, since human beings tend to attach more significance to that choice).

You have promised each other your lives, and I believe that promise is more important than any one decision about where to live. That is what our church leadership told us, and I believe they were speaking truth; I believe your marriage covenant is that important. I remember being disappointed not to hear a "go" or "no go for launch" from our church leaders, but only counsel to honor the marriage covenant. Focusing on our marital unity, however, ended up being one of the best helps in overcoming our difficulties.

I hope I made sense with as little pressure as possible. I never mean to push!

And truly, I have no vested interest in your staying or going. I simply want you and your husband to be united in whatever choice you make and however you choose to serve. I did want to give you some practical steps to take though, and I hope those made sense. Sending you love and praying you will find God when you seek him, and that even in the confusion and chaos and grief, you will experience the peace that passes all understanding.

# MOVING WELL

# How Moving Abroad is Like Giving Birth

*BY ELIZABETH*

IN THE FIRST TWO years that I lived in Cambodia, I wrote a lot about the ups and downs (or "yays and yucks" if you prefer). But as I prepared to return "home" after our first time Stateside, I asked myself, what was my overall analysis of those ups and downs? In the end, which wins out: The good, or the bad?

So I listed all the positive and negative things from my life in Cambodia and compared them. What I found in that list was that, in the final evaluation of the term, the good things won out. And here's why:

## Big Blessing #1: I have friends here

A seasoned-missionary-kid-turned-seasoned-missionary advised me to pray for a friend before I even got to the field. I did that, and I asked our prayer supporters to do the same. When I'd been living in this country only five days (and was still jet-lagged), I met the woman who would become my closest friend in Asia. I didn't know it at the time, but God had already answered my prayer. We go out for girl time about once a month, and I don't know what I would do if I didn't have her and our times together.

That's not all. Shortly after we moved here, a new family joined our team. Over the past year or so, we've gotten to know and love them. We take care of each other when we're sick (which is pretty often), and when we're not sick, we make each other laugh. They are our teammates, and they make life sunnier.

## Big Blessing #2: My marriage counselor was right

He assured us that we would be "just fine" on the field if Jonathan and I continued to love each other well. That if we really "got" this whole loving each other thing, we would be okay. I wanted his promise to be true. I wanted his claim to be right—but I didn't know if it would be.

Now, nearly two years in, I can say that he *was* right. This counselor has a special place in his heart for ministry and missionary couples and desires to strengthen their marriages so they can persevere in ministry. He showed us how to love each other better and how to invite God into the painful parts of our lives. Our marriage has not only survived the cross-cultural chaos, it's actually better now than it was two years ago.

## Big Blessing #3: My international church

I have a strong need for a good church. I have always loved the church, but I did not expect the international church we attend to be such a lifeline for me. Each week, I connect with God during the worship time. I need that special time of prayer and contemplation each week—I even take notes. And when I am forced to skip a Sunday because of illness in the family, I just don't feel as anchored the following week.

I met another dear friend in the church nursery here. She has been such an encouragement to me throughout this first term, as we shared our sorrows and struggles together, and as I learned from the wisdom of her decade in this country. I didn't know I could find all those things at a church, so soon after moving here. After all, I had been at our sending church for over fifteen years. I didn't know I could get the cozy feel of small-church relationships at a bigger church. I didn't know I could feel like I belonged so soon. I didn't know how universal Christ's church really is.

~~~~~~~~~~

In my doula training course, I learned that what creates a satisfying birth is not necessarily whether the birth plan was followed precisely or how the birth unfolded, medically speaking. No; how a mom feels about her birth is more closely tied to how well supported she was. If she was kept informed about the process and felt emotionally supported, generally she will consider her experience good, even if unexpected events occurred.

If you guessed I'm going to draw an analogy between birth and missionary life again, you'd be right. I realized that each of those three items on my list has something in common: I draw strength and support from them. My friends, my husband, and my church have all given me spiritual and emotional support during these past two years. In my final evaluation of this term, even though I've frequently cried, been regularly stressed out, and been tired nearly every day, I have been fully supported.

When I doubted, they listened. On down days, they were there. How I feel about this term is positive: I have been buoyed by my brothers and sisters in Christ. On this journey we call life, just what in the world would I do without them?

~~~~~~~~~~

*"Every good and perfect gift is from above" (James 1:17a NIV).*

# Ten Ways to Survive Your First Year Overseas

*BY ELIZABETH*

I WORKED AT A lot of summer camps before moving overseas. Camp work is hot, sweaty, and tiring, and I always loved that last shower before lights out. So before moving overseas, I told my husband that I'd be able to handle anything during the day in Cambodia as long as I had a clean shower and clean bed at night (with a fan!).

And for the most part, that's been true. Besides the nightly shower, however, I've picked up a few other survival skills from my first year overseas. My best advice still lies in the preparation phase, but today I want to share tips you can use once you get to the field. Here they are:

## 1. Figure out your absolute necessities, and do whatever you can to install them in your home or in your life

For myself, I needed curtains in my bedroom and gates on my stairs. I had to be able to dress and undress in private, as well as spend time with my husband in private. I needed curtains pronto! Thankfully a friend supplied me some hand-me-down curtains three weeks into our Cambodia adventure. They may or may not have matched my sheets, but they gave me the privacy I needed.

A close second for me was the safety gates on our treacherously steep concrete Asian stairs (for my then-one-year-old), obtained five weeks in to Cambodia life. Those were my absolute necessities. You may need something different. Certain kitchen equipment, perhaps. The point is, figure out your two or three absolute necessities, and obtain them if at all possible.

## 2. Funny YouTube clips are your best friend

Some weeks it was all I could do to get to Friday, when my husband and I would watch Fail Blogs on YouTube. Another favorite was Mitch Hedberg. (You can find compilations that delete his language.)

We're big fans of Brian Regan's "I Walked on the Moon" (mostly clean, with occasional language).

Of course who can't help loving Jim Gaffigan (also mostly clean)?

This is one of our family favorites: NFL Bad Lip Reading. Not all Bad Lip Reading is this kid-friendly.

## 3. Find spiritual nourishment

I can't tell you enough how much I love our international church and the spiritual food I receive there. But I know not everyone lives in a city that offers English-speaking church services like I do. Nowadays, though, overseas workers have access to sermons and podcasts on the internet. My husband, for example, likes listening to Andy Stanley sermons. Figure out which teachers feed *you*, and set aside some time to listen.

We all need to worship God in song, so if you don't have access to worship services in your heart language, remember you can purchase worship music on iTunes. (Artists like Bethel, Hillsong, and Matt Redman are some of my favorites.) I know some of this depends on your internet quality and won't work for absolutely everyone at all times; still, it's an improvement in resource availability over times past.

And don't forget your own personal morning quiet time – it's worked wonders in my life. So no matter what your options are, I do believe you can find the spiritual nourishment that you crave and that you need. You just might have to be creative about it.

## 4. Closely related to spiritual nourishment is finding community

You might be able to find this at an international church or on your team, as I've been thrilled to find. (Although I personally have had to guard against being *over*socialized.) Finding community might be trickier for you if you live in a really remote place, with few other workers.

One of the best things you can do is pray for God to bring you a kindred spirit or two. Yes, the goodbyes hurt, and sometimes God brings people into our lives only for a season, but I do believe God answers our prayers for friends. Sometimes we have to get creative in our search for community as well, and another option is online community. Velvet Ashes and A Life Overseas are two options for Christian expats.

If you're married, it's far too easy to forget that you and your spouse can provide built-in community for each other—but that only happens when you spend time together. Maybe there's no money to go out anywhere, or nowhere to go out, or maybe you don't yet have babysitters you trust. You can still have coffee at home. You can still put the kids to bed early. You can still find fellowship with each other; in fact friendship is a vital part of a thriving marriage. Our first year we went up to our roof after our kids' bedtime a couple times a week, looked out over our city and just talked to each other. It was peaceful and a time of great bonding, and I cherish those memories.

## 5. Your old coping mechanisms might not work at first— don't sweat it too much

I love to read, but my mind was too tired from language learning and culture acquisition to read much that first year. I've had other friends whose beloved piano playing went by the wayside their first year. Don't lose heart—these things will come back later, when your brain isn't so tired from the initial onslaught of culture and language.

## 6. Your body and mind may feel weaker than ever— take care of them

You'll probably get sick with strange illnesses. (The first two years are the worst for that, until your body adjusts.) But I'm not just talking about illnesses here. Before I moved overseas, I'd never struggled with mood swings, due to either hormonal shifts or low blood sugar. Now I deal with both, and not only do I need to be aware of them, but I have to be diligent in alleviating my symptoms.

Living cross-culturally (especially in a developing country or a very hot country) drains your body of its resources. So you'll have to feed and water it regularly. You'll need to de-worm regularly, take your vitamins, go to bed at a good time, and exercise. Exercise is not a coping mechanism you can afford to relinquish. You may have to get creative for this one too. A lot of people don't like using videos for exercise (you can access a lot online if you don't already own some), but if you don't have access to a gym or decent running paths, you may be forced to exercise in your home.

### 7. Fall in love with something in your host country

In the beginning it's too easy to love everything or to hate everything. But as with everything in life, the truth about your country is probably somewhere in between: a mixture of both good and bad. I can't tell you how many times I've encountered God in a sunset or a palm tree, in a rice field or a painted sky. When I need a reason for why I stay in a dirty, stinky, crowded city, I simply go to my roof and meet God in the clouds and banana leaves. You won't be able to love everything where you live, but if you want to stay, you can't afford to hate everything, either.

### 8. Some days you'll only be able to accomplish one thing— you might feel like a failure for that, but you need to celebrate that one thing

You might not be able to shop for furniture and groceries in the same day, and that's OK. You can always try again tomorrow with something else. You'll get more efficient at this life, and eventually daily living won't wear you out so much. You need to give yourself this grace. And you'll need to continue giving yourself that grace, because to a certain degree, living cross-culturally will always wear you out more than living in your passport country.

### 9. If you homeschool your children, don't be afraid to drop it for 3–6 months

Your kids will be OK, I promise. I didn't believe that at first, either, even when my missions coach assured me of it. But she was right; it turned out OK. Not only does it save you sanity (it's hard to homeschool kids and study language at the same time), but your kids really do catch up later.

Plus, they need to adjust to overseas life, too. We don't want to overload our kids with too many expectations.

## 10. And returning to my first point, if all else fails, don't be afraid to put yourself in time out in the shower

Go to bed early. You can try again tomorrow! Grace grace grace. You're gonna need to give yourself a lot of it this year, so just starting doling it out now.

# A Sorrow Sandwich

## BY *Elizabeth*

MOST OF THE TIME living in Cambodia, I don't feel like I am making huge sacrifices for God. In fact, I've found many things to love about living here.

I am so happy here that I sometimes forget that other people have made sacrifices for me to be here. Reminders come in the form of my children, when they miss the family and friends they've left behind in America. They come in the form of Skype sessions with my parents, when I realize anew how very much they miss us.

So I am sandwiched in the middle of two generations of people who have, in many ways, sacrificed more than I have—much more. My parents. My children. I have caused people I love to suffer. And I did it voluntarily. You might not hear many people talking about this. You are more likely to hear people talk about the sacrifices of the missionaries themselves (whether or not it's a missionary who is speaking). But I think that does an incredible injustice to the thousands of people in America who are sacrificing *right now* to send a loved one overseas.

My best friend in America was the kind of girl who dropped *everything* the day Jonathan's dad was diagnosed with brain cancer, just to sit with me in my shock and grief. She's the kind of girl who would drive to my house when my husband was out of town, so that after my kids were asleep, we could talk for hours and hours. She's the girl I laughed with and cried with for eight wonderful years. She's also a writer. So I asked her to write about how she felt saying goodbye to me. And this is what she wrote:

## A Letter from Home

### BY TERESA SCHANTZ WILLIAMS

Last year, Elizabeth and Jonathan and their foursome said goodbye to their families and friends and flew toward the adventure God chose for them. Those left behind, with none of the distractions of a new culture, slowly adjusted to their absence. The Trotters were missing from the daily landscape of our lives, and knowing this was going to happen didn't make it less painful.

At first when they left, I kept forgetting. I'd pick up the phone, punch in their number and sheepishly hang up. Or I would think I saw Elizabeth coming out of the library and wave too warmly at a confused stranger.

It was like when you rearrange the contents of your kitchen cabinets and spend the next four weeks trying to relearn where you store the salt. Things weren't where they were supposed to be.

Their pew at church was too empty. No squirmy bodies next to Elizabeth's mother, Mary, munching on grandma's snacks and vying for grandpa's lap. Those first few months were hard on the families stateside, especially as news of distress and health crises came their way. Powerless to help, family prayed.

A missionary wife once told me she hadn't understood what the extended family sacrificed when she and her husband left for the mission field. She had since come to see that they relinquished precious time with their children and grandchildren, forfeited shared memories of celebrations and milestones, and suppressed their instinct to rescue when things went wrong.

Some are called to go. Some are called to *let go*.

If you have to say goodbye, this is the century to do it in. My grandmother had a dear friend who was a missionary with her husband in Burma during the 1950s. Somehow they held their friendship together with letters and furloughs, and in the long silences between, they prayed.

Facebook, Skype, blogs, and email have closed gaps. Within the digital universe, both sides of the ocean can post photos and videos and updates. Elizabeth can share funny stories about the kids, so women back home can watch them grow. To celebrate their special days, one can browse their Amazon wish lists to find a gift, or select something from iTunes. Even international travel is more feasible than it once was. Visits are possible.

Nothing substitutes for presence. These days, I can't sit next to the bathtub and hold Faith while Elizabeth brushes the boys' teeth. I can't watch the boys wrestle or Hannah belly-surf down the stairs. I can't go to a girly movie with Elizabeth and rehash our favorite parts on the drive home. I can't watch her eat the frosting from the top of a cupcake and leave the rest because she only eats the part she wants. I can't hug her.

I concentrate on what I can do. I translate twelve hours ahead and try to anticipate what they might need. One p.m. here? Asleep there. I pray that the girls aren't waking them in the night, that their colds will soon be gone. I pray that they will be able to play outside every day this week. That Elizabeth can find hummus at Lucky's grocery store. I pray the details.

I can look over Elizabeth's shoulder and see the frontlines of world missions and watch God's plans unfold. I can see what the Holy Spirit has done in her, enabling her to do things I wasn't at all sure she could do. (Bugs, germs, smells, change in all forms.) And through her blogging, the special qualities I knew were inside her are out where others can see (humor, insight, modesty in all its expressions).

Perhaps it sounds overdramatic, but I've concluded that for me, missing my missionary friends is a standing invitation to resubmit to God's plans. My true and proper worship.

~~~~~~~~~~

"I thank God for you—the God I serve with a clear conscience, just as my ancestors did. Night and day I constantly remember you in my prayers. I long to see you again, for I remember your tears as we parted. And I will be filled with joy when we are together again" (2 Tim 1:3).

# How Do You Write Your Name in the Land?

## BY *ELIZABETH*

THE STREETS OF PHNOM Penh, Cambodia are littered with garbage. The garbage stinks, and the open sewers reek. The construction on my street can be deafening, and I sometimes tire of all these sights, sounds, and smells.

But in the middle of this assault on my (admittedly sensitive) senses, I catch a glimpse of perfection: palm trees, right in the middle of the city. Green and graceful, the most beautiful trees in the world.

Often, at the end of a long and draining day, all I can manage is to shovel a spoonful of hummus into my mouth and plop myself down on the corner of the couch that has the best view of the palm trees across the street. What happens inside my soul is beyond words.

Even better than my living room view is the view from my roof. It's a little slice of heaven, especially as the clouds roll in, the winds blow, and the afternoon rains start falling. The air is delicious up there, and the palm and banana trees are larger and leafier on that side of the house. And even though I'm so familiar with them by now, some days I just can't tear my eyes away.

So why do I share my love affair with palm trees? Well, because, in a very real way, palm trees sustain me. There is a power in their beauty that lifts my spirit, calms my anxiety, and releases me from the stress of all the rotting streets and invasive noises. What would I do without my daily dose of palm trees? They're a green paradise in an otherwise concrete jungle, and when I look at them, I stand in awe of my Creator.

They are how I write my name in the land. The idea of "writing your name in the land" comes from the movie *Skylark*, one of my favorite American pioneer movies. *Skylark* is the sequel to *Sarah, Plain and Tall*, another favorite of mine. (I have a lot of favorite pioneer movies.)

*Sarah, Plain and Tall* tells the story of a woman from Maine who moves to Kansas as a mail-order bride for Jacob, a widower with two children. Jacob and Sarah fall in love, and by the beginning of the movie *Skylark*, they've been married for a couple years.

The people of Kansas are now facing a drought. The prairie dries up a little more each day, and it has truly become a "dry and thirsty land." But Sarah comes from a place by the sea—a cool, wet place where drought is unknown—and she's never experienced a season like this before.

When the wells run dry, the people of the community travel to the river, hoping to find water there, but the river is nearly dry. In desperation, Sarah's closest friend Maggie, and her husband Matthew, tell Jacob and Sarah that they are considering leaving the prairie and settling somewhere else. Sarah is so frustrated by this possibility that she blurts out:

> "I hate this land. No, I mean it. I don't have to love it like Jacob, like Matthew. They give it everything, everything, and it betrays them. It gives them nothing back. You know, Jacob once told me his name is written in this land. Well, mine isn't. It isn't."[1]

Maggie replies in a thick Scandinavian accent:

> "You don't have to love this land. But if you don't, you won't survive. Jacob, is right. You have to write your name in it to live here."

Maggie winces at the severity of her own words, and Sarah walks away, not yet able to accept this truth. By the end of the film, though, we watch her take a stick, bend down, and literally write her name in the dust of the land. *Her heart has taken up residence in a place that is both overwhelmingly good and harsh.* And she has planted herself in it.

I still cry when I watch those scenes. Do I love the strange land I find myself in? Have I scrawled my name in it? I still get annoyed by daily life. I still struggle to understand many of the East/West cultural differences. I still get discouraged by the sin problems inherent in an exceedingly corrupt society.

But I love this land.

I love the rice fields in the rain, verdant and green. I love the banana trees, oversized and leafy. I love the palm trees too numerous to count—a sight that never grows old. I love the clouds, large and billowing, and the sunsets, pink and orange.

---

1. Sargent, *Skylark*.

So what sustains *you* in your host country? How do you plant your-self in the place God has called you to serve? When the earth under your feet seems to crack, when your life is dry and scorched, what do you hold on to? When the soil starts to disintegrate and your well dries up, where do you go?

When no rain falls, when the crops wither away, and there's no har-vest, what do you do? What is your anchor, and where are your roots? Where have you put your signature?

How do you write your name in the land?

# Remember that Humor Is a Spiritual Discipline

## BY *JONATHAN*

*"There are times when the most effective way to teach a certain truth is by laughing very hard."*[1]

~~~~~~~~~~

THERE ARE TIMES WHEN laughing very hard is brave defiance; a dare to the darkness impinging. Satan, the lying burglar, loves to steal joy. But Jesus, the rough-hewn carpenter, loves to give it back.

There's a difference between joy and happiness, between joy and laughter—I get that. But sometimes, we try to be so spiritual that we end up being too grown-up for God. Joy is richer and fuller than happiness. But joy does not exclude happiness. That's like saying, "I love her, I just can't stand her!" Really? "I'm joyful, I just look bitter and angry and like I want to kill a bunny!" Really? Is that all we've got to offer a world that's drowning in its own pessimism and rage?

Is some sort of hunkered-down holiness God's idea for the church? I don't think so. In such a world (which, it should be noted, is not too dissimilar from times past), laughter is a bright act of rebellion.

Seriousness is not holier than joviality. For many, though, it's much easier.

## Laughter as Prophetic Rebellion

I'm no stranger to sad things, or sad places. I worked in an urban hospital, in the emergency department. I watched people yell and scream

1. Belmonte, *Year with G.K. Chesterton*, 124.

until their bodies ran out of blood, their brains starved, and they. Just. Stopped.

Every week I sit in a counseling room and watch brave peoples' tears smack the floor.

My parents and my sister are still dead. And I still miss them.

So no, I'm not talking about a laughter that requires denial. I'm not talking about a laughter that's fueled by alcohol or idiocy. I'm talking about a laughter that is fueled by Christ. To remember the sun's existence on a rainy day is to remember reality. Dancing in the downpour is a prophetic thing: it will not always storm.

~~~~~~~~~~~

*"Optimism breaks through agnosticism like fiery gold round the edges of a black cloud."[2]*

~~~~~~~~~~~

*"Joy, which was the small publicity of the Pagan, is the gigantic secret of the Christian."[3]*

~~~~~~~~~~~

*"I have come into my second childhood."[4]*

We need a second childhood, to be born again into childlikeness.

A joyful heart really is wonderful medicine, healing the imbiber and others besides.

We must boldly remember that after mourning comes dancing, and gazelles still dance on mountains of spices.

## Humanism: Enemy of Happiness

Happiness without Christ relies on humanism. And humanism, as a source of joy, is simply not strong enough or deep enough for the long haul. It can produce flashes of joy and pleasure, for sure, but it is not durable. It is a plastic bag.

2. Belmonte, *Year with G.K. Chesterton*, 47.

3. Belmonte, *Year with G.K. Chesterton*, 95.

4. Belmonte, *Year with G.K. Chesterton*, 82.

The alternative, according to Chesterton, enables joy. Speaking of Robert Louis Stevenson, Chesterton said,

> "Stevenson's enormous capacity for joy flowed directly out of his profoundly religious temperament. He conceived himself as an unimportant guest at one eternal and uproarious banquet."[5]

The Christianized humanist stands on the edge of the sea and says, "*How great I am* that the God of all this would love me!" The Christian stands at the same sea and exclaims, "*How great God is* that he would create all of this and love me!" Though those two statements sound similar, they diverge sharply and, having diverged, end poles apart.

## So Rebel Already

Look for the wonder. Look for the humor. Laugh at the darkness as a child of the light.

Don't be afraid of the Godly Guffaw.

Read Chesterton.

Now, I'm not interested in ignorant bliss. I'm not promoting a happiness that exists only in the absence of pain. I'm advocating a worldview that views the world as it is, *and then keeps looking.* To see the world as it is, isolated and suspended in nothing, results in terror and too great a cognitive dissonance.

No, we must see the world as it is, without blinders, and then we must keep looking and see the great Actor who exists outside of (and inside of) the world.

His presence changes things. It must change things.

So look up.

Lift up your head and see the King.

> *Who is the King of glory?*
> *The LORD, strong and mighty;*
> *the LORD, invincible in battle.*
> *Open up, ancient gates!*
> *Open up, ancient doors,*
> *and let the King of glory enter.*
> *Who is the King of glory?*

5. Chesterton, in Belmonte, *Year with G.K. Chesterton*, 89.

*The LORD of heaven's armies—*
*he is the King of glory.*
*(Ps 24:8–10)*

~~~~~~~~~~

*You love him even though you have never seen him. Though you do not*
*see him now, you trust him; and you rejoice with a glorious,*
*inexpressible joy.*
*(1 Pet 1:8)*

~~~~~~~~~~

*Come, everyone!*
*Clap your hands!*
*Shout to God with joyful praise!*
*For the LORD Most High is awesome.*
*He is the great King of all the earth.*
*(Ps 47:1–2)*

# Our First Month Abroad: the Journal Entries

*BY* E*LIZABETH*

*He comforts us in all our troubles so that we can comfort others. When they are troubled, we will be able to give them the same comfort God has given us.* (2 Cor 1:4)

~~~~~~~~~~

I almost didn't publish the following journal entries, which I recorded during our first weeks in Cambodia. When I read them for the first time after a year, I was surprised by the intensity of my original feelings (although I'm nothing if not intense). I remembered that time as being bad, but not this bad. I'm sharing some of my journal here because I want 1) to give people hope, 2) to proclaim, along with Samuel, "thus far has the Lord helped us" (1 Sam 7:12 NIV), and 3) never to lose my compassion for those currently in the depths of despair.

I'm happy here now, and I'm no longer plagued by any of these yucks. We worked to correct some of them, while I simply became accustomed to others. The yays, however, persist—my dependence on worship, laughter, and a wonderful husband, haven't changed at all.

~~~~~~~~~~

Arrival Date: January 16th, 2012.

## Friday, January 20th

And there is absolutely nothing about this place that I don't hate. Can't think of any earthly reason why we shouldn't just pack up and go back.

So I pretty much don't know how I'm ever going to survive here, let alone be happy again.

[Theme #1: My overreactor is dialed ALL the way up. You'll see this repeated quite often.]

### Sunday, January 22nd

Church was so good for my soul. "My life is in you, Lord. My strength is in You, Lord. My hope is in You, Lord. In You, it's in You." In worship today I just declared this to God, that he is my strength, my life, that I'm depending on him to sustain me and only he can do it. We sang about going whatever the cost and up the highest mountain and through the darkest valley. God reminded me that I'm here to stay. Not just in Cambodia, but in relationship with him. I'm not leaving him. I'm stubborn on this point.

So tired. Can barely stay awake after 5pm every day. Up six times last night with one child. There is so much dust here that has to be swept and mopped every day, and that gets old. It feels so futile. Just get up the next day to clean it all again. Everything here is so stinkin' dangerous. Sharp corners on walls, slippery floors. So much more danger in general.

[Theme #2: My hope is dialed all the way down. Again, oft-repeated.]

[Theme #3: Worship music was my lifeline. You'll see this one again too.]

### Monday, January 23rd

Bought the wrong size diapers. Again. I can't get this kilogram thing figured out! But I am doing better in general. So is Jonathan. Can't wait to go back to church.

And good grief the mosquito bites. New ones each morning. So itchy. Jonathan had to fix some electrical wiring today. Plugs are never enough or in a convenient place. Can't flush in the morning. Showers don't drain well. The heat saps your energy. Driving saps energy—there seem to be no rules. The nationals and their police know the rules but we don't. Street signs don't exist and the roads aren't N-S-E-W. Dirt is everywhere and has to be cleaned. Laundry must be hung and dishes washed by hand. (Did I mention I can't wait to get a house helper?) The language barrier is huge and everything is in kg.

## Tuesday, January 24th

I'm not particularly happy. I'm not particularly unhappy. I am particularly exhausted. Everything is so hard here but I keep plugging away. "Whatever." That's how I feel much of the time. I can laugh, however. We laugh all the time. Mostly at the stupidity of living here.

Everything is so stinkin' dusty. Floors, furniture, stair railings. Even clean clothes smell like wood fire and spices. Annoying. One kid slept all night with the aid of Benadryl. Benadryl to another kid for his hundred mosquito bites. They were super bad in the house yesterday. Feet hurt excruciatingly badly. I need house shoes with arch support because I can barely walk. It's so humid here, even in air conditioning, that my hair doesn't dry at night.

[Theme #4: I can't survive without laughter. Experts claim that the beginning of laughter signals the slow ascent out of the abyss of culture shock.]

## Thursday, January 26th

Another day. Ugg. Why do I have to live here? I don't want to live here. I don't want to want to live here. And I don't want to keep living. Life is easier back home and I want it. Everything bothers me. Why does it have to be so hard? Nothing comes ready-made. You have to do it yourself, and even then the electrical wiring comes apart. I hate mornings. Reminds me how unhappy I am. At least at night I can look forward to sleep.

I suppose one of these days these pages will be happier. But I have never been unhappier. It seems so hopeless. I want to go home. I want to go home so bad that I don't even care that it would look bad, that my life story wouldn't mean anything, that it would go against everything we've ever said, that it would disappoint people, that we would have wasted people's money, that it might be hard to find a ministry job. But this life is so terrible. I can't stand it. I can't find meaning. I can't find pleasure. I can't find comfort. I can't find ease. I can't find understanding. I can't even find food I actually want to eat. And every morning I awaken to more needs from the girls. That is endlessly draining. Can't clean or cook or do anything b/c Faith needs me to hold her. I'm off to more house work now. Dirty, stinky, unending housework. Bartering is so hard, and you do it in two different currencies, two different languages, and never know if it's a good price.

So much to fix. I can't see the end, it goes on forever. This morning I wanted to die. I told Jonathan I wouldn't kill myself b/c I don't like pain, but all I wanted to do was to get on a plane alone and run away. Coming here really did seem like a good idea at the time. Not anymore. Plus Faith is sick with a fever, poor cranky baby.

[Repeat of Themes 1 and 2: High on overreactivity and low on hope]

## Sunday Afternoon, January 29th

Been sick for two days. Pain, chills, fever (flu-like) along with abdominal pain and diarrhea. Could barely move last two days. I missed church and hated to miss it. When will my heart take up residence in this place? I worry about never accomplishing anything. Never making a difference. To make a difference I'll have to learn this language (too hard).

[Themes 1 and 2 strike again: Overreactivity and hopelessness.]

Somehow I want to make peace with living here as Jonathan has. Being here makes me love my husband more than ever. He is so sweet to me, taking care of me when I'm sick, being patient with my depressed moods and angry outbursts. Seeing him in this setting reminds me how special he is, much more loving than most men.

[Theme #5 surfaces: I need my husband.]

## Wednesday, February 1st

I was so sick. Three days of diarrhea and pain, then went to a local clinic. (I thought I was going to die I was in so much pain.) I needed Cipro. Still not back to normal plus I have a terrible head cold on top of that.

Finding him is no longer fun and exciting. It's drudgery, fearfulness, pain, sadness. But I am determined to find him in this dark place. He is the light of the world and those who seek him will find him when they seek him with their whole hearts. I will find him. Yes.

## Thursday, February 2nd

One thing that's hard about living here (only one!) is that people like to touch my kids, and they don't like it. How to stop it politely? I don't know.

In a moment of frustration today I started singing Magnificat. I knew I had to praise, and sure enough, I felt better.

[Theme 3 (worship) to the rescue again]

## Sunday, February 26th

Church—great worship. "Your Grace is Enough." "How Deep the Father's Love." A Zoe Group song I listened to while pregnant with Faith and during her labor. I cried during "You are My Strength." Great a cappella song. Felt so good to sing. Made me homesick for heaven when we'll all be together again singing praises to our King.

[There I am, relying on theme 3 again (worship).]

## March 27th

A few weeks into Cambodia I realized it would be more difficult to pack up and leave for home than to stay.

And then, inexplicably, I stopped journaling. Apparently I didn't feel the need to journal my unhappiness anymore. So to anyone considering following God in a "big" way, no matter what that is, please do not give up hope that life will improve, that transition will pass. Do not believe that the rest of your life will be as dreadful as it feels right now. Hold on to hope.

~~~~~~~~~~

*We can rejoice, too, when we run into problems and trials, for we know that they help us develop endurance. And endurance develops strength of character, and character strengthens our confident hope of salvation. And this hope will not lead to disappointment. For we know how dearly God loves us, because he has given us the Holy Spirit to fill our hearts with his love. (Rom 5:3–5)*

# Romance, Science Fiction, and Missions

BY *ELIZABETH*

WHAT MOTIVATED YOU TO go into missions? What keeps you going?

## Romance

I don't know about you, but romance is what drove me into missions. The romance of being a great missionary, of changing an entire people group, of seeing a whole country turn to Christ. This romantic idea was first kindled during my children's homeschool studies of Saint Patrick—the man in the fifth century AD who took the gospel to Ireland, where practically everyone turned from paganism to Christ.

This dream of mine was further fueled when I learned about one of our organization's church-planting teams in South America. Churches have been planted that have grown to membership in the thousands. Those churches have planted other churches. Those churches have even sent out missionaries themselves. When I first heard of this field, I thought Cambodia was going to be just like that. Woo hoo!

Never mind the fact that those missionaries had been building a reality from *their* dream for over twenty years by the time I ever heard of them. And never mind the fact that all you experienced missionaries are laughing at me right now—I still believe it's those kinds of dreams that propel us forward, into missions.

## Science Fiction

Maybe today my initial missionary dream seems like unattainable science fiction to you: completely unrealistic, and completely out of reach.

But Ray Bradbury (notable author of the science fiction novel *Fahrenheit 451*) believed that science fiction actually *drove* real science:

> "I think it's part of the nature of man to start with romance and then build to a reality. There's hardly a scientist or an astronaut I've met who wasn't beholden to some romantic before him who led him to doing something in life."[1]

Ray Bradbury continued discussing the idea of romance versus reality:

> "I think it's so important to be excited about life. In order to get the facts we have to be excited to go out and get them, and there's only one way to do that—through romance. We need this thing which makes us sit bolt upright when we are nine or ten and say, 'I want to go out and devour the world, I want to do these things.'"[2]

Does the reality of life as a missionary start as a dream, somewhere deep in our pasts? In order to go out and teach Christ's love, do we have to be excited about it? Do we need something that makes us sit bolt upright when we are nine or ten and want to go into all the world? [Or perhaps, if you are like me, something made you sit bolt upright much later, more like age 29.]

Bradbury also said, "We may reject it later, we may give it up, but we move on to other romances then."[3] He clearly thought scientists needed something to motivate their work, even if they shift their focus. I wonder then, do missionaries need the same? To survive on the field, year after year after year, do we need a dream? But is it the original dream that keeps us going, or do our dreams change?

Science, like missions, is not all guts and glory. There are the countless experimental trials. There's the disappointment when your data doesn't support your hypotheses, or worse, it doesn't make any sense at all. And there's the frustration when your equipment breaks down, or not everyone interprets the lab results the way you do. Science is not mostly sudden breakthroughs—and working with the hearts of people isn't, either.

1. Bradbury, in Popova, "Mars and the Mind," lines 86–89.
2. Bradbury, in Popova, "Mars and the Mind," lines 90–94.
3. Bradbury, in Popova, "Mars and the Mind," lines 96–97.

My dream has changed, sort of. I'm still beholden to the romantic idea that the entire nation of Cambodia could turn to Jesus. But I no longer think that might happen simply because *I* showed up in obedience to his call.

It's true that some days seem like a never-ending clinical trial, but I do still dream of nationwide revival. I long for it, I pray for it, I want it, just the same as I did when I first studied Saint Patrick or learned of those thriving South American churches. That dream keeps me here, believing there's a purpose to living through countless, repeated trials.

So today, I want to invite you to reminisce along with me.

What missionary dream did you first dream? Is that still your dream, or do you dream differently now?

What happens if you've lost your dreams altogether? Do you keep going without one, or do you ask God for new dreams?

# My Search for Rootedness
# and the Temporary Intimacy of the Expat Life

BY *ELIZABETH*

IT'S NOT HARD FOR me to put down roots in a new place. Roots are all I want. That may sound unconventional coming from a Third Culture Kid, but Army life was unsettling, and even small tastes of stability were tantalizing to me. I'm always searching for roots.

Specific places can be very healing to me, but I almost wonder if the place itself doesn't matter as long as the place seems permanent. I could settle anywhere as long as it's forever. I know this need for stability points somewhere. It points to a longing for a forever home. A hunger for the new city. A desire that can't be completely fulfilled in this sin-tarnished world.

So whenever I move to a new place, I pretend it's a permanent home. I decide I never want to move away. I give myself, heart and soul, to this new place and to this new people. I make plans for future years, future decades even. I tell myself that I will settle here and live here forever. I imagine everything in the future taking place in *this place.*

While some TCKs want to move places frequently, that hasn't been my experience. I don't want to leave a new place after a few years of living there. I don't become unsettled at the thought of settling somewhere. Sometimes I tell myself that this desire I have for roots is good. I tell myself that it means I'm stable and secure. But then I have to ask, if I'm so stable and secure, why would I become so unmoored by goodbyes?

A desire to move frequently can be unhealthy, it's true. But it is equally true that this insatiable desire I have never to move or see life change can be unhealthy too. For you see, God is the God who is doing a new thing. And growth in Christ never happens without change—sometimes painful change. So I sometimes live in denial, for this overseas life is not, and can never be, permanent. I will have to move eventually. My friends, the dear people with whom I live my life and to whom I've pledged my undying love, must also move at some point.

I long for the kind of lifelong friendships I read about in books. I long for the kind of small-town community my grandparents experienced in rural Iowa. I want roots, and not sky. And I will put in the time and energy, doggone it. I will pour into friendships as though they were going to last forever. I want to be able to trust these relationships. I want them to become the structure of my life and of my heart. Always niggling at the back of my mind, however, is the fact that they can't be. That this marvelous intimacy we create with fellow expats is at best a generation's length: no one stays on the field forever.

We often lament that people in our passport countries don't fully understand us. Neither do the people in our host countries. But with our fellow expats, the friendship goes deep, fast. These friendships are deep and strong, yes, but alas, they remain short. They are not forever. The very thing that draws us together—our mobile lifestyle—is what pulls us apart. We move, or someone else moves, and the friendship is stretched taut. It was good, it was deep, it was real. And it was temporary.

Because one day all that precious intimacy goes poof. It evaporates. It dissipates. it's not that we won't keep in touch—in this internet age we probably will—but our daily and weekly fellowship will be severed. Love may not wane, but shared life must and will. This small, tight-knit community is practically perfect, except that the closeness isn't here to stay. It's not long-term in real life the way it is in my imagination. And for now, this is a tension I carry with me in all my nonfamilial relationships.

I live with the unwanted understanding that this place cannot be my forever home. I can't settle here for all time. I know I must leave someday. I must say goodbye to the people and the place, and I don't like it. Not one bit. In these times I tell myself it's okay, that all I really need is my relationship with God.

But that attitude tends to isolate me from others. I retreat into my protective shell and cut off life-giving relationships. But doesn't God set us in physical places, all the way from the garden of Eden to Canaan to southeast Asia to the new heaven and earth? Christ is central to our rootedness, yes, but physical places and physical people are important too. Fellowship and space-time were his idea, after all.

So where does this leave me, unable to settle permanently in a space, unable to live continually with the same people, unable to depend solely on Jesus for companionship? It leaves me in a place of temporary intimacy with people and temporary settledness on the map. It leaves me in a place of desiring more permanency than I can currently claim. And it leaves me waiting for a better day and a better country, for a time and place when temporary fades away and I'll be given eternal roots.

# Culture Days

*By Elizabeth*

IN THE EARLY DAYS of living in Cambodia, a high school student came to my house for math tutoring. I noticed the neighbor children pestering her as she waited for me to unlock the gate. When I let her in, one of the girls grabbed a handful of my stomach and yanked. As my student pushed her moto into my house, a boy followed her inside and began examining some of our stuff. I told him, "ot tay, ot tay," which means "no, no." Then I tried to lead him out of the house—I had not, after all, invited him in. He just laughed, repeated my request in falsetto, and shuffled out slowly.

A day like that makes me want to lock my doors, hide myself in my bedroom, crank up the air conditioning, and watch a movie.

It's what I call a "bad culture day."

The next few days I didn't want to go outside, or even unlock the gate for our house helper in the morning. In fact, I asked Jonathan to unlock it. I just couldn't handle another neighbor kid violating my house or my body. (These neighbor kids live in the orphanage next door—and I had never seen those two before. They don't have normal social boundaries, even for Cambodians.)

But today I had errands to do, so I called my tuk tuk driver and walked out my front door. I paid the bill that was due and bought the items on my list. I even talked to my driver.

Fast forward to this evening. This evening our children begged us to let them play outside on the street. We initially created a play space for them on our roof in order to *avoid* playing on the street, where children and adults alike touched them too much. We've spent a lot of time on the roof in the last several months. Lately, though, they don't want the roof.

They want the street. (That desire in itself is a huge step forward *into* the culture for them.) So out we went, culture-avoiding-me included.

First, Jonathan stopped by a local Khmer restaurant to pick up some supper. We love their fried rice (and its price!). We started eating it in front of the house while the kids played. That's a very Khmer thing to do. They cook in front of their houses over an open fire, just like they've done for thousands of years, and then eat outside as well. Nobody touched me or my children rudely. We talked with the older ladies. One of them particularly likes our children, and told us tonight that it makes her happy to watch them play. Later, when a child slipped on the wet pavement, they were very concerned for him to clean his scrapes well.

Even my shy little daughter played and laughed with the girl next door. (That was a first, by the way.) We felt a sense of belonging in what we did tonight—eating Khmer food, speaking the Khmer language, and playing with our Khmer neighbors.

It was what I call a "good culture day."

A day like today gives me the courage to go back out and try again. It gives me the courage to interact with the people—unwanted touches included.

God, give us more good culture days.

# A Good Day

BY *ELIZABETH*

I HAD A GOOD day today. Yes, it's true. I had a good day yesterday too. And not just "good for Cambodia," but honest to goodness, downright good.

The November before I moved here, I climbed a twenty-foot pole. And jumped off it. (I know you're all asking yourselves if this is the same nonathletic Elizabeth Hunzinger you thought you knew.) I climbed it with no fear. But when I got to the top, I froze. The transition from crouching at the top of the pole to standing on the top of the pole was incredibly frightening. It's the shortest part, about one second of motion, but it's the most difficult. And I needed Jonathan to coach me through it. Once I was standing, I felt fine again.

It's the same in labor. Transition, that part of labor just before full dilation, is the shortest part. It's also the most intense and the place where a mom doubts herself. She needs help to get through it. (Jonathan claims that since he did this for me four times, I owe him four doula fees).

In training we learned about the "Chaos Bridge," which is an analogy for transition. We start out settled and stable, move into a period of unsettlement with all its farewells, and then into the bouncy bubbly transition. We start to come out of it while resettling, and then finally reach a new settled state.

When I was neck-deep in missionary transition, friends on both continents supported me with prayers and encouragement. I couldn't have made it through without their *doula-ing*, as all my birthie friends would say.

Transition. The most terrible part. The shortest part. Now I know with certainty that it doesn't last forever. And I can assure the next person

I see experiencing transition that it does indeed end. It's painful, but it won't last long. Not much longer now. I promise.

~~~~~~~~~~

*"Even though I walk through the valley of the shadow of death, I will fear no evil, for you are with me; your rod and your staff, they comfort me"*
*(Ps 23:4 ESV).*

# C'est la Vie

BY *ELIZABETH*

SOMETIMES LIFE SURPRISES ME. Like that time when Jonathan was sick with typhoid fever, and I was in the school room, and suddenly the light bulb burst into flame. Literal two-inch orange flames.

That never happened to me in America.

Or that time when Jonathan was recovering from middle *and* outer ear infections, and he went up to our beloved roof, with its three square meters of peace and tranquility (and several potted plants), only to discover that someone had painted those pots. And the rocks in the pots. And even the plants themselves.

That never happened to me in America either.

Don't get me wrong—plenty of surprising things did happen to me in America. Like the time a Canadian goose blew itself up when its wings touched two nearby power lines in our yard. Or the time a different Canadian goose attacked my leg while a dog the size of a pony jumped on my back. (That was in my neighbor's yard, by the way.)

But back to surprises in Cambodia.

Our boys wailed about our painted plants. I was at the end of myself. That week I had dealt with more sickness in the family and fought off more discouragement than is usual for me, and now, my roof, my precious stronghold of sanity, had been vandalized.

But with Otto Koning's *Pineapple Story* at the front of my mind, we set out to solve the mystery of who, and more importantly, why.[1] Next

---

1. Otto Koning was a missionary who planted pineapples in his yard. They took three years to grow, but before he could eat any of them, the nationals stole them all. This happened several times, and he was always angry about it. Only when he gave up his "right" to eat those pineapples to God could he stop being angry. The nationals noticed his change in behavior, and he started to have success in ministry.

door to us is an orphanage, and there is an old man who lives there. All day long he lounges on a hammock on the roof, watching television and smoking cigarettes. Occasionally he does some odd jobs around the place.

The neighbor children told us that this man painted our pots and plants and rocks, but none of them seemed to know why. The adults were a bit more helpful, laughing embarrassedly at our questions. This man is apparently bored and likes to make things look nicer. While we were at the seaside with my parents, he took the opportunity to improve our rooftop view.

I thought it would be common courtesy to ask before forcing home improvement projects on someone else. But it wasn't very long until I could see the humor. "My neighbor painted my plants," I'll say. And when you ask me why my neighbor painted my plants, I'll say, "Oh, because he thought it would look better." You might ask if it did look any better, and I'll say, "No, not at all."

The neighbors asked us if we wanted him to paint them again, perhaps all one color? (He originally painted them yellow and white.) We said yes, white is best. (Actually, *un*painted is best, but. . . .) And I did have some hope that our pots would get better when we saw him outside this week, painting three tables white.

We played badminton and frisbee on our roof today. And those pots, they were one color, all right. They were one hundred percent yellow. (Surprise! A darker shade of yellow.) But we enjoyed our roof just as much as we did before our neighbor painted our plants.

# When Friends Do the Next Right Thing

*BY ELIZABETH*

WHAT DO WE DO when the people we love do the next right thing? What if that next right thing leads them *away* from us?

When we say yes to God, we must often say no to the places we already know. And when God leads us overseas, we enter a communal life that is punctuated by goodbyes. Just like an airport, the missionary community endures constant arrivals and departures. But God is the travel agent here, and he hardly ever places anyone on the same itinerary. Perhaps we knew this uncomfortable truth before we said yes; perhaps we didn't. Either way, though, we must now live with the consequences of our obedience.

And I, for one, sometimes grow weary of it.

These expatriate friendships of ours tend to grow swift and deep, and ripping ourselves away from those friendships is painful. This summer, I have to say goodbye to two friends whom I love and respect and will miss terribly. *And I am still somewhat in denial.*

I have never had any doubts that they are following God where he leads them next. They are doing the next right thing. Even in the leaving, they are doing the next right thing. They are honoring their friendships and saying their goodbyes thoughtfully and tenderly. They are setting up ministry for the workers who will follow them. They have listened to God, and they are doing what he says. But they will leave a gaping hole in my heart and in this city, and they can never be replaced.

*What am I supposed to do when my friends do the next right thing?*

I actually don't know what I'm supposed to do. But I know what I *do* do: I grieve, because when a member of the international community leaves, all hearts bleed. The hearts of the leaving, and hearts of the staying. There is just no stopping that.

So I grieve for myself: it's hard to say goodbye to people I love. I grieve for others in the community who must also say goodbye: these goodbyes are their losses too. I grieve for the ones leaving: they must say goodbye to a life they know in order to build a brand new life somewhere else.

And I also grieve for people who have not yet come to this area of the world—people who are making plans to live and work here, and even people who haven't considered it yet, but will someday. I grieve that they will never know the wonderful people who have been such an integral part of the international community here.

So what can we do, as the body of Christ? We are *all* involved in sending, receiving, and being his workers. *How can we provide smooth takeoffs and soft landings for our brothers and sisters?*

When our friends leave, can we say goodbye with love? Can we send them on their way with our blessing? Can we give ourselves the space to mourn these losses? Can we keep our friends in our hearts, our minds and our email inboxes, no matter where they live in the wide world?

When we leave, can we accept loving goodbyes and understand how utterly we will be missed? Can we depend upon God—and His people—to help us settle in our new home? Can we open our hearts to new people and new places, while still remembering those who love us from afar?

When new missionaries arrive, can we welcome them wholeheart-edly, even though we know we will most likely have to say goodbye to them some day? Can we tell them where to set up their utility bills and show them where to buy furniture and help them fill their refrigerators?

When churches send out new missionaries, can we send them with our love and with our support? Can we resist the temptation to pull our hearts away too soon, in an attempt to ease the coming pain? Can we never cease to pray for them?

When missionaries return to their passport country, can we wel-come them? Can we open our arms, hearts, and homes wide to returning workers? Can we listen to their stories without judgment, and extend much grace in a time of great unsteadiness?

We were never meant to walk alone. So can we, as the global church, *be* Christ to each other? Can we need each other, and can we be needed? Can we cushion each other's pain during goodbyes and hellos? Can we do these dreaded transitions with bodies spread across the world, but with hearts beating as one?

# GRIEVING WELL

# Outlawed Grief

BY JONATHAN

LIVING ABROAD IS AN amazing adventure, but it comes with some baggage. And sometimes the baggage fees are hidden, catching you by surprise, costing more than you planned. You thought you had it all weighed out, you could handle this, squeeze right under the limit.

But then it got heavy. Your new friends moved away, or your child's new friend moved away. Far away. Like other continents away. And your kid's broken heart breaks yours.

Someone died and you didn't get to say that last, fully present, good-bye. Family members celebrate a birthday, or the whole family celebrates a holiday, and you're not there because the Pacific's really big, and you're on the wrong side of it.

Or your child can't remember her cousin's name, and she doesn't even know that's sad. And you realize there are just some things Skype cannot fix.

And you grieve, and your kids grieve. Maybe. But what if all these things happen again? And again. You have another round of airport goodbyes, another holiday season with sand. Another Christmas with crying.

What if grieving gets old and annoying and time-consuming and exhausting? What if it becomes easier to just *not* grieve? To not let others grieve? I'll tell you what happens: grief itself gets outlawed and a curse descends. And everyone learns that some emotions are spiritual and some are forbidden.

Has your grief ever been outlawed? Have you ever felt that your sadness or grief was wrong and not very spiritual and you should be over this by now? If so, I am very sorry. The prohibition of grief is a terrible, terrible curse.

Sometimes it's outright: "Don't cry, it'll all be okay." But oftentimes it's more subtle (and spiritual) than that. It's the good-hearted person who says, "It's not really goodbye, it's see you later," or "You know, all things work together for good."

What if your kids miss Grandma and McDonald's and green grass, and someone tells them, "It's for God," or "It'll be okay someday; you'll look back on this as one of the best things that ever happened to you." What if you tell them that? Grief gets banned, and what was meant as a balm becomes a ticking bomb. The intended salve starts searing.

When loss happens, why must we minimize it? Why are we so uncomfortable with letting the sadness sit? Are we afraid of grief? We sometimes act as if you can't have grief and faith at the same time. Sometimes, shutting down grief seems spiritual. We tell ourselves and others, "Forget the past and press on. God's got a plan. God is sovereign." We use Bible verses.

But banning grief is not biblical, and it's not spiritual.

Maybe we feel that grieving a loss of something or someone shows that we don't have all our treasures in heaven. Perhaps we delude ourselves with the twisted notion that if we had all of our treasures in heaven, our treasures would be safe, and we'd never experience loss. And although this is crazy talk, we speak it to ourselves and others.

Does grieving really signal a lack of faith? Would the truly faithful person simply know the goodness of God and cast themselves on that goodness? No one would say it, but we sometimes treat the sovereignty of God as an excuse to outlaw grief. I mean, how could we question the plan of God by crying?

We may feel that grieving a loss that was caused by someone else (through neglect or abuse) shows a lack of forgiveness. And although we know it's not true, we act as if once a person's truly forgiven an offender, the painful effects and memories disappear forever.

What if the loss was caused by parents or a spouse who decided to become an overseas missionary? Does the goodness and holiness of their decision negate the grief? Of course not, but sometimes we feel that the truly spiritual would recognize the godly sacrifice and be grateful. As if gratefulness and grief are mutually exclusive. As if a decision has to have one hundred percent positive or one hundred percent negative results. Gray exists, after all.

Maybe you made the decision to move overseas and it was a God thing and your call was sure, but now it's just really, really hard. How will you deal with your own grief? Will it threaten you, or will you coura-geously allow yourself to feel it?

Remember, grieving isn't equal to sinning.

Sometimes, outlawed grief goes underground. It becomes a tectonic plate, storing energy, swaying, resisting movement, and then exploding in unanticipated and unpredictable ways. A tectonic plate can store a heck of a lot of energy. Sort of like grief, once outlawed. It descends below the surface. And sometimes heaving tectonic plates cause destruction far, far away. It takes highly educated people with technical machines to pin-point the actual location of the destructive shift.

Have you ever experienced an earthquake like this, caused by bur-ied grief? It might not be obvious at first, but after a little bit of digging, you realize that the pressure and tension had been building for a long, long time.

So please, allow grief in your own heart and in the hearts of your family members. If you're uncomfortable with other people's grief (or your own), you might want to look deep, deep down in your own soul and see if there's some long-outlawed, long-buried grief. If you find some, begin gently to see it, vent it, feel it. Begin talking about it, slowly, with a good listener.

And if you come across someone who's grieving a loss, please re-member that they probably don't need a lecture, or a Bible verse, or a pithy saying. But they could maybe use a hug.

# When Grief Bleeds

*BY JONATHAN*

GRIEF IS A POWERFUL thing, echoing on and on through the chambers of a heart.

Loss singes the soul, and death does indeed bite.

We are not the only ones who grieve, to be sure, but those who've lived abroad certainly know this to be true: it hurts to leave. It hurts to return. And when others leave, whether by death or call or transfer, that hurts too.

Our stories are the ones written with contrails, straddling continents and seas. And these stories, the good and the bad, the ones that heal and the ones that hurt, must be written, and remembered.

Some would say to get over it. Stop crying. Some might accuse: *Too little faith. Too little thought of heaven. Too much focus on the past.* As if holiness requires Novocaine. Numbness. But grief is an indelible part of our story now. Grief bleeds through the pages of our lives, marking the pages and stories that follow.

Failing to acknowledge these chapters is to censor, to edit out, to delete plot twists and main characters, to murder history.

So we leave the pages as they are, splotched and imperfect. Because on every single ink-stained page, he remains. Comforter. Rock. Shepherd. God. He remains the God who grieved, the God who understands, the God who comforts. He remains, and he is enough.

So we keep feeling, refusing to numb. We keep sketching out these life pages, confident that he knows our stories. He loves our stories. He redeems our stories. And we keep trusting that in the end, our stories are actually a part of his story.

And he's really good with words.

# C. S. Lewis, Sadness, and What Eternal Hope Looks Like

*BY JONATHAN*

SOME CALL IT PESSIMISM, unspiritual, a sickness best treated with peppy music and cliché-riddled Christianese. They caution and guard against sadness, considering it a rabbit hole (or a worm hole) leading nowhere good. Others call it holy, Jeremiah-ish, defending it with the label of realism—open eyes that see things as they truly are.

It is a fundamental sadness.

Do you know what it feels like, this fundamental sadness? The sadness that seems to be part of all things? Sometimes the sadness is very personal; it's the loss of a sister or a father or a good friend. Sometimes it's the loss of a country or long-treasured plans.

Sometimes the sadness is more global. It's the emotional darkness that comes after you hear about Las Vegas, Mogadishu, the Yazidis, Paris, the Rohingya, or Raqqa. Sometimes its triggered by hashtags like #MeToo or #BringBackOurGirls.

~~~~~~~~~~

It is the blazing sunset that sears, not because of who's present, but because of who's absent.

It is the baby's cry in a mother's arms that taunts your empty ones.

It is the background sadness, fundamental and seemingly underneath all things.

It's the threat of miscarriage behind every pregnancy.

It's the one who sees the beauty of the dawn, but feels deep in his gut that the dawn comes before the dusk—that sunrise precedes sunset.

It is the lover who knows, at the beginning of a beautiful kiss, that it will end.

~~~~~~~~~~

For me, this foundational sadness is not necessarily depressing, but it is always pressing: exerting force, demanding to be heard, demanding to be observed.

Do you know this feeling?

People get scared when I talk like this. I sort of do too. What will people think? This doesn't sound right, or mature, or holy.

And yet Jesus wept.

"And yet." A powerful reminder, hinting at the deeper magic.

Jesus knew Jerusalem would destroy the prophets, and he knew Rome would destroy Jerusalem.

And yet.

Though the sadness feels fundamental, the deeper magic is there, waiting, pulsing. It absorbs the sadness, bears it, transforms it, then re-births it.

## The Deeper Magic

> "'It means,' said Aslan, 'that though the Witch knew the Deep Magic, there is a magic deeper still which she did not know. Her knowledge goes back only to the dawn of time. But if she could have looked a little further back, into the stillness and the darkness before Time dawned, she would have read there a different incantation.'"[1]

Witches never know the deeper magic. They know only winter and death, sorrow and pain. Half-truths all. But the deeper magic persists, refusing to be overwhelmed. It is older than death and wiser than time. The deeper magic knows that there is more.

There is hope.

And when hope is born (or reborn), the thaw begins. Without the deeper magic of hope, we might stop our story at the table of sadness and end up with an eternal winter and a dead lion. And that truly is horrible.

---

1. Lewis, *Lion, the Witch, and the Wardrobe*, 163.

But the deeper magic must be got at, not through escaping sadness or loss, but through fully embracing it. Through laying down. I don't think we need less lament, I think we need more lament, more tears.

So I invite you to the paradox of life bittersweet. Life's not *either* bitter *or* sweet. But it's also not neither. It's both.

I invite you to make room for the person who is totally happy and deeply clappy.

I invite you to make room for the person who is frozen in sadness and depressed.

And I invite you to make room for the person who feels all of those things at the same time.

## Why Do We Forget?

I sometimes wonder why others don't see it or feel it. Life is sad. People are hurting. Why aren't more people sad? But sadness doesn't sell well, and it doesn't seem to preach well either. But it's there. It's there in our families and ministries. It's there in our churches and friendships.

Truth be told, it's much easier to be angry. And so instead of being sad, everyone is angry. All. The. Time. And anger *does* sell well. (It seems to preach well too.)

Maybe you don't believe me, maybe you don't think sadness is there. But do you think that anger is there? That it's in our families and ministries? That it's in our churches and our friendships?

As a pastoral counselor, I see a lot of anger. But anger's just a fire alarm, alerting us to the real problem. People don't have an anger problem. People have a pain problem. And that pain is most often unlabeled, unwelcomed, unprocessed sadness.

Of course, sadness by itself isn't the solution. (That'd be depressing.) But insofar as sadness prepares us for hope, it is the solution. And although I do not like it and I wish it weren't so, deep sadness is often the mechanism for drawing our hearts and souls back to God and the eternal intimacy he's promised.

When we're unwilling to hold space for sadness, when we can't handle the unwieldy truths of mystery and paradox, we block the very pathway that leads to hope. And hopeless people are dangerous people, willing to hurt themselves and others without measure or limit.

If we stop at sadness, without digging deeper, many terrible things become imminently rational. But the deeper magic shouts out and ushers in what only it can. Hope.

~~~~~~~~~~

*I know the Lord is always with me.*
*I will not be shaken, for he is right beside me.*
*No wonder my heart is glad, and I rejoice.*
*My body rests in safety.*
*For you will not leave my soul among the dead*
*or allow your holy one to rot in the grave.*
*You will show me the way of life,*
*granting me the joy of your presence*
*and the pleasures of living with you forever.*
*(Ps 16:8–11)*

## The Shock of Magic

The beautiful and shocking deeper magic meant that, in the near future, "the Table would crack and Death itself would start working backward."[2]

Hope still means that.

The instrument of pain, the actual place of loss, which seems so strong and immovable, will move. It will be redeemed and transformed by the deeper magic; what has broken us will break, shattered by the love of the Lion.

There is hope!

The altar will be cracked, and where blood and sadness once flowed, will soon be sunrise and Aslan's roar.

May we never forget.

---

2. Lewis, *Lion, the Witch, and the Wardrobe*, 163.

# For the Times When You Hold Back the Tears

BY *ELIZABETH*

I'VE SPENT MOST OF my life locked in my head, keeping my emotions at bay, and not even realizing I was doing so.

I still do this, even though I know by now what's going on inside of me. I can feel tears rising up inside me, begging to be poured out. But I shove them down and don't engage.

I swallow the lump in my throat. I blink back the tears. I'm so good at this that I don't even have to blink sometimes.

I can literally watch myself do this. It's like an out-of-body experience. I can say to myself, "She's locked in her head right now, refusing to deal with those pesky emotions. Why is she so stubborn?"

Why? Because emotions take *time*. They take *energy*. And after I engage my emotions, I seriously need a nap. So it's easier for me to detach from them. It's easier to ignore them.

It might not be easier in the long run, but in the short run, it's certainly *faster*, because I've got things to do. People are depending on me. I can't take the time to deal with this. Crying won't help my situation.

No, crying might not help my situation, but it might help *me*. When I'm done crying, my problem might not be better, but *I* am better. My problem might not be solved, but I no longer feel like it's insurmountable.

I don't always let myself do that. I'm afraid that if I start crying, I won't stop. I'm afraid it won't fix my problem. And I'm all about solutions, people.

But. What if the tears *are* the solution? What if the tears allow my soul to say something that words can't?

I need to feel.

I don't always *feel* like feeling.

But I need to feel.

So today, if you're like me, and you have a hard time accepting the fact that you're human and that you have feelings in the midst of all the goals and tasks of life, I give you permission to feel.

And if it's easier to shove the tears down your throat than to let them flow freely, I give you permission to cry. Cry as hard as you need, for as long as you need. Use all the tissues you need.

And if too much is going on in your life, and you don't think you have the time to stop and cry, I still give you permission. After you've cried a little, or even a lot, you just might find you have the strength to carry on.

And when you're finished, you can look up and remember that if I were with you today, I'd be sitting right beside you, with a tearful smile and a warm hug.

I promise.

# When You Just Want to Go Home

BY *JONATHAN*

I SWIM IN THE abyss of memories. People and places I cannot return to, and few know. It is a morass I voluntarily enter, knowing it will hurt, but needing it still. *Someone* should remember these things.

Birthdays used to be happy occasions, full of cake and memories of years gone by. Now, birthdays are just full of memories of years gone. And places gone. And people gone.

Home, once lost, can never be regained. Another home can be built, to be sure, but what has been cannot be again. It is gone. There is hope. But hope for the future does not remove loss from the past.

When does one grow up and forget their childhood? Thirty-five? Eighty-five? I think never. Something deep and strange happens when the heart goes back. When pictures show you things you remember feeling more than seeing. Like the faded painting on the wall—of water fowl and cattails—that I haven't thought of in decades. My mom loved that painting. It feels peaceful, silently watching a family grow up and then leave.

Another picture shows my late mom and dad in the kitchen, but what I see is the blue metal bowl with white speckles. It was part of the country kitchen I grew up in, the one with glass doors looking out upon green, or brown, or white, depending on the season. I see that bowl and hear the clank of metal spoon upon metal bowl, and I feel at home. No one else had metal bowls.

Oh how mysterious is the snapshot that elicits such emotions!

I look at the photos slowly, seeing the details. Looking for the background. The memories swarm, and I let them. Something deep within is washed by these shadows of what was. I need this cleansing. I need to remember my moorings.

I won't be getting a call from my mom on my birthday. She won't be telling me she's proud of me, or asking about the grandkids. I won't hear about how her journey with God is growing and changing.

My dad won't ask about my work or ministry. We won't talk about books or hawks or how tall the grass is.

The Pacific Ocean separates me from siblings. Time separates me from everything else.

For now.

For the time being, I am time's subject. Moving at its pace, regardless. But time is God's subject, and at the end of all things, time itself will be changed, and we will reign with him forever and ever. Time's thermodynamic authority will be renounced, along with its painful propensity to separate. No longer will time rob and decay, slowly pulling like gravity on the soul.

God will finally do something I never could, although I was told to often enough. He will redeem time.

And he will relocate. In a physical, undeniably earthly way, he will come home. "Look, God's home is now among his people! He will live with them, and they will be his people. God himself will be with them" (Rev 21:3). And when he gets here, "He will wipe every tear from their eyes, and there will be no more death or sorrow or crying or pain. All these things are gone forever" (Rev 21:4).

He's longing for home too. So, in my drownings and darkness, perhaps I am brushing up against the heart of God. Perhaps I am tasting his tears too.

I will never go home again until I do, and that home will last forever, and not just in snapshots and pixels. It will last forever, in three-dimensional space, because of him. And all those longings, elicited by memories of home, will in turn be satisfied.

I will belong, with my own place at the table. I will be at peace. I will be wanted. There will be a mutual desire for presence. I will desire to be with God, and he will desire to be with me.

And then I'll find my mom and dad and a blue metal bowl, and we'll sit and talk forever about work, and grandkids, and maybe even grass.

And we will be home.

# Grief on a Spindle

*BY ELIZABETH*

Will You draw out my grief,
Spin it on Your spindle?
For my grief is hard to spin,
I always resist it.

It lies in wait, it's been misplaced,
Matted up with rage and fear.
The coil's too tight, the thread's not right
There is no bending here.

This wool's unfit for weaving,
My heart is unprepared for healing.
And my pain demands disclosure:
Is Love enough to form my skein?

So spin my grief upon Your spindle
Gently draw out yarn afresh.
Spin my grief upon Your spindle,
For my soul, it needs to stretch.

Spin my grief upon Your spindle,
I want to learn Your love anew.
Spin my grief upon Your spindle,
Clear out the muck that sticks like glue.

Spin my grief upon Your spindle,
Coat it with Your oil of Love.

Spin my grief upon Your spindle,
Weave a tapestry above.

# The Gift of Grief and the Thing
# I Heard in Portland

## BY JONATHAN

*"If we honestly face the sadness of life in a fallen world, then only
our hope in Christ can preserve us from insanity or suicide."*[1]

THAT'S AN INTENSE STATEMENT, and I sort of choked when I read it
for the first time. But the more I chew on it, and the more I ponder my
own life with its episodes of emotional and intellectual crisis, the more
I think it's correct.

## Honestly

I spent three years working as an ER/trauma nurse in an urban hospital
in the States, and that bloody, chaotic trauma room forced me to "honestly face the sadness." Those were dark days indeed; I was ill-prepared,
psychologically and theologically, to deal with the darkness and the
depth of the pain I witnessed. I was far outside the Christian bubble, and
reality bit hard.

For many people, moving across cultures, often to developing places, serves as their wake-up call. Missions becomes their trauma room,
where they see suffering and poverty and grief up close and personal.
People often move to Cambodia bright-eyed and in love, and then after a
few months, or perhaps a year, the accumulation of the poverty and the
corruption and the darkness forces them to "honestly face the sadness."

Have you seen that happen? Of course, the sadness was present in
their affluent passport countries too, but money and familiarity have

1. Crabb, *Inside Out*, 212.

a way of disguising and hiding pain, like gold lacquer on cardboard. But when the suffering is really seen, honestly, it does what Martin Luther wrote about nearly 500 years ago; it "threatens to undo us."[2] Of course, it doesn't *have* to undo us, but it certainly threatens.

## The Gift of Grief

> "[W]hen we are able to maintain the fiction that life is tolerable at worst, and quite satisfying at best, we sacrifice an appreciation for the two center points of our faith: the Cross of Christ and his coming. The Cross becomes the means by which God delivers us from something not really too terrible, and the coming is reduced to an opportunity for a merely improved quality of life."[3]

In other words, when we blind ourselves to grief and the real sadness of the world, we risk turning the glorious reality of eternity into a nice upgrade instead of the radical salvation of the universe and the epic righting of all wrongs that it certainly is.

Now, I hate grief. I really do. I don't like being sad and I don't particularly like listening to peoples' sad stories. But for whatever reason, God has brought me to a place where I now regularly get e-mails from people that say, "Hey, I was told that you were the guy to talk to about my recent traumatic loss." Awesome.

I think it's because I don't flee the feelings, and I don't flee the feelings because I know that God can do amazing, restorative, centering, maturing, focusing, healing work *through* them. Not after the feelings, not around the feelings, but *through* them.

I am absolutely convinced that grief is a gift that the church needs to learn to deal with. Grief has the potential to refocus us on the eternal, if we'll let it. Grief and loss guard us against the temptation to degrade heaven into a distant and entirely nonapplicable theory, instead of the life-altering reality that it is.

~~~~~~~~~~

"When hints of sadness creep into our soul, we must not flee into happy or distracting thoughts. Pondering sadness until it becomes overwhelming

2. Luther, "A Mighty Fortress Is Our God," in Howard, *Songs of Faith and Praise,* Hymn #10.

3. Crabb, *Inside Out,* 212.

can lead us to a deep change in the direction of our being from self-preservation to grateful worship."[4]

~~~~~~~~~~

Worshipful grief is potent, with eyes wide open to the realities of life. It's also evangelistic.

Worshipful grief communicates to those outside the church that we're not morons whose faith completely disconnects us from reality. We are, in fact, in tune with the way things are precisely *because* of our faith. And because of our faith, we can grieve with hope, something that secular philosophy and humanism simply cannot provide.

## What Happened in Portland

Portland is a beautiful city in the Pacific Northwest of the United States. It's also where my sister lives, so last year I left a very hot, dirty, and brown Phnom Penh and landed in a cool, beautiful, and green Portland. I bought blueberries by the gallon and ate them by the handful. And I was angry.

Why do these people get to live here? In this place that's so safe and gorgeous? Why do they get berries and public services and English? And why are they all in shape and appear to have just disembarked from a travel magazine? (To be clear, I realize that not all of Portland fits this image, but my sister lives in a suburb, and yeah, it pretty much all fits.)

There's a public park close to her house, and they've got a fully shaded state-of-the-art playground with grass and towering pine trees. The whole place smells like a pine forest because the whole place *is* a pine forest. And did I mention it was also just a small city park?

Anyways, there was a trail around the lake and I of course took it. I passed picnics and happy people on stand-up paddle boards. I passed ducks and geese, and I swear they'd all read the book *How to Pose for a Postcard*. I heard laughing kids. And I was angry.

And then I got to a waterfall, clear and sharp, loudly mocking me with its falling waters. It was astoundingly beautiful and embarrassingly infuriating. And so I cried. I cried to myself and I cried to God.

I mourned the loss. I grieved the fact that I lived in a concrete box with bars on the windows and karaoke and neighborhood cats that liked to work out their differences very loudly and very after-hours. I did what

4. Crabb, *Inside Out*, 213.

I counsel people to do: I named the losses, I felt the losses, and I talked with God.

And in one of those rare occurrences when I sense God speaking back to me, I felt God say, "Yes, you have lost something. Yes, you have given up some stuff. But what I have asked you to sacrifice I have not asked you to sacrifice forever. I have asked you to postpone."

Now I was listening.

"I will bring you back here, on the New Earth, in eternity, and all that is good and lovely and beautiful about this you will experience again."

And then I cried some more, but different tears. Sweeter tears.

His words, had they been preached to me by a hard-nosed theologian, would have grated and rubbed raw. But on that day, in a city park somewhere north of Portland, his words were like falling water, cooling and calming and stirring deep peace within me.

And his words still resonate. His words reminded me of truth my heart desperately needed—all is not lost. There will be a resurrection and the restoration of all things.

## Why it's a Gift

This oxygenating reminder, this reminder of eternity, did not happen in spite of my grief; it happened *because* of it. It didn't come through an attempt to erase grief or diminish loss. It came through mourning and boldly naming the loss.

And although I do not like it and I wish it weren't so, grief is often the mechanism for drawing our hearts and souls back to God and the eternal intimacy he's promised.

## An Unforced Gift

Don't miss out on the focusing ability of grief. It is a gift. But remember, like most gifts, this gift is best received without force. These are not truths to preach *at* someone in pain.

There are times for nonpreaching, when grief bleeds and souls mourn. For these times, I still just recommend a gentle hug, quiet presence, and the often ungiven gift of silence.

Preach heaven to the church. Preach hope to the church. But watch your timing. Preaching to someone in pain is an awfully cheap and cowardly substitute for simple incarnation.

## The Gift of Music

Music can give voice to the soul, especially in the areas of grief and eternity. In fact, mourners and poets often instinctively connect feelings of grief with longings for heaven. One researcher, in his essay entitled "Recovering the Theology of the Negro Spirituals," showed the connection: "The eschatology of the spirituals emphasized heaven. Roughly forty percent of the compiled spirituals dealt with heaven as a primary theme."[5]

Likewise, for me, music is often a balm and lifeline. Here are a few songs about heaven that have ministered to me in my grief.

- "Heaven Song," by Phil Wickham
- "Your Arrival," by Phil Wickham
- "In Your City," by Phil Wickham

~~~~~~~~~~

*"We are citizens of heaven, where the Lord Jesus Christ lives. And we are eagerly waiting for him to return as our Savior" (Phil 3:20).*

*"I heard a loud shout from the throne, saying, 'Look, God's home is now among his people! He will live with them, and they will be his people. God himself will be with them. He will wipe every tear from their eyes, and there will be no more death or sorrow or crying or pain. All these things are gone forever.' And the one sitting on the throne said, 'Look, I am making everything new!' And then he said to me, 'Write this down, for what I tell you is trustworthy and true'" (Rev 21:3–5).*

*"My Father's house has many rooms; if that were not so, would I have told you that I am going there to prepare a place for you? And if I go and prepare a place for you, I will come back and take you to be with me that you also may be where I am" (John 14:2–3 NIV).*

5. Faithful, "Recovering the Theology," 6.

# Naming the Missing Pieces of Our Souls

## BY ELIZABETH

I GREW UP IN a faith tradition that sang a cappella. Worship could arise in any place and any time: our voices were all we needed. We didn't need advance planning. We didn't even need songbooks, for the words were written on our hearts.

The songs of my childhood held such depth and resonance. There were four-part harmonies and four-part songs, echoes and counter melodies, descants and rounds. There were the "Greatest Commands" and the "Magnificat." There was "Lord, Be There" and "Someday."

There was singing in the stairwell after Sunday night church, where the acoustics were best. There was singing in the dirt at summer camp, amongst the bugs and under a canopy of stars.

No one could sing "On Zion's Glorious Summit Stood" or "O Lord, Our Lord, How Excellent Thy Name," like the Kansas camp counselors of my youth. And no one could sing the seven-fold amen of "The Lord Bless You and Keep You" like the Arkansas camp counselors I later worked with.

The singing of my childhood was like none other. These days, however, I worship with an interdenominational fellowship that uses instruments. (And I love it.) But somehow when I'm there, the a cappella tradition of my past seems distant indeed. That is, until some friends invited us to share a meal with them this past spring.

As part of their family tradition, they sing the "Doxology" before they eat. (They have an a cappella heritage in their past too, though it's different from mine.) My husband and I joined in, adding extra parts. Upon hearing the beloved four-part harmony of my youth, I had a sudden longing to return to the days of old. To the days of unspeakably beautiful singing, to the days when God seemed so close and touchable, to the days of simple faith and abounding joy.

I yearned for those days. I longed to join my voice with others as we sang "Pierce My Ear" and "Unto Thee O Lord." I wanted to hear the tight harmonies and the moving parts of "Holy, Holy, Holy" and "It Is Well." I hungered for a time in my life when singing to God was all that really seemed to matter.

The desire I felt was so strong it almost knocked me over. It stayed with me all that week and on into the next. For a while it went with me everywhere I went. I missed the campy a cappella music of my past so much that it hurt.

Sadly, I can't go back to those places and those times. For one thing, I live in Asia and no longer attend the camps of my childhood. And for another, the singing of my religious heritage isn't what it used to be. It's incorporated more mainstream songs and morphed into something more modern. In the process, it's lost some of the magic of its four-part harmonic past.

Which means all I'm really left with is a vague happiness at the thought of those memories and an ache for what once was. There's actually a name for this feeling, but you can't find it in the English language. Rather, it's the Portuguese word *saudade*, which, according to Wikipedia, "describes a deep emotional state of nostalgic or profound melancholic longing for an absent something or someone that one loves."[1]

One of the better-known descriptions of *saudade* comes from Aubrey F. G. Bell's book *In Portugal*, where he explains it as "a vague and constant desire for something that does not and probably cannot exist, for something other than the present, a turning towards the past or towards the future; not an active discontent or poignant sadness but an indolent dreaming wistfulness."[2]

This is what *saudade* does: it links us to the past and infuses us with longing for the future. What we're really longing for when we long for the innocence of our past is the fulfillment of our final future. What we're really aching for when we ache for some long-lost era is the eternal not-yet when Eden will be restored and all will be redeemed.

*Saudade* can give us a proper longing for a better country, a true-north ache for our real home. *Saudade* can root us in the purity of our

---

1. "Saudade," Wikipedia.
2. Bell, *In Portugal*, in Emmons and Lewis, *Researching the Song*, 402.

past, yes, but more importantly, it can point us to the future of our heavenly home.

So my question for you today is, what do you long for? How have you experienced *saudade* in your life? What is it that you can't get back, can't seem to recreate? What traditions from your past do you miss intolerably while living overseas? How do you cope with the missing pieces of your soul?

# Two Words for the One Who's Far from Home

## BY *ELIZABETH*

I FOUND A NEW word on the Facebook profile of a writer, and it's the best new word I've heard in a long time.[1] It's called *fernweh,* and it's a German word that means "a longing for faraway places."

The feeler of *fernweh* carries a desire—whether met or unmet—to travel to distant countries, to visit new places, and to have new experiences. Its nearest English equivalent might be the idea of wanderlust. When transliterated, *fernweh* means "farsickness," in much the same way that *heimweh* means "homesickness."

*Fernweh* and *heimweh:* these sister words draw me in. Ever since I found them, I cannot get them out of my head, for I live in a faraway place. At least, it's far away from the Europe and North America in which I grew up. It *was* far away, but now it's near. I find now that the faraway place has become home, and home has become the faraway place.

The sense of home I get when I see a palm tree is so deep that I think the Maker must have inscribed it on my heart when he made me. For me there is both longing and fulfillment in a palm tree.

I travel through the city in a *tuk tuk* (open carriage), and I pass by a *wat* (temple). This Asian architecture seems so familiar now and not far away at all. I crave these sights. I want to see them my whole life.

The place I live is both far and near, and somehow I have *fernweh* and *heimweh* all at once. But how can something be both foreign and familiar at the same time? It is this way for all of us global nomads, I suppose.

---

1. Many thanks to Amy Peterson, whose Facebook post inspired this chapter.

And perhaps, in the kingdom of God, *fernweh* and *heimweh* are really the same longing. Whether we ache for something new, or whether we ache for something known, all our aches point us to God.

All our longings—even the unholy ones—are for the true water that quenches our thirst and the true bread that satisfies our hunger.

So when I desire this place, it's really God I'm longing for. And when I desire another place, it's God I long for there, too.

Jesus, the One who formed us from the dust and breathed the breath of life into us, knows this about us. That's the reason that, right before he dies, he tells his disciples to "Make yourselves at home in my love" (John 15:9 MSG).

So whether I am at home, or whether I am longing for home, what I really want and what I really need is my true home in Christ. And when I feel *fernweh*, or when I feel *heimweh*, can I find in these yearnings the God who created them in the first place?

Can I truly find my home in his love?

# Worthless

## BY *JONATHAN*

I FEEL WORTHLESS.

The feeling rises and crests like an impending wave barreling toward the surface of my heart. And with each wave of worthlessness comes an intense weariness of soul, a near drowning.

The breakers seem to rise from nowhere. I can't predict them, and that makes me mad. They're not tied to whether my work or ministry is going well or faltering. They don't seem to be related to whether or not folks approve of (or agree with) me. They just come and break.

I wonder if I'm alone. Am I?

I don't know enough of this language. *I'll never know enough of this language.*

I don't know what I'm doing. I have fewer skills than I thought I had. I have fewer skills than they think I have. *I wonder when they'll find out.*

I haven't accomplished what I came here to do. I'll never accomplish what I came here to do. *What did I come here to do?*

This country doesn't need me. There are a lot of workers here already. *What can I do?*

My passport country doesn't need me. There are a lot of workers there already. *I have nothing to offer. I am worthless.*

And the waves of worthlessness crash. And then I crash.

Do you know the feeling? I wonder how many of us know the feeling. I wonder how many of us have drowned in this feeling.

So now, I speak to the drowning ones, those gulping for air under the waves. To you, and to myself, I say "Remember your God who descends."

"I love the Lord because he hears my voice and my prayer for mercy. Because he bends down to listen, I will pray as long as I have breath" (Ps 116:1–2).

Allow these truths to wash over your soul:

God not only hears your prayer, he hears your voice. He hears *you*, not just some list of words strung together in the form of adoration or petition or whatever. He is *near enough* to hear your voice, and *loving enough* to care.

He descends. He bends down to listen, to hear you. He's not a distant, aloof dad who requires his children to "speak up and for goodness sake enunciate." He bends down to love you. This is your God.

He is not a God hidden away in a holy place, high on a hill. He is not sulking behind a giant curtain in a temple, coldly demanding allegiance "or else." He is a God who takes that temple curtain, that holiness, and wraps it around his own flesh and blood and bones and joins you. And wonder of wonders, he wraps you up in his holiness, covering your worthlessness, calling you worthy.

Worthy of his affection.

Worthy of his love.

Even worthy of his dance.

So if you find yourself drowning in worthlessness, remember. Remember the King who descends. Remember the Father who sings. Remember that he loved you before you even accomplished breathing.

# TAKING CARE OF YOUR HEART WELL

# When Missionaries Starve

BY JONATHAN

IT'S SOMETHING THAT'S CAUSED the rise and fall of kingdoms. It's confused the most erudite of the educated and been understood by the most childlike of children.

It's been cherished and treasured by some, burned and ridiculed by others, and it's absolutely necessary to your emotional health while living and serving abroad.

It is the Word of God.

The more pastoral counseling I do with cross-cultural workers and missionaries—and the more I get to know myself—the more I believe in the power, beauty, and absolute necessity of the Word of God.

Many of us study the Bible as part of our jobs. We read it, parse it, argue about it, and teach it. But sometimes, in the middle of all of that, we forget to eat it. We end up trying to feed ourselves with yesterday's manna, and we starve. We need to return to the slow chewing of the word for our own sustenance.

We need so much more than yesterday's manna, so much more than the gorging of conferences or the regurgitations of famous teachers. We need time with God and his Word. Today.

Each bite will not be Instagrammable. Each bite will not be magnificent and earth-shattering and memorable, and that's as it should be, because sometimes you just need the calories.

Regular, non-crisis reading of the Word may seem to make zero difference in your life today or even tomorrow. But I promise you, in a year or ten or fifty, the consistent ingesting of the Word will make all the difference.

*"The unfolding of your words gives light; it gives understanding to the simple" (Ps 119:130 NIV).*

So let's remember what we already know: the Word of God is powerful, and beautiful, and necessary. And after that, let's consider a couple of cautions.

## The Word of God is Powerful

An American friend of mine recently visited North Korea as a tourist. I don't know if you read the news much, but North Korea and the United States aren't exactly buddy-buddy.

He told me he brought his Bible with him, and you know what? They let him in. They let him in with his English Bible, but they inventoried it at the border, and they made sure that he knew that when he left North Korea, that Bible better leave with him.

Why? Because they recognized what we often forget: the Word of God is powerful, and can transform nations and families and hearts. The Word of God empowers the weak and gives hope to the hopeless. And hopeful people are dangerous people.

*"For the word of God is alive and powerful. It is sharper than the sharpest two-edged sword, cutting between soul and spirit, between joint and marrow. It exposes our innermost thoughts and desires" (Heb 4:12).*

## The Word of God is Beautiful

It is beautiful because it shows us Christ. The Scriptures reveal the heart and mind of our glorious Creator. In the Scriptures, we see his character and his wisdom. And through the Scriptures, our Father reveals his plans from ages past and into eternity.

*"The grass withers and the flowers fall, but the word of our God endures forever" (Isa 40:8 NIV).*

*"Heaven and earth will pass away, but my words will never pass away" (Matt 24:35 NIV).*

The Word of God is more desirable than money and sweeter than high-fructose corn syrup. It magnifies his magnificence, redirecting and refocusing us on the Almighty.

Imagine what would happen if we consistently opened the Word and invited the Spirit of God to show us the mind of Christ and the heart of the Father. It would be amazing. It would be absolutely beautiful.

## The Word of God is Necessary

*The instructions of the Lord are perfect, reviving the soul.*
*The decrees of the Lord are trustworthy, making wise the simple.*
*The commandments of the Lord are right, bringing joy to the heart.*
*The commands of the Lord are clear, giving insight for living.*
*(Ps 19:7–8)*

Too often, when we want revival or wisdom or joy or insight, we don't look to the Scriptures. In fact, the Word is typically the last place we look. If we're looking for wisdom or insight, we're likely to Google something. If we're looking for refreshment or joy, we're likely to ogle something. (And I'm not just talking about porn; there are many, many other things we stare long at, believing that "that thing would solve my problems or at least make me feel a bit better.")

But there is a better way, and Jesus knew it. Jesus spent a lot of time in the Hebrew Scriptures, directly quoting from every book in the Pentateuch, and many others besides.

In what seems to me to be a fascinating move for the Son of God, Jesus refused to solely rely on a direct connection with the Father for fresh revelation. Particularly during the hard times, Jesus relied on the Scriptures. This is sobering.

You know the story, Jesus is tempted three times, and three times he responds, "It is written."

*"It is written: 'Man shall not live on bread alone, but on every word that comes from the mouth of God'" (Matt 4:4 NIV).*

## The Word is Necessary Because God Loves to Echo Himself

Have you ever heard people use the God Card? I think it happens a lot in our line of work. Folks say, "Oh, God told me to do this," or "God wants me to do that."

Sometimes, God really does lead people (amen!) and speak to people (praise God!), and sometimes people hear him wrong. In my pastoral counseling practice, I often lead people in listening and healing prayer, where we bring issues before God and invite him to speak truth and healing to their specific situation. But how can we be sure it's God?

It's a valid question and it's one we must ask. I answer my clients by telling them that we're listening for the echo. We're asking, "Where has God said this before?"

Here's my simple two-part test in determining whether or not God has spoken:

1. Is it biblical?

2. Is the fruit good?

If there is biblical support for what the person thinks God just said, and if the fruit in their life (more peace, a desire to forgive, increased love, repentance, etc.) is good, then I'm okay with saying they heard from God.

But before we can answer the question, "Is it biblical?" we've got to spend some time in the Scriptures. Before we can say, "Yeah, this sounds like God," we need to hear regularly what God sounds like.

## CAUTION: Two Things to Watch Out for

Some folks read the Scriptures without the Holy Spirit. Others want a relationship with the Holy Spirit but without the Scriptures. Both are dangerous.

I grew up in a tradition that was all about the Word. We taught it and knew it and loved it, but I don't think I ever heard anyone mention the Holy Spirit. That's an absolute travesty! On the flip side, I come across folks who are desperate for a prophetic word from God, passed down through a prophet or gifted teacher. They're hungry to hear from God, but they're not opening their Bibles. That too is terribly sad. So can I just say this? If you're hungry for a special word from the Lord, but you're not spending much time in the Word, you're not as hungry as you think you are.

*"Like newborn babies [you should] long for the pure milk of the word, so that by it you may be nurtured and grow in respect to salvation."*
(1 Pet 2:2 AMP)

## CONCLUSION

The Scriptures teach us what God sounds like. They help us to hear his voice, see his hands, taste his wine. The Scriptures show us his character as warrior and Lamb. The Scriptures, while certainly not a fourth member of the Trinity, help us to know and love and serve the God who is three in one.

May we be a people who praise God for the gift of the Scriptures. May we be a people who view the words of the King with deep reverence and overwhelming joy. May we be a people, a diaspora even, who love to come home and sit together in the Father's house, under the Word of God, in the presence of the Holy Spirit, through the blood of the Son.

# Go to the Small Places

*BY JONATHAN*

THERE ARE THREE PLACES that make me feel very small.

1. Standing at the edge of the sea, watching the never-ending motion as water is pulled by the unseen and unrelenting forces of gravity and wind and planetary motion.

2. Standing at the foot of a mountain, pondering the historical shifting and breaking that pushed stone into sky.

3. Sitting with a client during pastoral counseling, listening as they delve into the deepest parts, the pains and hurts that few see.

In the small places, I feel inferior and inadequate, unable to change much or make an impact. Do you have those places? Truth be told, those feelings of "smallness" are why I love the sea and mountains; that's why I seek them out. But I don't typically welcome those feelings on the job, with clients. Maybe I should.

Maybe we all need to go to the small places on purpose.

Sometimes we do long for the small places, for a reminder about our place in things, for context. But sometimes the small places break in upon us uninvited: a diagnosis, an accident, a betrayal, a terror attack.

The small places cause us to remember reality, whether we like it or not. They are sobering splashes of cold water. When we overdose on our own importance or the magnitude of evil in the world, the small places are the antidote. Narcan for the soul. Or at least they can be.

Lately, God has been asking me to go to the small places and to remember who he is. It's fairly easy to do that by sea and stone, but I have to work at remembering him in the other places.

But I will go to the small places. I will embrace my smallness and remember the One who makes mountains skip like a calf. The One whose voice is powerful and majestic, splintering cedars and twisting oaks. The One whose voice thunders over the very depths of the sea.

I will go to the small places.

I will stand and be small and point upward.

I will go to the places where my ego and abilities are rightly overwhelmed.

I will go where my ambition slams up against the reality of my inadequacies.

For it is there that I remember: *I am not God.*

And in the small places, I will shout the only thing that makes sense: GLORY! Whether by the edge of seas or mountains, or in the presence of the wounded, I will remember him. I will remember my place in the scheme of things, refusing to bow to the news or nature or narcissism. I will remember my place before the throne of God, and I will join the ongoing chorus: "In his temple everyone shouts, 'Glory'" (Ps 29:9)!

~~~~~~~~~~

What is your small place? Where do you feel inadequate and over-whelmed? Language school? Your ministry job? Reading international news? In your role as a parent?

Is God asking you to go to the small places? To remember to say the only thing we can say in such places? Glory! What would change if, in those very places, we looked up?

Now, sometimes we say "Glory!" and we're all jumpy thumpy happy clappy. Other times not so much. Sometimes we pause and remember and say "Glory!" through tears and valleys. Sometimes we say "Glory!" through protest, arguing with God.

We must remember our calling. Our invitation, really.

For we have been invited to enjoy God forever and ever. We have been invited to look at the world differently. Yes there's pain, and yes there's political turmoil, and yes there's suffering on a massive scale. That is all true.

And there is God.

And yes, he has called us to respond to the pain around us with love and compassion, and with cries of justice for the poor and oppressed.

But in order to do it, in order to maintain a Christlike posture toward the people around us, we must visit the small places. And there, aware of our size and his, we must say, over and over and over again: "Glory be to God the Father, God the Son, and God the Holy Spirit. As it was in the beginning, so it is now and so it shall ever be, world without end. Alleluia. Amen."

# Jesus Loves Me This I Sometimes Know

*BY ELIZABETH*

I USED TO THINK trusting God meant trusting him for the circumstances of my life. I used to think it meant trusting God for my future. But this past year God has completely overhauled my understanding of trust.

I'm married to a man who has all the gifts. Seriously. You name it, he's got it. And as he and his gifts grew more public these past few years, I began to believe nobody valued my gifts or even noticed them. Nobody saw me, I told myself; they only saw him. I convinced myself the world didn't want anything I had to offer; they only wanted what he had to offer.

I felt myself disappearing, fading into nothingness. Very soon, I told myself, I would be invisible. Am I important? Do I matter? Does anybody see me, truly see me? In agony I flung these questions into the cosmos, only to have them answered time and again with a resounding NO! No, you're not seen. No, you don't matter. No, you're not important.

I was certain the problem was my marriage. If only I weren't married to such a massively talented man, I wouldn't feel this way. If only he would stop shining, I would feel better about myself. I accused him of erasing me and told him I wanted to die. We kept repeating the same irrational conversations.

Then one Sunday morning I awoke with the sudden realization that the bitterness I held toward my husband was actually directed at God. None of this was my husband's fault—it was God's. He was the One who hadn't given me the desirable gifts. He was the One who was withholding from me. This was no longer about my marriage: it was about my trust in God's goodness.

Why does the giver of gifts seem to pick favorites? Why are some people more highly favored? If God loves us all equally, why are his blessings so unequal? Since (by my reckoning) God hadn't given me the good gifts, I concluded that he must not love me.

That sounds ridiculous, I know. Learning that Jesus loves us is one of the first things we do in Sunday school. When we belt out "Jesus loves me, this I know, for the Bible tells me so," we're supposed to believe it. Except here I was, and I didn't believe it.

I prayed a half-hearted prayer: "God, please, meet me at church today." I'm not even sure I meant it. Then at church the speaker began talking about how God doesn't pick favorites. From my seat I remember hearing, "He doesn't like Ernie more than Ann." I looked up in astonishment and told God, "I think You just answered my prayer."

God had spoken to my mind that morning, but my heart still had its doubts. My solution was to try grunting my way into belief. I thought if I just tried hard enough, I could force myself to believe God's love for me. But head knowledge has a hard time filtering down into heart knowledge, and I was groping in the dark.

A few months later I found myself in a counseling office to debrief my first few years overseas. Conversation soon came to a standstill. I was stuck. The counselor wisely handed me some colored pencils and asked me to draw. I'm an abysmal artist, but I did as she asked: I drew a purple mountain's majesty, a part of creation that draws me closer to God.

The counselor asked me what that mountain might say to me. The first words that came to me were: "Just Sit." Then she asked what else that mountain might say to me, and the word "Believe" immediately flooded my soul.

"Believe what?" she asked. Through tears, I croaked, "Believe that God loves me as much as he loves my husband."

And with that one word from God, months of striving to grasp his unconditional, all-surpassing, nonpartisan love evaporated. God used a poor colored-pencil sketch to short-circuit my rational brain and reach inside my heart. It was a breakthrough of belief that took me deeper into the love of God than I ever dreamed I'd go.

Shortly after my time with the counselor, I encountered 1 John 4:16 in the New International Version: "And so we know and rely on the love God has for us." I stopped cold. For me, knowing God's love came first, and relying on it came afterwards. How could this verse so perfectly sum up my experience of God's love when it had been written some 1,900 years earlier?

I loved this verse so much I looked it up in other versions. The English Standard Version reads, "And so we have come to know and to believe the love God has for us." When I looked it up in the Greek, I discovered that "know" implies a personal experience, and "believe" means to trust. First John 4:16 is most definitely my story. First I had a personal experience of God's love, and now I find I can trust it.

My Brute Force Method had failed. Trying to trust had failed. It was only when I let go and stopped striving that I could actually trust his love for me. So maybe trust is more of a release than a grip. Maybe it's more of an invitation than an instruction. Maybe radical trust in God isn't about my circumstances, but about his love.

Psalm 13:5 declares, "I trust in Your unfailing love." Trust in his unfailing love is life to me now. I no longer believe the lies that tell me my husband is more valuable than I am. I know I'm loved, and I no longer need to slice through my husband's heart with my perfectly practiced, precision-cut lies. The most broken part of our marriage has been made whole. I never thought I'd be able to proclaim that.

I am daily living Paul's prayer in Ephesians 3:17–19. I'm experiencing the love of Christ, and he is filling my life with his love. I'm trusting in him, and he's making his home in my heart. I feel my roots growing down deep into God's love, and I trust its width, length, height, and depth like never before.

This is the cry of my heart for you today. I pray along with Paul, that "Christ will make his home in your hearts as you trust in Him. Your roots will grow down into God's love and keep you strong. And may you have the power to understand, as all God's people should, how wide, how long, how high, and how deep his love is. May you experience the love of Christ, though it is too great to understand fully. Then you will be made complete with all the fullness of life and power that comes from God" (Eph 3: 17–19 NLT).

~~~~~~~~~~

Further resources that helped me know and rely on the love God has for me:

The life and ministry of Rich Mullins, especially his song "The Love of God."

Anything by Brennan Manning, especially *Reflections for Ragamuffins.*

# Learn Your Triangle: A Tool for Discipleship (for You and Others)

*By Jonathan*

Sometimes you stumble across a tool that you didn't know you needed, but as it turns out, you really do. (Like pretty much everything Steve Jobs ever created.)

I've creatively titled this tool "The Shapes Diagram," and I use it with ninety percent of my pastoral counseling clients because it takes complex ideas (like emotions and inner healing) and makes them a bit more concrete.[1] As you continue this journey of cross-cultural living and serving, I think it could help you too.

This diagram basically designed itself as I was trying to communicate some core emotional health ideas to Cambodians in Khmer. It wasn't that my clients were dumb, it was that I lacked enough language skill to accurately describe these ideas. So I did what any former youth pastor would do, I started scribbling. This is what I came up with:

---

1. You can view a video walkthrough on our website. Just search "trotters41" and "shapes diagram."

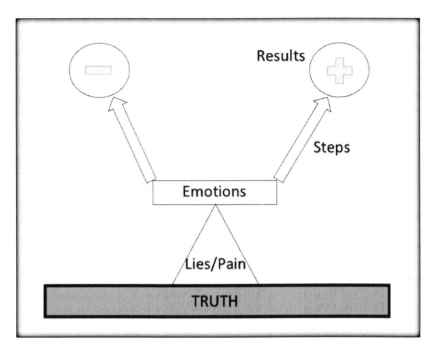

Basically, we all have emotions, and most people end up seeing me because they're experiencing some emotions they don't like. In other words, most people don't come in happy (except the premarital clients, they *do* come in happy, and usually they leave happy too, but that's not a given).

We start in the middle rectangle. For many, the rectangle (emotions) includes anger or sadness or anxiety. Now, many pastors hear the story that led to the unwanted emotions and immediately start looking at what *steps* the person needs to take (or avoid) in order to get to the positive result (and avoid the negative one).

For example, someone might tell the really sad person, "Exercise, read your Bible more, pray!" They might continue, "Don't drink when you're sad, don't do drugs, don't watch *Gilmore Girls*. Those would be steps in the wrong direction and would lead to a negative result."

Here's the thing: that might all be good advice, and maybe people need to hear it, but pretty much every depressed person I've ever talked to already *knows* those things. What I've come to believe (and experience with my clients) is that for the most part, all of that top part (the emotion box, the steps, and the results) is future-oriented. That is, the top half forces the client to ask, "What will I do now?" And that's certainly a very valid question.

The thing is, that top half of the diagram (emotions plus steps plus results), often balances precariously on the triangle that consists of emotional pain and lies from the past.

Often, past painful events in the client's life have caused him or her to believe, deep down in their core, lies. Lies like "I'm worthless," "I'm unlovable," and "I'm broken beyond repair."

It takes a lot of energy to keep everything steady on the tip of that triangle, but people try and they try and they try. They never deal with the emotional pain and the lies. We do them a tremendous disservice if all we do is give them steps.

I want to ask the question, "What's in the triangle? What's the pain that this is all balancing on?" In practice, about half of my clients see this diagram and immediately say, "Oh, I know what's in that triangle!" They then go on to list the traumatic event or the emotional trauma and the lies it planted. The other half typically says, "Well, I think this is probably true, but I'm not sure what's in there." That's fine too, and so with their permission, we just continue the conversation.

If we can help a client to see what's in the triangle and label it and maybe find the lies, then we can encourage them to invite Jesus into that specific place for healing. We can invite the Truth in and he can counter the lies and heal the emotional pain. The triangle can be erased, and it's not nearly as mystical as it sounds.

Then, with the triangle gone, the client's emotions are simply resting on the Truth (Jesus). The emotions are still there, because the client is still a human, but the whole thing is much more stable.

Now some people try to bypass the triangle and jump straight to the Truth. But that's not as effective. In fact, it's just terrible. You can't skip the triangle and jump straight to Jesus. You want to meet Jesus *in* the triangle. And he wants to meet you (and your clients) there too.

If you jump over the triangle (the pain/lies) you also jump over the healing.

I ask people to imagine that someone's drowning in the middle of the Mekong. What if I see them drowning and I ride my boat over to them and I give them five gallons of good, clean water. Do they need that water?

Well, sort of. I mean, people need clean water to drink. And the Mekong in Phnom Penh, Cambodia is filthy. But is it helpful to them?

No. It's also not very kind. When someone's drowning, I don't want to just throw clean water at them, I want to actually help them.

We do that to folks who are depressed or anxious or experiencing a lot of difficult emotions. We give them good clean "water" of Truth and throw a Bible verse at them and stuff. The verses are true and good, but the timing is way off. Help the person *not* drown—that's what the church has to get better at doing, not just throwing water bottles to drowning/depressed people and telling ourselves we were helpful.

## Conclusion

When your emotions start teeter-tottering—and they will—ask if there is a triangle worth considering. Why does your teammate's behavior trigger you *like that?* Why does this event trip you up more than the next person? Maybe it's nothing, but maybe there are past pains, past lies. If there are, Jesus would love to help you identify what's in the triangle and then meet you right there in it.

~~~~~~~~~~

Caveat: I'm all for medication if it's necessary, and I would *never* tell someone who's depressed to stop their meds or go off their meds. I'm talking about a holistic approach here. So maybe someone's on meds, fine—they should still be looking at what might be in the triangle. Maybe there's nothing, but maybe there's something. Maybe it really is just a chemical imbalance that needs intervention. I believe that happens. But I also think exploring past painful events and asking around for deep-seated lies can expose someone to healing and greater self-awareness.

# Distractions and the Voice of Jesus

BY *ELIZABETH*

FOLLOW ME.

Jesus whispered these words to me a few months ago. I was in church. It felt like he was right there in front of me, pointing his finger at me and saying, "Elizabeth Trotter? Yes, you. I want you to follow Me. You—just you—follow Me."

Rarely does Scripture come to me fast, strong, and seemingly out of nowhere like this. I knew this phrase came from John 21, so I opened up my Bible and read it. I hadn't been reading this story lately, and it wasn't a story that had ever meant much to me before. So I knew I needed to pay attention to this message from God.

Over the next few weeks, I read the story and reread it and then read it some more, because the truth was, I *was* distracted, and I desperately needed to hear its message.

One morning after the resurrection, Jesus and his disciples are by the sea, eating bread and fish. Jesus starts talking to Peter and asks, "Do you love me?" Peter answers, "Yes, Lord, you know I love you." Jesus tells him, "Then feed my sheep."

A second time Jesus asks Peter, "Do you love me?" A second time Peter answers, "Yes Lord, you know I love you." And a second time Jesus tells him, "Then feed my sheep."

Yet again Jesus asks Peter, "Do you love me?" Peter's feelings were hurt, and he answered again, "Yes Lord, you know I love you. And again Jesus tells him, "Then feed my sheep."

Jesus then tells Peter what kind of death he is doing to die. Peter turns to look behind him and sees John. Peter then asks Jesus, "What about him, Lord?" Jesus replies, "If I want him to remain alive until I return, what's that to you? As for you—follow me."[1]

I get distracted by so many things. I get distracted by feeling sorry for myself. I tell myself I'm such a terrible missionary because I don't speak the language very well. I tell myself I don't measure up and I'll never measure up, that I will never be good enough or worthy enough, and that *everybody is rejecting me.*

I get distracted by jealousy. I'll see someone else who's been given amazing ministry opportunities, and I wish I had those opportunities. Why can't that be me, God? Why can't you let me do that? Why does she get to do that when You *know* I want to do it? Whether it's teaching math and chemistry, or attending births as a doula, I can get distracted by what I *don't* get to do instead of finding joy in what God *has* assigned me to do.

But the biggest distraction for me, by far, is controversies within the American church. Since I've moved overseas, I've kept up on hot-button issues in the United States. I tell myself I do this so that "I'm not out of the loop when I return," but I'm not just informing myself when I read controversial blogs; I become emotionally embroiled in them.

I read what all the online voices are saying, and I become very worried over the direction of the church. I have intense intellectual and emotional reactions to inflammatory blog posts. I formulate arguments in my head to combat them. ABC is right, and here's why; XYZ is wrong, and here's why. Surely that's helpful, right?

Wrong. It doesn't help. All it does is agitate and depress me. It distracts me from doing what God has already clearly told me I need to be doing with my time. Which means I'm wasting a lot of the time he has given me. It means I'm squandering his gifts.

Distractions, distractions, distractions. Not a single distraction is helpful for ministry, or my own personal spiritual life. Each distraction keeps me from doing what God has called me to do in this season of my life. When I get distracted by feelings of jealousy or inadequacy, or by worry over the future of the church, I don't have the time or energy to do any of the things he *has* called me to do. I cannot fulfill his purposes in my life if I spend all my time reading other people's angry words.

The truth is, it's not my job to guide the global church. That's the job of Jesus, and he can handle it. Hearing from God and writing out of my own relationship with him does not in any way require that I be

---

1. My paraphrase. See John 21 of the NLT.

up-to-date on church controversies. It just doesn't. I can follow him without regard to what he is doing in anyone else's life but my own. The truth is, I don't have to know about religious debates in order to love my husband and children well, and to love women and teen girls well.

The truth is, I can do what God is calling me to do, right now, and I can be joyful in it, instead of being jealous. The truth is, I will never measure up as a "perfect" missionary or a ministry wife, because *no one measures up*—and that is actually the good news about Jesus's sacrifice.

But when I'm distracted by any of these things, I'm not paying attention to God. When I'm distracted by these things, I don't notice the person right in front of me. And I won't be able to love them if I can't *see them*. If I allow myself to be distracted, I won't be able to follow the greatest commands to love God and people.

The day Jesus reminded me to follow him only, I had been sitting in church, emotionally twisted over yet another American church issue. And I suddenly felt he was saying to me, "You—follow Me. Stop turning your head to look at other people. Look at Me. Regardless of what anyone else around you is doing, I want you to follow Me." In that moment, I realized I had been wasting my life on distractions. I wasn't following; I was worrying.

Hearing the word of God on this issue made me reevaluate my life. I can't waste my time reading controversial blogs; instead, I must protect my time by staying away from online debates. I must say "no" to them— and I'm learning to. Refusing to read certain kinds of blogs releases me from the internal pressure to "save the American church."

I must simply focus on what I can do, today, to serve God and others. I remind myself of Jesus' words quite often. If I want to follow Jesus, then I, along with Peter, can't look around at other people. I have to look at Jesus. I have to follow him alone.

# Please Stop Running

BY *JONATHAN*

IN MY FORMER LIFE (and I mean that in a totally non-Buddhist way), I worked as a trauma nurse at an inner-city emergency department in the States. One of the first rules new hires had to learn in the ER was that No. One. Runs. Even if someone just got shot or stabbed or is actively dying, no one runs. Even if you have to go to the bathroom really bad, no one runs.

Even in the middle of taking care of a trauma victim, it was better to be calm and methodical than stressed out and in a hurry. So many times I heard a senior physician or nurse tell the newbie, "Slow down. Breath. Think."

The slowness of the attending physician didn't mean she cared less about the patient. It didn't mean she was lazy. It didn't mean she was worn out. It meant she was experienced.

## Oh, How We Run

And then I joined the "overseas worker club" and I realized, *we're all running*. Oh, how we run. We run to get here. We run to learn language. We run to get stats and photos that we can e-mail back to our senders. And when we return to our passport countries for a furlough, we run even faster! So much of overseas work seems to involve running and running and trying and striving.

There's so much to do! There's so much need! We need more money! We need more people! People are dying! If we don't help, no one will! Go! Go! *Now*! Hurry up! Time's short!

It's exhausting. Yeah, we're running, but we're also tired. So, can I invite you to slow down for a second? Could we just push pause for a second and invite the Prince of Peace to teach us what it might look like to live in peace, even in the ER? Even on the field?

Perhaps this is simplistic, but I really believe that overseas workers would last longer and be healthier if we could learn a bit about rest. After all, God doesn't give extra credit to workaholics.

In God's economy, obedience isn't measured by how much work gets done; it's measured by whether the work we did was the work God asked us to do. Sometimes, it's simply measured by a cup of cold water, lovingly given.

Jesus doesn't call us to work in his fishers-of-men-factory until we drop dead from exhaustion. He is not like that.

## Jesus, Our Example

Jesus, the guy who could have died from exhaustion long before he died on the cross, is our teacher. He provides a wonderful example of rest. After all, he had a pretty important job to do, a high calling if ever there was one, and only twenty-four hours in a day, just like us.

He spent lots of time with people, loving, serving, healing, confronting, and teaching. He spent lots of time coaching and traveling and discipling.

But he found rest in solitude. Often. He found rest in the presence of his Father, on a mountain, away from demanding crowds and disbelieving disciples. He needed those times of refreshment; he needed rest physically, and I believe he needed this regular rest spiritually. So do we.

Jesus perfectly balanced exterior, people-focused ministry with deep rest. Jesus rested in the peace, security, love and acceptance of his Father, and then turned around and loved people like crazy.

May we do the same. May our time with the Father, resting in his presence, drive us to love people. And after a time of loving and serving people, may we take our bone-weary souls back up the mountain to rest with our Father.

Rest is not a bad word.

Rest is not a waste of time.

Rest is holy, and commanded.

Rest forces me to admit my humanity.

Rest reminds me to agree, once again, that he's God and I'm not.

## Not All the Same

I grew up thinking that the only correct way to rest was by spending time reading the Bible and praying. Of course, those disciplines are healthy and necessary, but they're not everything. Some of us have souls that resonate with music, and the rhythm and poetry of a song can transport us into the presence of majesty. If that's you, then you may need to invest in some good headphones and a robust iTunes account.

Some of us require the deep colors of open space, or ocean. If that's you, you may need to carve out time in your schedule, as a friend of mine has, to escape the concrete jungle and visit a national park. (If you live in the jungle, you just might have to visit a city and enjoy the thing called Starbucks, or electricity.)

The way you rest will be unique, so resist the urge to compare or judge. For example, my wife reads science magazines and the periodic table of the elements and is awed by the Creator. I just get a headache (and a B minus). She's also found that a long *tuk-tuk* ride (think moto-driven carriage) through the city does wonders for her soul, giving her space to reconnect with the Father without the clamoring of four small children.

I don't know what rest looks like for you, but I know it will be something that connects you to Jesus. It will be something that stirs your soul and lifts your heart. Whatever that is for you, find it, guard it, schedule it, do it.[1]

Allow your love of people to drive you into the deep embrace of the Father, and allow his heartbeat, his thoughts, to drive you back to loving people.

We do, all of us, work in an emergency department. There is death and trauma and pain and suffering all around. And yet, in the midst of the storm, in the middle of it all, there is peace. His name is Jesus.

So if you must run, then run hard, straight to him. He'll catch you.

---

1. *Sacred Pathways,* by Gary Thomas, was an excellent resource in my journey to discover what healthy rest looked like for me. I highly recommend it.

# Margin: The Wasted Space
# We Desperately Need

## BY JONATHAN

*"Staying alive is not about how fast or how slow you go; it's about
how much margin you have."*

THAT'S WHAT A FRIEND of mine here in Cambodia says when asked
about how to *not* die while riding motorcycles in our little corner of
Asia. And since he's been riding and racing motorcycles since before I
was born, I listen.

Going slow with no margin can be more dangerous than going fast
with tons of margin. It's true with motorcycles and it's true with missions.

Your speed is not necessarily what determines your safety; your
margin does.[1] Margin takes into account all sorts of variables: How far
can you see? How much space is between you and the next vehicle (or
cow)? What are the road conditions? Is this even a road? How likely is it
that the large pig strapped to the back of that bus in front of you will stay
strapped to the back of that bus in front of you?

## Margin and Missionaries

Some of us overseas folk like to move quickly, flying through life and
ministry at the speed of *fast*. Others prefer to plod, smelling the frangipani and lingering long. And it's easy to judge.

The plodders judge the quicksters: "Oh, they're definitely going to
crash. They need to slow down or they're going to burn out." And maybe

---

1. I'm grateful for the work and writing of Dr. Richard Swenson. Particularly, I'm
thankful for his book, *Margin*.

136

that's true. But maybe they've built in rest and Sabbath and margin and maybe they'll be just fine.

The quickies judge the plodders: "Good grief! They don't do anything! When are they going to actually get off their bahookies and get to work?" And maybe that's true. Maybe they are lazy. Or, maybe they've built in rest and Sabbath and margin and maybe they'll still be around decades after the *fast* people fizzle out.

I've often thought the plodders were inherently healthier, but I realize now that if they lack margin, their speed is irrelevant and their risk of crashing (burning out) remains high. Remember, it's not about speed as much as it's about margin.

So, whether your preferred speed is warp or waddle, we need to talk about margin. How much do you have? How much relational margin? Emotional margin? Financial margin?

Margin is wasted space that we desperately need. It's space that's not accounted for and produces no obvious, easily quantifiable profit. However, margin is extremely important, creating a zone of safety, giving you time and space and emotional capital to react safely when something unexpected (on the road or in ministry) happens.

Often, we make margin a liability: "You're not busy? What in the world are you doing? Think of all the needs!" I used to believe this was primarily an issue for those of us from the West; however, I'm realizing that this is very much an issue for many of our brothers and sisters from the East too. The truth is, we all need to devote some serious attention to how we deal with margin, because the costs of living marginless are extremely high.

## Airlines and the Bourgeois

Many of us absolutely hate the idea of waste. In fact, the title of this chapter might have been an extreme turn-off for you. I'm sorry about that. I feel ya, really. Hear me out just a little bit longer, because with our strong aversion to wasted space, I believe we're kind of like airlines.

Airlines can't stand wasted space, and we all know what that feels like. Remember the last time you crossed an ocean in sardine class? It's like living without margin: you can do it for a bit, but after a while, things start to hurt that aren't supposed to hurt, and your mind begins to drift to thoughts of revolution and a bourgeois uprising against the folks sprawled out behind the curtain.

Margin, like leg room, seems unnecessary at first; but then you live without it for a while, things stiffen up, and you realize just how necessary that wasted space really is.

## Wasting Trees and Asphalt

Do you have any idea how much paper we waste with margins? Neither do I, but I think it's a lot. Think of all the trees we could save if our magazines and books and newsletters were printed from the very top of the page to the very bottom and the words bled out onto the edges. People might lose their minds, but hey, at least we wouldn't be wasting space!

Even my Kindle has a margin. Why is that? Would you read a book or a website that had words all the way to the edges of the screen? Probably not. You'd probably have some sort of visceral turn-that-thing-off reaction. I know I would. Would you live a life all the way to the edges, without margin? Many try.

In the United States, the average interstate highway has fourteen feet (4.3 meters) of wasted pavement.[2] You can't drive on the shoulder. It's just there, wasting space and asphalt. It's road margin. US interstates have enough wasted space to pave a road fourteen feet wide around the entire planet. *Twice.* That's a lot of wasted pavement.

Many of us live in countries where the main roads aren't even fourteen feet wide! So why do they do that? Why do they waste so much money on so much asphalt that's not even part of the road? To save lives, I guess. Because road margin is a great idea.

## Why We Need Wasted Space

I need wasted space. My family needs wasted space. My relationship with God needs wasted space. And I need to realize that, in reality, some of the best moments of my life happen in the wasted spaces.

The stuff I remember on my deathbed will probably be the stuff that happened in the margins: The dance I shared with my little girls in a hillside bungalow while the ocean extinguished the sun. The man talk with my brother about deep stuff that happened in a tree house in a field,

2. "Interstate Highway Standards," Wikipedia.

doing "nothing." The unrushed joy of losing a game of Stratego to a small child. Sipping coffee with my soulmate, pretending to be tourists in our own town, listening to each other's hearts.

The moment shared with God, unhurried, among trees and grass and falling water. The silent listening.

The moment of sitting still, letting one word or phrase from him sink deep and heal. And comfort. For me, those moments are life, and they almost always happen in the margin.

## When Margin Isn't

Now, if you're straight-up lazy, this chapter is not for you. Don't use this as an excuse to continue being lazy. A blank page doesn't have a margin; it's just a blank page.

Margin indicates activity, not the absence of it. And it's not called rest if it's all you do. The dowager countess, Lady Grantham, perfectly illustrates this with her pointed question: "What is a weekend?"[3]

Sabbath only occurs after work. Sabbath is God's margin. It's God's wasted space, if you will, that of course isn't wasteful at all. It's restorative. And protective. Are you keeping Sabbath? Why not?

## The Great Destroyer of Margin

What destroys your margin?

- Distractions that crowd out the voice of Jesus?
- Smartphones with all the apps you never knew you needed in order to stay tethered to the world you never knew existed?
- News that'll keep you discouraged or angry or depressed every hour of the twenty-four-hour news cycle?
- Blogs with never-ending comparisons and measurements and opinions?
- Personal insecurity that won't allow you to rest, for fear that you won't accomplish something, and you not accomplishing something will cause others to judge you, and others judging you will actually make you less valuable or more vulnerable?

3. Percival, *Downton Abbey*, "Episode One."

Take note of the destroyers. For a season, I deleted the Facebook and Twitter apps from my phone. It was a great decision that allowed me to reset and rediscover some margin that I had pretty much lost.

What could you do today to reclaim some margin?

Rein in Netflix?

Learn to say "no"?

Banish the TV or internet from the bedroom?

See a counselor?

## Conclusion

Margin is the wasted space we desperately need. So, spend some time in the margins. Waste time with your friends, your spouse, your kids. Waste time with your God, just being with him. No agenda. No checkbox. Just love and relationship and coffee.

If you have a strong reaction to the idea of "wasting time," ask yourself, "Why?" Remember, being busy all the time could be avoidance. Avoiding Sabbath could be idolatry.

Close the computer, delete the apps. Dance with your daughter and remember:

*Life is a breath,*
*Breathe deep and slow, and*
*Savor the moments in the margins.*

*The glorious unpressured time of not-work.*
*Remember, Jesus slept.*

*God remains on his throne, after all.*
*He was capable before you showed up, and*
*He'll remain imminently capable after you're gone.*

So work hard and rest well. And remember, wasting time just might be the most productive thing you ever do.

# Let Me Tell You About Kassiah Jones

*BY ELIZABETH*

RECENTLY, MY HUSBAND AND I took our kids to the local home school co-op's spring performance. Some of our friends were in the play. It was called "The Race" and was an original play based loosely on the story of "The Tortoise and the Hare."

Every character in this play was modeled after an animal. There was a bear and a sparrow and a fennec fox (among others), but the character that most captured my attention was the character modeled after the ant. Her name was Kassiah Jones, and she never knew when to quit.

When it was time for the village inhabitants to prepare for the annual race, Kassiah trained harder than all the rest. She worked hard and never knew when to stop.

On race day, Kassiah was in the lead, far ahead of the others, for the first three laps. But on the fourth lap she didn't come back around the curtain with the rest of the runners. At the end of the race, after somebody else had won, the villagers went in search of her. They found her, collapsed from exhaustion, and had to carry her out on a stretcher.

I so identified with Kassiah Jones. I work, work, work, and never take a break. I know I need to. But I forget.

The week I attended "The Race" was, to be honest, brutal. We'd gone three days without refrigeration and had lost the entire contents of our fridge to Cambodia's hot season. We'd gone a couple days with a puking child and half a night's power outage with said puking child. I got to the end of that week completely exhausted and out of sorts.

So that Friday I took the first of what I'm now calling a "Kassiah Jones Day." I canceled home school. I played games with my kids. We watched science videos in the air conditioning. I read more than usual to them. I'm with them all the time, but I don't always share enjoyable activities with them. Instead I focus on finishing our lessons, and then in my "free time," I work.

But I now have a vocabulary for what my soul needs and for the way I'd been treating it. I have a symbol, a simple phrase that encompasses a world of meaning for me. It's true I forget to Sabbath. It's true I forget to breathe. It's true that all too often, I *am* Kassiah Jones.

But I think that needs to start changing, and I think I know just how to try.

# Anger Abroad

### BY JONATHAN

TWO FRIENDS WERE PLANNING to meet for lunch one day when one called to cancel, stating that she had a terrible headache. This wasn't a typical headache, and it hurt badly. Her friend admitted that she too had a horrendous headache, and suggested they go to the ER together. (This is just one step beyond going to the bathroom together.)

They showed up at triage and told their stories, grimacing through the pain. They were ushered to separate rooms, placed on various monitors, and examined. The first friend was treated for mild dehydration and sleep deprivation. She was told to sleep more and drink more water and less coffee. (They told her that her symptoms were consistent with a condition called "parenthood.") She was released the same day, terribly discouraged; she really liked coffee.

The second friend was examined and immediately transferred to the operating room for emergency brain surgery. She was diagnosed with a brain aneurysm and spent the next week recovering in the critical care unit.

## Anger as a Symptom

Both women had hurting heads. Both wanted to find the cause, and both were helped, although the interventions were very different.

Like the headaches in the story, anger is a symptom, and we need to pay attention to it. I see a lot of missionaries wrestling with anger, but I don't hear a lot of missionaries talking about it. I'd like to change that.

As a symptom, anger points to something. It doesn't necessarily point to something massive or exceptionally unhealthy, but it might.

Ignoring the symptoms of anger is very risky, and the stakes are high. Unresolved, unaddressed anger will hurt you and those around you.

In our example above, one lady's pain came from easily addressed, easily fixed factors (drink more water, sleep more, get a babysitter). For the second lady, however, treating her pain required expert care and plenty of time. Some of us may just need a holiday (preferably on a beach, with ice cream). Others may need to consult with someone who really knows what they're doing—someone who's skilled enough to ask the right questions, to probe, to help diagnose.

Some might say, "Wait, anger can be holy and righteous." Yes, that's true. But when I experience anger, either my own or another person's, it is very seldom holy and righteous. And honestly, I think the anger exemption is usually applied too liberally. When Jesus faced the greatest injustice of all time—the most heinous crime ever committed against the most innocent of victims—he responded with love, not anger, saying "Father, please forgive them."

## Peaceful Missionaries?

"Missionaries are some of the most peaceful people I know; they really seem to have figured out how to seek peace and pursue it."

"Overseas workers are good at letting the peace of God rule in their hearts."

What do you think of these statements? Have either of these been your experience? Yeah, me neither. I think we'd *never* use the word "peaceful" to describe ourselves or our coworkers. And I think that's really, really sad. But anger's not the problem. Anger's the symptom that points to the problem. So I'd like us to pause and ask, "Where is our anger coming from? What's going on under the surface of our souls?"

Often, the ones who don't show anger just bury it. And then, like other negative emotions we're not too fond of, it bubbles up. Like the deepwater oil rig in the gulf, something blows, and black tarry stuff explodes from the deep and ruins paradise (or Florida).

## Why So Angry?

Sometimes, we're angry at our spouses who dragged us here. We're angry at God for calling us here. We're angry at teammates who stay here. We're angry at the churches who sent us here: "They're just so monocultural and ethnocentric and don't understand what it's like here."

We're angry at nationals who live here because they just won't respond to *the amazing good news that God is love!*

We're angry at organizations that issue directives from comfy offices in comfy cities that smell nice and have green space and are nothing like here. We're angry at the traffic, the corruption, the instability, the injustice.

Maybe we're angry at our children who don't like it here. Or maybe we're angry at ourselves for bringing them here.

The tricky thing is, we know we're not *supposed* to feel anger at those things. And since being angry at those things is not always socially or religiously acceptable, we find a "safe" receptacle for our anger. We act on our anger in places no one sees. With people who can't get away.

Please hear me on this. I'm not saying that being angry makes you a bad person. I *am* saying that if anger is part of your normal daily routine, you need to pause and assess your symptoms. What's really going on? Where's the anger coming from? From wounded pride? Traumatic past events that inflicted deep pain? Fear of failure?

Doctors love to ask about symptoms. Why? Because symptoms are crumbs on the trail to diagnosis. Are you willing to follow the crumbs? The next time you feel anger rising up inside your chest? Are you willing to ask, "Where is this coming from?" Are you willing to sit down with a good listener and say, "Every time xyz happens, I get really angry." Are you willing to give the listener freedom to ask questions?

Are you willing to look for slow-burn anger? Maybe you think, "I'm not an angry person, I never yell or throw stuff." Slow-burn anger is a favorite among Christians because it allows us to have intense feelings of anger on the inside without showing the world (or our church) how angry we really are. We have the same feelings on the inside, but we don't show them on the outside.

We hide the burning coals of repressed anger deep in our bosom, and it destroys us from the inside out. A house will burn down just as easily from fire on the inside as fire on the outside. We must deal with anger. The church must deal with anger. The cost of persistent, unaddressed anger is much higher than the cost of a few counseling appointments.

## The Anger Alternative

It is my heart's cry that we would be people of peace.

People who adore the King of kings *and* the Prince of wholeness.

People who know what it feels like to rest in the presence of the Almighty.

People who believe, deep in our souls, that his yoke is easy, and his burden is light.

~~~~~~~~~~

*"I am leaving you with a gift—peace of mind and heart. And the peace I give is a gift the world cannot give. So don't be troubled or afraid"*
*(John 14:27).*

*"I've told you all this so that trusting me, you will be unshakable and assured, deeply at peace. In this godless world you will continue to experience difficulties. But take heart! I've conquered the world"*
*(John 16:33 MSG).*

*"Are you tired? Worn out? Burned out on religion? Come to me. Get away with me and you'll recover your life. I'll show you how to take a real rest. Walk with me and work with me—watch how I do it. Learn the unforced rhythms of grace. I won't lay anything heavy or ill-fitting on you. Keep company with me and you'll learn to live freely and lightly*
*(Matt 11:28–30 MSG).*

*"For a child is born to us, a son is given to us. The government will rest on his shoulders. And he will be called: Wonderful Counselor, Mighty God, Everlasting Father, Prince of Peace"*
*(Isa 9:6).*

# Angry, Mean, and Redeemed

BY *ELIZABETH*

I LOST MY MIND this hot season. Became unglued. Went a little nuts. Whatever you want to call it. Yes, everyone's crabbier and more uncomfortable this time of year, and it would be mighty convenient to blame my meltdown on the heat. It would also be unfair, for I can't in good conscience blame the external temperatures for my roiling internal mess.

I'd been angry at some disappointments in my life for a while, and it was spilling out into irritability and rudeness with my husband and children, who did not deserve my unkindness and snappiness. I refused to talk to God about these things because I was convinced he couldn't change any of the circumstances anyway, and I didn't want to be even more disappointed by his lack of intervention. So I just kept getting angrier and angrier, more and more irritable, and more and more distant from God.

One Sunday morning I hit a breaking point. I sat down with the question, "How did I become such a whiny witch?" (You can substitute more colorful language if you want; it would still be true.) I actually locked my door so my kids couldn't walk in on me. I got down on my knees—something I rarely do while praying—and confessed and repented to God.

Then I did something I hadn't been able to do for weeks, because I'd been staying too angry: I cried. I cried and cried. I lamented the terrible person I still am, how ugly my heart still is, how much sin I still have, how badly I was reacting to seemingly everything. I implored God, "What are you going to do with me?"

His immediate reply: "Forgive you."

147

Forgive me? That's what he was going to do with me? He wasn't going to give up on me? He wasn't going to punish me? No, he said he was going to forgive me. But I suppose there's nothing else to do with a sinner like me, but to forgive. I almost couldn't believe how badly I needed absolution. When I received forgiveness, I suddenly found I could forgive those who had sinned against me. And my evil attitude toward my family dissipated.

In the end, I found it was unforgiveness that was keeping me from God. I had been avoiding the pain of repentance. Feeling the weight of my own sin *hurts*. I'd rather stay angry at someone else's sin. But I was continually frustrated by my angry outbursts toward the people I wasn't actually angry with. I kept asking myself, "Why can't I get it together?" The answer was simple: because I hadn't gone to God.

Going to God was such a relief. It's the only way I can describe it. It was a relief to know that after all these years, when I act like a witch for weeks on end, God still forgives. A relief to know my sin was not the end of me. A relief to know that no matter what, I can go back to the cross, back to my Savior, back to my Lord. I got off my knees a forgiven person, lighter and freer, and ready to live again.

# How to Avoid Burnout

BY *ELIZABETH*

I FLIRTED WITH BURNOUT. I was camping out along its edges, and I didn't even know it. Only after some conversations with my husband and with a spiritual director did I recognize what was going on and how I'd been complicit in my own spiritual sickness.

These are the things I'm doing to carve out rest and Sabbath in my life and to move farther and farther away from burnout. I'm no expert, and this is by no means a comprehensive list. They're just things that seem to be working in my life. Some are deceptively small and simple; others are larger and more extreme and took more courage to do.

## 1. In the midst of the chaos, choose to breathe

God formed us from the dust and breathed the breath of life into us. There is life and peace in our breath. Why then do we go about our days neglecting this very curative gift God gave us?

In fact I've described breathing as a "free drug" before:

Some drugs are free.
Like breathing.
I love breathing. It's my favorite.
I recently announced this to my kids.
Some of them thought I was crazy, but one agreed.
It's true though. I just love breathing.
Pause.
Inhale, exhale.
Breathe in, breathe out.

Release, receive.
When I stop to close my eyes and breathe deeply and slowly, I
immediately calm down.
My body relaxes.
My thoughts stop swirling.
My emotions stop pressing.
So take a deep breath. Maybe take three.
And remember, some drugs are free.
If only we will use them.

## 2. Open my hands in surrender

Even better than simply taking some deep breaths is to sit in a quiet place,
place my hands in my lap, and open them up to God. As I do so, I release
my hurts and concerns to God. I give him my frustrations and trust him
to keep all of them, because I'm too weak and tired to hold onto them
anymore. I'm not as consistent in this practice as I want to be, but when
I participate in this small act of surrender, it makes a huge difference in
my day.

## 3. Grab hold of awe and wonder
## in ordinary moments and days

I'm inspired by the idea of ordinary time, which I first read about in Kimberlee Conway Ireton's *The Circle of Seasons: Finding God in the Church
Year*.[1] Ordinary time encourages me to ask, "Where is the glory of God
hiding in my life right now?"

If I can cultivate a sense of wonder and joy in the everyday things
of creation, then I find miraculous little moments hidden in my ordinary
days. When I purposefully take the time to notice these things:

I can explore space-time with my son
and delight in a sunset with my daughter.
I can drink in the clouds and rooftops
from a fourth-floor, downtown city window.
I can breathe in the blue sky on my way to a dinner meeting.

1. Ireton, *Circle of Seasons*.

I can be captivated by a bright yellow full moon.
I can delight in a downpour so strong
the palm trees are engulfed in white gauze.
I can inhale the heavenly fragrance of the frangipani flower.
I can marvel at our daily game with gravity,
at the blue-scattered sky,
at a photosynthesizing palm tree.

I used to think I needed long periods of time away in order to truly rest. In truth, little mini Sabbaths are often available to me. But they only happen if I'm willing to stop rushing around and pay attention.

## 4. Fast regularly from technology

I fought this practice for a long time. I believe I have what might be called a "soft addiction" when it comes to the internet. I go to it for comfort—though comfort can't be found there—and I have a hard time turning it off when I'm tired or overwhelmed.

Last year I began by fasting from the internet during family vacations and team retreats. I was sensing God's invitation to fast from technology on Sundays, but I ignored it for several months. When I finally started obeying a couple of months ago, Sundays suddenly became much more restorative. Now I read, sleep, or spend time with my husband on Sunday afternoons. My relationships are better, I'm more rested, and I avoid the "computer haze" that starts to set in after too much time zoning out in front of a screen. This practice makes me much better prepared for Monday.

Additionally I try to keep technology out of the bedroom on weeknights, turn off the screens by 9 pm, and keep the computer closed until *after* I've talked to God in the morning. I often pray for strength to resist the pull of work before I even get out of bed.

## 5. Get creative with Sabbath

When you're in ministry, Sundays are often too intense to be considered restful. But Sabbath doesn't have to happen on Sundays, and it doesn't have to be a full twenty-four hours, either. Creativity in carving out Sabbath is especially important if you have young children, and you may have to alternate childcare between parents and only take half days at a time.

My husband, for example, takes Wednesday mornings off. First he takes a child out to breakfast, and then he takes a few hours for his own Sabbath. After lunch he comes home to do office work so that I can get out to a coffee shop to work on my own creative projects. My Wednesday afternoons are not, strictly speaking, Sabbath, but they provide the space to write and think and be separated from the never-ending needs of our home. Too often last year, I let these precious pockets of time slip through my fingers, and I felt the strain. Now I try to guard them much more carefully.

## 6. Get brave and quit something

This took me a long time to do. I could not bring myself to quit *any* of the ministry activities I had committed myself to. I thought each and every one of them was essential and all-important, and I was afraid I would let people down if I quit. But in the end I realized I was so overloaded I had to do it—and it really was hard to do. I had to accept both that the ministry would go on without me and that my identity wasn't tied up in those particular ministries.

But getting brave and quitting things isn't just about ministry. It's about social gatherings too. Where I live, there are so many invitations. So many good things to do. And so much fear of missing out—on community, on friendship, on educational and recreational opportunities. It's still hard to say no and miss out on wonderful opportunities, whether they're for myself or my children. But I simply can't do everything, and I'm getting more comfortable with the fact.

## 7. Participate in regular confession, repentance, and worship

Tears cleanse the soul and make space for God. I don't know why this is true, and I almost wish it weren't, but it is, and it's the way God has designed us. We are created to humble ourselves before him and others and admit we are wrong.

When I'm running too fast and seeking solace in false comforts, my heart hardens, my tears dry up, and I become deaf to the voice of God.

But I find rest for my soul in confession, repentance, and tears. My most recent experience of this was at an Ash Wednesday service, but I've told similar stories before.

## 8. Be faithful in caring for body and soul

Last year I knew I was distant from God and that I wasn't taking care of my body. Why is it that when I'm too busy, the first things to go are exercise and time with God? Those are the things I need the most. But in times of stress, it's all too easy to sleep in and skip talking to God altogether, or to get up and start working during that sacred morning hour instead. And when I'm tired, it's all too easy to eat junk food, watch Netflix, and skip exercising. But after I started cutting stuff out of my life, it became easier to stress-eat less, to exercise more, and to approach God more honestly and more consistently.

I like to call these things "soul care" and "body care," because even after all the "self-care" propaganda we have, that term still sounds selfish to me (and a lot of other women I talk to). But soul care and body care? That's worship. That's stewardship. It's taking the soul God gave me, and reconnecting it to its Creator. It's taking the body God gave me, and moving it and nourishing it so it can feel better and give more. So don't forget to take care of your soul and your body.

## 9. Seek counseling or other outside help

At the beginning of this chapter I mentioned my meetings with a spiritual director. I knew 2016 had been brutal; I just didn't know why. My counseling sessions helped to pinpoint the motivations behind some of my poor choices and prompted me to begin making better choices. We missionaries can be really driven, unhealthy people sometimes, and counseling can help us figure out both why we are so driven and how to move forward in health.[2]

2. Further reading: *Crazy Busy* by Kevin DeYoung, and *Leading on Empty* by Wayne Cordeiro.

## 10. And finally, take a longer break

Sometimes you need a longer time away from regular life. After taking pretty much no breaks during our first term, our family now takes a two-week Sabbatical in the middle of each two-year term. This extended time is for getting into nature, getting away from work and technology, nurturing our family relationships, and getting debriefing or counseling.

I know it's not always feasible to get away for longer periods of time, but if you can, it's great preventive medicine. And if you find yourself drained so low that you can't continue living life the way it is, taking a longer break may be more of an emergency measure. Just don't be afraid to take that step.

# My Low-Pressure Approach to Cultivating Intimacy with God

## BY *ELIZABETH*

THIS IS A STORY about getting away with Jesus and how it transformed my life. It's a story of hearing God whisper, "Come away with me," and it's the story of how I said yes—not perfectly, but repeatedly. It's a story that might seem really elementary to some of you, and you've been living this for years, but for me it was groundbreaking, and it happened in Cambodia.

Our international church was a watering hole for me right from the beginning of my time in Cambodia. It was a spiritual oasis, a weekly time to refresh and renew and meet with God. I remember walking into the church's auditorium four years ago, feeling something inside me take a deep breath, and just *knowing* I was home. I met God that first Sunday, and every Sunday after.

But about a year and a half ago I felt God drawing me into deeper communion with him. I felt him calling me to a more daily commitment to meet together. Before then, I'd never learned to be consistent in my time with God. I had tried, but my attempts never lasted more than three to six months at a time. And they were never in the morning. (And I'd kind of always felt guilty about that, actually.)

But I was suddenly finding that Sunday mornings were not enough for me. They weren't enough to get me through my week. My cup was empty. My well was dry. I didn't have the strength I needed to thrive. Maybe in my passport country I could have survived like that, going from Sunday to Sunday, with maybe a Wednesday Bible study thrown in. But in Cambodia, I couldn't live like that anymore. Life in this country was taking more out of me, and that meant that in turn, I needed to take more from God.

I knew, deep down in my spirit, that this was what God was calling me to. I knew I needed this, and I knew I *wanted* it. But I have *never, ever* been a morning person. Left to my own devices, I would prefer to sleep.

So I had to start with really small steps. And I do mean really small: ten minutes. I woke up ten minutes early. In the beginning all I did was read a daily selection of prayer and Scripture from a prayer book. I got a notebook, and I started writing out my own prayers and recording the Bible verses that really stood out to me.

I knew I wanted this to be a long-term commitment, so there were several things I decided not to feel guilty about:

- I didn't let myself feel guilty if I skipped a day because I was too tired to get out of bed. I just woke up the next day and started over again.

- I didn't let myself feel guilty if I couldn't keep up with some pre-scribed Bible reading plan. I didn't try to catch up when I missed. I just slowly worked through whatever section of Scripture I was in.

- I didn't let myself feel guilty if I got sidetracked with other Scrip-tures or devotional books and deviated from "the plan."

- And I didn't let myself feel guilty about my short times. I just slowly increased my morning time, usually by ten minutes at a time.

Each individual meeting with God doesn't always *feel* very fruitful, but the seconds add up to minutes, and the minutes add up to hours, and every moment with God means something. When I look back over the last few years, I see that these times with God have been the source of some of my greatest spiritual breakthroughs. And that's not to say I didn't experience God before coming to Cambodia, because I did. I really, really did.

But here is where I discovered that God's love for me is much deep-er than I ever knew before. Here is where I discovered he loves me as much as he loves everyone else, and I didn't use to be sure of that. Here is where I learned who I am in Christ in ways I'd never known before. And I've had various seasons where God says, "Okay, we're going to work on this particular sin now, or this particular lie."

I know I can get really excited when I talk about intimacy with God. But I also want to be very careful how I talk about it because

- the last thing I want to do is heap more guilt and shame on you or give you something more to *do*.

- I don't want to give the impression I think I somehow "earned" God's intervention in my life by deciding to spend more time with God. I didn't earn his gifts of healing and freedom; everything is a gift and comes from him alone.

- I don't want to give the impression a morning quiet time will solve all your problems. I still walk through difficult times. I still sin—and that still discourages me. I still sometimes skip my morning devotional time. And I still sometimes have a hard time connecting with God.

- I also know some of you may be walking through a desert right now, or a fiery trial, and thriving may seem far from possible. So I want to be really sensitive to your pain and your weariness.

When we talk about needing to steal away and spend time with God, it can sound legalistic, like this is what you have to do to measure up. But that's *never ever* my intention. All I want is for people to get away and be with God. All I want is to see people healed and set free. Our time with God is *not* where we prove what great followers we are, it's where the healing happens.

And we will still have trials. Our relationship with God can't inoculate us against difficulty. And we will still have times in the desert, seasons of winter when we can't see the fruit or feel his presence.

If that's you today, if you're in a difficult or dry season, I want to encourage you not to give up hope. Seasons don't last forever. Hold out for another season. In the big picture, over the whole course of our lives, if we are drawing near to God and he is drawing near to us, we can thrive even in a dry and weary land where there is no water.

And that is the truth about my story: I'm no longer barely surviving in Cambodia. Cambodia is actually the place I learned how to thrive in my walk with God. Cambodia is where I learned how to abide with him and to commune with him. I found God here, and I'm not the same person I was before. In fact, God isn't the same God I thought I knew. He's so much bigger and better than I ever thought.

And I'm thankful for that, thankful that I was so needy that it drove me to get more of God. What I was on my own wasn't enough to handle life on the field. What was inside me wasn't enough. I didn't have the reserves or the strength the way I might have had in my own country.

I still hear God on Sunday mornings—I'm so thankful for Sunday mornings! Now though, I hear God throughout the week too. (And since I'm a human and kind of dense and hard-headed, it helps the lessons sink in better if I hear them on Sunday *and* during the rest of the week.)

So if you are like me and you're only haphazardly meeting with God, perhaps only on Sunday mornings, and if you're ready to go deeper into God and into his love, I want to gently suggest that maybe it's time to make more space for him in your life, maybe it's time to invite him into your busy, stressed-out schedule and into your worried, overwhelmed heart.

I promise you that if you get away with Jesus, it's going to change your life because the time we spend with God is what helps us thrive— whether you're in Cambodia like me, or somewhere else. Only God's love is enough to fill our hearts for our days, for our marriages, for our friendships, for our work, for our children, for our ministries. When we're connected to God, we can be like the trees in Jeremiah 17:7–8, the ones planted by streams of water, flourishing and bearing fruit, even in the dry, desert places.

~~~~~~~~~~~

*God, you are the only one who can make us flourish in the desert. You are the only one who gives life to our lifeless souls. God, plant us in you, that we may know you, that we may know your heart. Give us your life abundant, and help us thrive in whatever land we find ourselves. And we acknowledge that when you do this, when you make us thrive, it is not our doing, it is* your *doing, and the glory goes to you alone. Thank you for being enough for us. Amen.*

# Surviving the Field as an Introvert

BY *ELIZABETH*

I'M AN INTROVERT. I'm also a missionary. According to a recently popularized definition, an introvert is someone who is drained by being with other people, and who is energized by being alone. But missions is a rather people-intensive lifestyle, right? Is it possible for an introvert to be a missionary? For me, the short answer to this question is yes, introverts can be missionaries. But the story of how I arrived at this answer is not so short.

A few months into my life in Cambodia, I realized I was not like the rest of the ex-pats I met who seemed to have boundless energy to get together with other people on a regular basis. I did not possess that same energy. I enjoyed meeting new people and welcoming them into my home, but it made me tired. This tendency to be worn out by social events means I am an introvert (although I had never before considered myself to be one).

By all means, I am a very social introvert. I love people. I love getting to know them, and I love spending long periods of time with them. But I generally enjoy people one-on-one more than I enjoy large group settings (a typical introvert characteristic). Group settings where I am forced to meet several new people are especially difficult (and have been known to make me want to run away).

So how did I not know I was an introvert for the first three decades of my life? Especially after having been in ministry (something you do *with people*) for a third of that time?

I have two very sensible explanations for this. First: I was having babies. And as anyone who has ever had a baby in the house knows, being a mom makes you (very) tired. So if being with people ever wore me out,

I would not have been able to distinguish it from the exhaustion I faced on a daily basis.

And second: we rejected social life entirely for several years, starting when Jonathan added a full-time hospital job to his part-time ministry job. His working hours each week totaled over sixty, and there was so little time margin, that he devoted the rest of his time to our family. We didn't really do social events, so I wouldn't have known if they made me tired.

After we moved to Cambodia, we attempted to reenter social life. We soon realized that a social meeting on a weeknight completely wiped us out for (at least) the rest of the week. We learned that having more than one social event per weekend ruined us for the entire next week. (I use the pronoun "we" because Jonathan, like me, is also an introvert.)

In our desperation, we instituted a personal rule: no weeknight meetings (with few exceptions), and a maximum of one social event per weekend. Sometimes we've turned down social invitations out of respect for our family's introvertedness. Other times we've broken our rule (for very good reasons), and we've paid the consequences of fatigue and general discouragement for the entire next week. Language learning and cross-cultural living are hard enough without adding that to the mix.

I may not be like the extrovert who thrives in large group settings (on the contrary, I thrive in close relationships), but not all mission or ministry work is done in large groups. Relationship-building is often done in small groups or individually. And I happen to believe God has called me to that kind of ministry—loving other women, one-on-one, in the friendships he brings to me.

So, can a missionary be an introvert, and can an introvert be a missionary? Yes, if we avoid large gatherings (since we are drained by too many people). Yes, if we avoid too many gatherings (since we need sufficient time to recharge between events). Yes, if we plan enough solitary time.

I, though I am an introvert, am not anti-social. I want to enjoy my time with you. I believe you deserve to be enjoyed. So I choose to pace myself socially, to rest when I'm worn out, and to give you the best I am able to give.

But probably not this weekend.

# The Art of Pressing on in Our Rhythms

BY *Elizabeth*

I USED TO STUFF and starve. I'd stuff myself with food, and then deprive myself of it. Or I'd fast in preparation for a big meal. I didn't want those binges showing up on my body.

Unfortunately, stuffing and starving doesn't work for weight control in the long run (or so I remember reading somewhere). It's also not very comfortable. I was always ravenously hungry or painfully full, never moderately hungry or pleasantly satisfied. I was stuck in a cycle of feast or famine.

I used to do the same thing with sleep. When my high school homework kept me up late, I'd sleep in on the weekends. My physics teacher Mr. Carmichael told me the engineering students at the university I was planning to attend also studied late into the weeknights and then tried to catch up on the weekends.

But, he said, the science showed that this approach doesn't work. Habitually depriving ourselves of sleep and then sleeping in on the weekends doesn't give us quality rest. Our bodies aren't made for that rhythm. (Though of course his wisdom did nothing to prevent me from succumbing to it again in college.)

I think I used to stuff and starve in my relationship with God, too. I'd subsist on crumbs from Sunday morning services and on predigested meals from Bible class. Then I'd spiritually pig out at conferences and camps.

Stuff and starve. Feast and famine. It's not a healthy cycle, whether we're talking about food, sleep, or our relationship with God. It's taken me *years* to learn how to pace myself in these things. How to eat when I'm hungry and (mostly) stop when I'm full. How to (mostly) get up early to meet with God and how to (mostly) go to bed on time. My rhythms aren't perfect by any means, but they're much healthier than before.

I remember hearing in prefield training that a break needs to be at least two weeks long in order to be effective. You need that much time to decompress from the stress of cross-cultural living, they said. But it left me wondering, just how reasonable *is* that expectation? Can everyone get away for that long? And how badly might my mental, emotional, and spiritual health deteriorate in between those long rests?

I personally cope much better when I have shorter, more frequent breaks. I don't have to freak out if I miss a regularly scheduled exercise session or early morning devotional. My times of refreshing are no longer scarce; I know I can pick them up again tomorrow. This is the art of pressing on in our rhythms, of forgetting yesterday's failed rhythms.

I'm not saying an extended period of rest is bad—far from it! In the Old Testament God commanded his people to observe a Sabbath year every seven years and the year of Jubilee every fifty. But he also commanded a weekly Sabbath, and we humans need shorter, more evenly-spaced feeds of both God and food.

So we plan our daily and weekly rhythms of work and rest. We can also add monthly and quarterly rhythms to the mix. For example, our family needs a ministry and cultural break about every three months, and we take a few days outside the city to rest, unplug from work, and play together as a family.

We've discovered that if we don't take a weekend away every quarter, if we try to stretch it longer than that, then we start disliking our host culture. And if we wait too long, all the stress of daily life that I've been stuffing down over the past several months tends to explode all over my family as soon as we reach our destination. So we're diligent in taking that quarterly respite.

This year I began a rhythm I learned about in Wayne Cordeiro's book *Leading on Empty*. It's called a personal retreat day, and it involves going away by yourself for a half to a full day and meeting God in nature, in prayer and journaling, in his word, and in other good books. Personal retreats don't have to be all that frequent—maybe just a few times a year—but I've found they renew my hunger for living and working overseas and provide some space for the junk to start filtering out of my soul.

As much as I love my rhythms, I have to admit they sometimes get off-kilter. For instance, I stayed up much too late to write this. And, I'm currently visiting my passport country—something we all know can disrupt our soul care. But here's the thing about rhythms: they don't have to be rigid. We can always start again tomorrow when mercies are new.

So if your rhythm is flagging and your soul is suffering, take heart: you can always start again. God will be right there waiting to commune with you. He's not mad about waiting. So let's not beat ourselves up when our rhythms aren't perfect; they will never be.

Instead, let's resolve to let the dawn reset our rhythms. Let's choose not to stuff and starve. Let's choose not to oscillate wildly between feast and famine. Let's commit together to regular rest and renewal—for ourselves, for our families, and for the ones we serve.

# TAKING CARE OF YOUR MARRIAGE WELL

# Three Ways to Care for the Heart of Your Wife

BY JONATHAN

MARRIAGE CAN REALLY BE a drain on missions.

Marriage on the field can be a constant source of distraction, discouragement, and pain.

But I hope it's not.

~~~~~~~~~~

Marriage is a complex thing (two into one) entered into by complex people (humans) who have to do complex stuff (live).

And you all know this already, but missions is a hard gig for marriages. You've got sky-high stress levels, extreme temperatures, lots of broken things, financial tightness, the fishbowl of fundraising, and a rewarding but very hard job. Sounds like fun, right? Well, if you add all of that to an unhappy marriage, I can tell you the one thing you certainly won't be having is fun.

So, onward! What are three things you can do to care for the heart of your wife? And for the record, I'm trying all these too, man, and learning as I go.

## 1. See her

Your wife needs you to really see her. She's not touched up and airbrushed and two-dimensional. She's not a product of Photoshop. She's real, with a body, mind, and soul, and she needs you to see and value *all* of her.

She's the one who shares your memories, your children, your bed. She's also the one who shares your future. You chose her. So brother, *keep choosing her*. She is, after all, a daughter of the King.

Now, here's the deal: it's very hard to turn toward your wife and really see her when your face is glued to the porn screen. Watch two-dimensional fakeness, body parts flying for your pleasure, and try to see your wife as anything more than disconnected pieces. It'll be really hard.

Porn kills love. And watching porn keeps you from seeing your wife.

Porn is really expensive. Even the free stuff. Want a reminder of the cost? Check out Matthew 14 or Mark 6. The story of Herodias's daughter dancing for Herod reminds me of the old anti-drug campaign in the States: "This is your brain. This is your brain on drugs [porn]." Herod was willing to give away half his kingdom (or behead a prophet that he didn't actually want dead) because he thought a teen girl was hot. Yikes.

Turn to God, man. Repent. Get some strong accountability. Yeah, it's scary, and costly, but the price you're paying is way higher, and climbing.

## 2. Listen to her

Listening is an extremely validating gesture. It feels good to be listened to. It's like someone cares. So yeah, you want to care for the heart of your wife? Listen to her. Want to see how you're doing? Complete this short quiz[1] and then have your wife do it too. Then compare scores.

If your scores are vastly different, that's probably worth noting and may indicate that one or both of you aren't really listening (or communicating) very well.

Most people never feel listened to. Our wives shouldn't be most people.

Need help? Check out *Why Marriages Succeed or Fail: And How You Can Make Yours Last*, by John Gottman.[2] He's got decades of experience helping couples listen (and hear!) each other. By the way, his research indicates that healthy couples devote at least five hours per week to specific, focused, I'm-paying-attention-to-you time. If you're too busy for five hours per week, you're too busy. Find some margin.

Not interested in a book? Check out this short article[3] with some basic (but important!) info on listening.

---

1. Find the quiz here: https://www.gottman.com/how-well-do-you-know-your-partner/quiz/.

2. Gottman, *Why Marriages Succeed or Fail*.

3. https://www.gottman.com/blog/the-digital-age-the-first-duty-of-love-is-to-listen/.

Not interested in research? That's cool. Check out 1 Corinthians 13 and ask how a patient, kind, nonboasting, humble, nondemanding, nonirritable, nonrecord-keeping husband would listen to his wife. Then listen to your wife like that.

## 3. Touch her

Not like that, dude. Chill. This one's last, but not because I want you to *see* her and *listen* to her so you can sleep with her. That's just crude. No, that's not the kind of touch I'm talking about. I'm talking about the kind of touch that tells her you're there for her. I'm talking about comforting touch. Intimate touch.

I'm talking about touching her with your heart. I'm talking about holding hands and long hugs. I'm talking about a soft kiss that has nothing to do with a proposition. I'm talking about loving her with your arms. I'm talking about showing affection in a culturally appropriate way. Often.

Ladies, if you're reading this (and I hope you are), please help us out. We're not really very good at reading minds. Tell us what kind of touch you want and don't want. And ladies, can I just say one more thing? It's OK to want nonsexual touch and ask for it, just like it's OK to want sexual touch and ask for it.[4]

## Conclusion

These are generalities, I know, so I won't feel too bad if your wife reads this and says, "That's not me at all!" Cool beans. Just make sure you ask her what *is* her? What is it that will help her feel loved and cared for?

For our fifth wedding anniversary, I bought Elizabeth a large, framed periodic table of the elements. My dad warned me that might not be such a good idea. He was so wrong. I knew my wife, and although most folks wouldn't find that sort of gift endearing, it was a slam dunk.

If you really took the time to see your wife, to listen to her, to touch her, would she feel cared for? Loved? Probably. If not, then ask her what *would* help her feel cared for and loved. Easy peasy.

You might be thinking, "OK, remind me again why this is in a book on cross-cultural work?" Well, because you take yourself (and your

4. For more, read "On Making Love" at https://trotters41.com/2017/11/25/on-making-love/.

marriage) with you. And because it matters. And because we're most likely working with people, and people often get married, even in other countries. And because marriage is "The Beautiful Hard."[5] Oh yeah, and because I really, really like seeing husbands "love [their] wives just as Christ loved the church" (Eph 5:25 NIV).

May God help us all to love our wives like that!

~~~~~~~~~~

*Ladies, I know that many of you feel loved and cared for already. That's wonderful! However, as a pastor and lay counselor, I also know that many of you don't. You feel widowed by missions, unheard, unloved, and alone. That really breaks my heart. If that's the case, perhaps this chapter could spark a conversation between you and your husband. If he doesn't want to budge, or if he thinks everything is just fine, please reach out to a trusted pastor or counselor or member care person. You're not alone, or at least you don't have to be.*

5. For more, read Rachel Pieh Jones's article here: http://velvetashes.com/marriage-is-the-beautiful-hard/.

# The Purpose of Marriage is NOT
# to Make You Holy

*BY JONATHAN*

Before we moved abroad, we did some marriage counseling. What I mean is, we sat in an old guy's office for fifteen hours and cried. It was amazing.

He told us our marriage could be a safe haven on the field. Or not. He said we could strengthen and encourage each other on the field. Or not. He said that our marriage could bring peace and stamina and even joy to the mission field. Or not.

He was right.

## Some Questions

If you and I were chatting at a local coffee shop and I asked you, "Hey, I'm curious, how would you describe marriage?" In general, what words would you use? Would you say, *"Marriage is. . .*

Hard?

Wonderful?

Good?

&#^$? (That could mean good things or bad things, I suppose.)

How do you describe your own marriage? Often, the first word I hear people say is "hard." And after they say "hard," they quickly follow up with, "but it's good." Now, think about your relationship with your best friend. How would you describe that relationship? Would you say, *"Our friendship is. . .*

Fun?

Easy?

Intimate?

Hard?

Would you call it "hard, but good"? Honestly, what would you think of someone who spoke of their closest friendship, first and foremost, as hard? Um, weird.

What about your relationship with God? Is it, first and foremost, hard? Is that really what we're going for? Is our chief end to endure the hard, with God and our spouses? On a gut level, I think we know there's more. There has to be more.

## A Dangerous Idea

*"The purpose of marriage is to make us holy."*

*"Marriage is hard, but it's okay, because it makes us holy."*

*"My marriage is really difficult. But that's good, because marriage is supposed to make me holy."*

Have you ever heard a variation on this theme? Often, people don't say it so explicitly, but I've heard this a bunch, and I think it's dangerous. It's almost like we looked around and said, "Well, marriage is really difficult, and a lot of folks never experience intimacy or joy or happiness in their marriages, so let's just tell them marriage is supposed to make them holy instead."

We sound so spiritual when we talk like this, and we think we're elevating the institution of marriage when in fact we're simplifying it and cheapening it. We're robbing it of beauty, and we're insulting people.

We're insulting the people who aren't married. How are they made holy? Are they doomed to a life of less holiness due to their marital status? Are they holiness-deficient? Are we implying that our single brothers and sisters, widows and widowers, or folks who've dealt with the trauma of divorce, don't have access to the thing that can make them holy? Namely, a spouse?

*Can* marriage make you holy? Sure. Any relationship with another human has the potential to wear off rough edges, point out selfishness, expose our sin, and through the work of the Holy Spirit and the sacrifice of Jesus, make us holy. (See: parenthood.) But saying "marriage *can* make you holy" is very different than saying "the *purpose* of marriage is to make you holy."

The real-life implications of this belief are what scare me the most. If marriage is to make me holy, and if what I really mean by that is that the hard parts of marriage make me holy, then I'm actually completely justi-fied in *staying* in the hard parts, without any hope of or desire to change. There is no impetus to seek deeper intimacy with the one I've promised to be with forever.

You know, sometimes marriage is hard because we've got issues that need to be worked on. But instead of acknowledging the emotional pain, or the fear of intimacy, or the past offenses, we deflect and avoid, consol-ing ourselves, "Well, at least it's making me holy."

This is not God's plan for marriage.

Instead of hitting conflict or hardships and deflecting to "holy," we need to start asking the tough questions, like "Why are we having this conflict?" or "Is there deeper emotional pain that's making this so hard?" Can we stop using the idea of holiness as an excuse to avoid the hard questions?

And more to the theological core, I think we believe marriage can't be pleasurable and enjoyable, because then it wouldn't be as spiritual. This is an ancient discussion. Pause and analyze for a second if any of these fallacies have crept in to your thoughts on marriage:

Marriage can't feel good.
Marriage can't be good unless it's purely spiritual.
Spiritual intimacy is the most important part of marriage.
Physical and emotional intimacy in marriage are inherently "less than" spiritual intimacy.

Again, we don't really talk like this, but it is often our meta-message. Marriages are not meant to be endured.

~~~~~~~~~~

*Marriage is for intimacy.*
*The sharing of souls and dreams and flesh.*
*The first taste of summer.*

~~~~~~~~~~

Marriage, the joining together of two unique persons, predates sin and exists beyond it. Marriage satisfied Adam. It excites Jesus.

The first marriage was designed by a loving Father, for joy and com-panionship. Closeness. It was good. The last marriage, a proclamation of

Love's victory that echoes in eternal joy and companionship and glory. A celebration such as the cosmos has never seen.

Marriage is the mysterious coming together of two people; the blending of heart and vessel and marrow. The tearing of the veil. Intimate. At least, that's what it's supposed to be. But intimacy can be a scary thing. It's vulnerable and exposed and leaves us naked. It's also amazing.

The opposite of intimacy is withdrawal. Distance. Disconnection. Ask yourself or ask your spouse, "Are we close? Are our hearts even in the same room, communicating easily? Have we settled for a dull disconnect?" It's worth talking about. And for the record, if one spouse feels like there's distance and disconnection but the other spouse thinks everything's great, the first one's right, and the marriage needs help. If you're the spouse that's denying distance, I beg you to stop. Now. Listen to the heart-cry of your husband or wife.

Every relationship will have seasons. Seasons of grandeur and awe and warmth, and seasons of darkness and winter. But there's a big difference between a *season* of winter and an ice age. If you're living in an ice age, please get help. It doesn't have to be that way.

## A Blessed Arrangement

Intimacy with your spouse is a gift, a fountain of youth. Treasure it, protect it, and fight for it. Here are some ideas:

- Explore the relationship between Christ and the church.
- Study Ephesians 5.
- Read the Song of Solomon. Slowly.
- Find a marriage counselor, even if you don't have any "issues."
- Pursue emotional healing.
- Say no to good stuff so you can say yes to better stuff. Do not embrace your mission so much that you lose your marriage. Keep porn far, far away. Porn will destroy intimacy faster than you can click "delete browser history."
- Read good books about marriage. Trade babysitting. If at all possible, when someone comes to visit you on the field, let them get over jet lag and then leave the kids with them so you and your spouse can get away overnight. When you've got little munchkins

at home, even twenty-six hours away (our last getaway) can be awesome. (And someone please tell me I'm not the only one who counts those getaways in hours!)

You may be in a place where getting away is impossible, or unsafe, or just really stupid. So, change your definition of "a date." Putting the kids to bed early and catching up with your spouse over coffee (or tea, I guess) can be romantic, if you want it to be.

## Regarding Sex (A Word for My Brothers)

Sex and intimacy are not synonyms. But still, a marriage characterized by emotional intimacy will include some form of healthy physical intimacy.

Men, we think we know a whole lot more about sex than we actually know. And that's a problem, because we think we don't need to learn, or even worse, we think that we've learned about sex already, you know, because we watched some porn once or listened to guys in the locker room. Yikes. Our wives deserve better than that.

Having sex doesn't take much skill or special knowledge, but really making love to your wife's heart and body, now that takes some practice. And research.

I think you should research sex. I know you think about it a lot, so why not study it from a healthy source? Have your wife do some research, and read whatever she thinks you need to read. And if she thinks you need to read something, then you need to read it. However, if she doesn't want you reading about sex, she's probably got a very good reason, and you should look into that before you start calling her names. For example, if you've violated her trust, or pressured her in the past, she's probably not going to be too excited about this paragraph. And she's probably right.

That being said, a pretty basic book that might be a good place to start your research is *A Celebration of Sex: A Guide to Enjoying God's Gift of Sexual Intimacy*, by Dr. Douglas Rosenau.

A longtime missionary and medical doctor once told me something interesting about sex. (And I always listen when someone tells me something interesting about sex.) He said, "Often, the sex life of a missionary couple is a barometer for the health of their marriage in general."

Sex doesn't create intimacy, and you can't fix an unhealthy marriage by having more sex. That wasn't his point. He was just saying that emotional distance, or a lack of emotional intimacy, will show up early in a couple's sex life. It's a warning sign. And if the emotional intimacy between a husband and wife begins to diminish, it should be addressed sooner rather than later.

It should be noted here that a healthy sexual relationship has nothing to do with frequency. It has to do with intimacy. Do you, as husband and wife, regularly connect with each other both physically and emotionally?

Husbands and wives, enjoying each other physically and emotionally, is very pleasing to God.

## When One Partner Doesn't Care

Maybe you hate this chapter. Please, hear me out. For most of this chapter, I'm assuming that both husband and wife want to grow closer. I'm assuming you both want a healthy marriage characterized by deepening intimacy.

However, I realize that many people live in marriages that aren't like that. Maybe that's you. Maybe you're in a marriage that's missing something and you already know it and it's breaking you. Maybe you wish things would change, but they haven't, and you don't think they ever will. If that's you, I want you to know that I totally believe you. I see you, and I'm so very sorry.

It is not good to be alone, but being married to someone and still alone, now that might be worse still. If that's you, you may find yourself in a valley of grief, and that might be right where you need to be for a time. Grieving the loss of dreams. Grieving for the broken places, and the broken things.

If you're in that hurting place, may the Lord of peace surround you with his love. May you find friends and confidants who will walk beside you, encourage you, and strengthen you. May you find the church to be a welcome and warm place, full of people who care about you, about seeing *you*. Not you, the part of the "bad marriage" or the "failed marriage," but you, the child of the King, who is worth so much. May you know intimacy, with your God and with his people. And may he bring you safely home.

## Conclusion

Marriage is a great gift, and we honor the Giver when we accept the gift with joy and excitement. We honor him when we treasure each other, respect each other, know each other.

We miss the Father's heart when we think he gave us marriage "to make us holy."

Yes, marriage is sometimes hard, and life is not all peaches and cream, but if your default description of marriage is "hard," I'm telling you, there's more. Look for that. Pray for that.

## A Marriage Blessing

May your marriage be beautiful. May it remind you often that God gives good gifts. Very good gifts.

May people look at your love and see that there is a God and he is awesome.

May you show the world—and the church—that it's not about submission or obedience or "who's in charge," that in your love and mutual submission, you will race each other to the bottom. And when you get to the bottom, may you find love, wholeness, joy, peace, and life. In other words, Jesus.

May you laugh often. At each other, with each other, because of each other. And if and when God fills your home with children, may you sit around the table and laugh and laugh and laugh.

May you taste heaven when you taste each other.

And when you walk through the shadowlands—and you will walk through the shadowlands—may the One who led you together continue to lead you together. He is the Creator of the soaring mountaintops and the scary valleys. May he sustain you and remind you.

May this year be the best year of your marriage. Until next year. And may next year be the best year of your marriage. Until the next year. May you experience the intense joy of being known deeply, and the great honor of knowing another.

May your love, promised and given, echo into eternity.

May people hear your stories, witness your love, and say from now until forever, "Look at what the Lord has done!"

# Our Journey to Finding Joy in Marriage, and the Things We Lost Along the Way

## BY *ELIZABETH*

WE WERE IN A diner eating pizza. The young couple sitting across the table from us had just asked us how we've sustained the joy of our relationship over the years. I wasn't exactly expecting that question, so my first answer was pretty simple: we spend a lot of time together. Talking, dreaming, laughing, debriefing. Companionship and intimacy require time, and lots of it.

When we were first married, we retreated together to cheap lawn chairs overlooking bushes that barely shielded us from the highway on the other side. We walked all over that university town, in all kinds of weather, for our date nights. We might walk to the library for a free movie and share an order of breadsticks from Papa John's, where even with the sauces, our meal totaled a mere $3.69.

Later we added children—and enough disposable income for Jonathan to buy me a porch swing. We'd sit in that thing and talk while our children played. At night, we'd tuck them into bed and sneak back out to talk some more, with hot chocolate or bug spray as our companions, depending on the weather.

Even after losing both the yard and the porch swing in our move to Cambodia, we found a way to escape together. We'd head up to our roof and sit in bamboo chairs (with bug spray as our definite companion), watch the city skyline, and share soul secrets. These days you'd be more likely to find us sipping coffee at our kitchen table, the kitchen door conveniently locked behind us.

But the more I pondered this young couple's question about joy in marriage, and the more I traced our marital history over the years, the more I realized that finding joy was about losing things too. On the journey to find joy in marriage, we've shed some surprising baggage.

## Who's in Charge Here?

I went into marriage spouting ideals of male headship. My husband Jonathan would be in charge and make the final decisions, and I, as the wife, would submit. In any disagreement, his opinion would count for more. We thought we believed that premise, and because we didn't have a lot of conflict, we thought we were pretty good at following it.

In real life, however, I don't think we ever actually *practiced* male headship (or what is sometimes called complementarianism, a term I didn't know at the time). We thought we did because we loved God and wanted to obey his word, and male headship is what the Bible instructs, right?

But Jonathan never pulled the "I'm in charge" card on me. Never. Not even once. Not even when he felt led overseas and I didn't. I put pressure on myself to submit to his call, but it never came from him.

## A Little Premarital Advice from My Mom

Growing up, I watched my mom honoring her husband, and she taught me to do the same. When it came to practical advice, though, she focused on "talking things out." She told me that in her marriage to my dad, if one of them cared about something more—whoever it was—they went with that. The next time it might be different, and that was okay, because nobody was keeping track. She said if they didn't agree, they just kept talking until they did agree. Practically speaking, my mom and dad were on equal terms in their marriage.

One day my mom told me about a conversation with some other Army wives. One of the women turned to my mom and told her that *she must really love her husband.* Mom was a bit confused; she hadn't been raving about how wonderful Dad was or how much she loved him. But something in the way she talked about him (or did *not* talk about him, as the case may have been) spoke her love loud and clear to those fellow Army wives.

Now I know that the type of marriage my mom was describing follows the mutual submission outlined in Ephesians 5:21: "Submit to one another out of reverence for Christ." Now I know that people call this type of relationship "egalitarian," but it's almost as if back then we had no vocabulary for the biblical marriage conversation.

## The Priesthood of All Believers

Even in the early days of our marriage, whenever we needed to make a big decision, Jonathan and I would always pray together. We assumed that God would impress the same thing on our hearts, and that we would be united in both seeking God and obeying him.

Looking back now, I can see that the path to egalitarianism begins with the priesthood of all believers. We went into marriage saying we believed in male headship, yet in decision-making, we fully expected God to speak to both of us. We believed we could, and would, both hear from God, and that God would say the same thing to both of us. Blame it on the *Experiencing God* craze of the 1990s if you want, but this is how we approached God from the very beginning of our marriage.

## Love and Respect?

Several years into our marriage I heard about the idea of love and respect, which claims that a woman's biggest need is to be loved by her husband and that a man's biggest need is to be respected by his wife. That seemed like good, solid, biblical advice. In our marriage I felt loved, my husband felt respected, and we were happy. "Hmm," I thought, "love and respect must be the key to marital happiness."

Then I read a book about the idea (the book is long for being built on the foundation of only one verse). About halfway through, I had to put it down. It was so tedious I couldn't finish it. How many more stories and examples could there be? The book seemed to be repeating itself.

Besides, I felt like something was missing. I need my thoughts, ideas, and intellect valued: I need respect. Almost as much as love. And my husband needs love, perhaps more than respect. He can't survive without my compassion, empathy, and listening ears.

(In all fairness to the author of these ideas, he has elsewhere stated that men and women need both love and respect, though in differing amounts. It's just that I didn't get that impression from reading his book or from watching his videos.)

Lest you get the wrong idea here, let me make one thing clear: I deeply respect my husband. I value his opinions and consult him on everything. I turn to him for counsel, guidance, and perspective. I trust his advice and regularly defer to him in decision-making. He most certainly has my respect.

But for him, although my respect is nice, if I did not also care about his feelings, his dreams, and his deepest longings, and if I did not tenderly take care of him, he would shrivel up and die (his words, not mine). He needs my open-hearted love. And if he loved and cared for my deepest hurts and feelings, but did not also value my gifts and abilities, I'd be crushed. In fact, if I didn't have his respect, I wouldn't actually feel loved by him.

Receiving only love or only respect isn't good enough for Jonathan and me. We need both love *and* respect. The teaching of "love and respect" was a nice start, but for us it didn't go far enough. As a wife, yes, I respect my husband, and as a husband, yes, Jonathan loves his wife. It's in the Bible; it's good. But God isn't going to be offended if wives also love their husbands, and husbands also respect their wives.

In the book of Ephesians, Paul was improving upon the pagan hierarchies of the day.[1] Neither Paul nor Jesus—who demonstrated both love and respect for women *repeatedly* in the Gospels—is going to be upset if we take these instructions that much further, if we add more love and respect, and more *imago Dei* (the belief that our Creator made us in his image, and that we have inherent value and worth), to our relationships. On the contrary, I think it pleases him.

~~~~~~~~~~

*"A marriage where either partner cannot love or respect the other can hardly be agreeable, to either party."*
—*Jane Bennett in* Pride and Prejudice[2]

~~~~~~~~~~

1. Trotter, "Paul the Mysogynist?"
2. Wright, *Pride & Prejudice.*

## Encountering Jesus as Healer

The more I considered this young couple's question, the more I kept coming back to the same answer: emotional healing. Emotional healing is what happens when Jesus walks into our pain and binds up the wounds of our hearts. Emotional healing is what draws us closer to each other than ever before. Emotional healing shows us both *why* we hurt each other and also, how to *stop* hurting each other.

Pursuing emotional wholeness is a journey Jonathan and I have been on for years now. And though we walk together, our paths look different. The healing Jonathan needed came in the form of expressing long-hidden grief. For me, it meant beginning to feel long-hidden feelings.

For both of us, the path to healing has trodden straight through pain, but it's been worth it, for the healing we've found has deepened our intimacy and intensified our joy.

Perhaps the honeymoon should have worn off by now, but it hasn't. We have more joy and intimacy after eighteen years of the daily grind than we ever dreamed possible. Along the way, we've shed strict interpretations of gender roles and lost deep emotional wounds. In their place, we've welcomed emotional healing and embraced mutual love and respect.

We are co-heirs with Christ and co-leaders in our home. We lead each other closer to Jesus, closer to love, closer to wholeness. We give each other space to grow, and we say the hard truth to each other, too.

This is what our joy looks like.

# When Ministry and Marriage Collide

BY *ELIZABETH*

JONATHAN AND I HAVE been married eighteen years now, and I can honestly say being married to him is the best thing that has ever happened to me. We were friends first, then fell madly in love our senior year of high school. Even our first year of marriage—considered by some to be quite difficult—was pure bliss. And I can honestly say that every year after that has grown more joyful and more intimate. This is not to say, however, that we haven't ever struggled.

I've shared before about two of the major struggles in my marriage. I've talked about how I didn't want to move overseas in the first place and how Jonathan and I were at an impasse until God got a hold of me. I've also shared my struggle to believe God loves me as much as my husband, since he seemed to have so many more gifts than I have.

There was another difficult season in my marriage. The two stories I mentioned earlier represent enormous works God wanted to do in my heart and in my spirit. They also had enormous implications in the way I lived everyday life alongside my husband. The struggle I'm going to talk about in this chapter might seem more earthy than spiritual, but it still looms quite large in the landscape of my memory.

Some of you know we served in youth ministry in the United States for ten years. At one point we lived in a parsonage next door to the church building, and we hosted summer youth meetings in our house. Initially we only invited juniors and seniors to our house on Tuesday nights for Bible study, and I thoroughly enjoyed it. Later we started hosting all ages in our house every Wednesday night during the summer. And every Wednesday night without fail, teenagers trashed my house.

This went on for two whole summers. My house was a disaster every Wednesday night, and I had a breakdown every Wednesday night. Jonathan and I could not see eye to eye on this issue and often fought over it. He felt we needed to have the teens in our home, and that I needed to *want* to have them in our home, and that furthermore, he believed the teens would perceive my reluctance to welcome them into our home, so I needed to check my attitude.

This, as you can imagine, led to lots of stress in our marriage. I wasn't confident enough to instruct the teens how to throw trash in the trash cans or how to avoid spilling Coke all over my white living room carpet. I'm more confident now and would be able to teach teenagers in that way, but I was too intimidated back then. (Also I was much more uptight about cleanliness when I only had two kids as opposed to now, with four.) I just wanted my husband to kick the teenagers out; I wanted him to do it for me. At the same time I felt an intense pressure to let them in my house every Wednesday, or else I'd be a "bad ministry wife."

Conflict can happen, even when you're married to your best friend, even when you are absolutely convinced he's the only one for you, even when you love practically everything about him. We shouldn't be surprised when we have disagreements with our spouses. We're different people, and we'll see the world differently. And when we feel our own point of view so strongly, it can be difficult to imagine someone else's point of view.

For any of my old darling youth group members who may be reading here today, please know I love you. And I want you to know I miss you all so dreadfully. I'm recounting a problem that was *mine*, not yours. Probably any of you who still like me enough to read my book wouldn't have been the ones tearing my house apart in the first place, but either way, it doesn't matter. This conflict wasn't about you.

Two years and many, many fights later, we finally got creative in our problem-solving. We finally thought outside the box. This wasn't either/or. It wasn't: have them at our house, or they won't feel the love. It wasn't: have them at our house, or I'm a failure. It was: let's have them *at* our house and not *in*. We didn't cancel Wednesday nights at the parsonage. Instead, we invited teens into our yard (but outside our house).

We gathered around the fire pit for hot dogs and marshmallows, for long chats and pyromaniac adventures. We played volleyball with the teenagers and let all the youth volunteers' kids play in our kiddie pool. We swung on the bag swing and climbed up the rope on the oak tree. And it was a great compromise. It was hotter outside than in, that's for sure, but my husband didn't have to give up teens at his house, and I didn't have to give up my sanity, my privacy, or my clean house.

I share this story to illustrate that compromises around ministry stressors are possible. For a long time, I saw the problem one way, and Jonathan saw it another way, and as long as we did that, there was no meeting in the middle. We had to get desperate enough to think about things in a different way, desperate enough try something new. I'm such a black-and-white thinker that our eventual solution never occurred to me (or my husband). In the end he must have figured he had to do *something* about his unhappy wife, no matter the ministry cost.

Now I look back and think how silly we were that we couldn't find a compromise sooner. At the time, though, it didn't feel silly at all. It felt deadly serious, as I'm sure all marriage conflicts do at the time. It took me a long time, but it was a good lesson to learn: sometimes there's a solution that isn't either/or. Sometimes there's a solution that meets both spouses' needs at the same time. Sometimes we just need to consider other options.

# Intensity and Intentionality

BY *ELIZABETH*

TWO WORDS COME TO mind when I think about marriage and motherhood on the field: intensity and intention. After living internationally for over four years, my experience has been that everything about living overseas is more intense than living in your passport country.

It's more physically intense. It's wildly hot where I am, with no central air conditioning. Housework takes longer as there are fewer automated devices. Electricity and water are sometimes unreliable, and food and water supplies aren't as clean. That meant that in the beginning especially, we were ill more often—and more severely—than we were back "home." Life in another country is also more mentally and emotionally intense. Learning a strange, new culture and doing everything in a new language is hard work. You make mistakes and misunderstand things every day.

Anyone crossing cultures must deal with these changes and stressors, but as a parent, I also bear witness to the strain of crossing cultures on my children. They get annoyed by aspects of life here: it's loud, it's crowded, and we have no yard or playgrounds nearby. They don't like the way local people touch them or stare at them, and they don't particularly like the local cuisine (or at least, not all of it). Life here is transitory, and the friends they make often move in and out of their lives with little advance warning. On top of all that, they miss friends and family back home—especially grandparents.

In light of the intensity of missionary life, I have to be more intentional about marriage and motherhood. I need to care for my children's hearts in a way I wouldn't if we lived in America. Of course we have the same preschool and preadolescent emotional turmoil that children and parents have in their home culture, but we also have more potential issues. I have to keep my own heart soft toward my kids, and I need to take the time to validate their feelings. This is difficult to do as I am already emotionally, physically, and spiritually stretched to the max myself. Practically speaking, it means I also need to carve time out of our schedule so they can communicate with friends and family back home (usually that's through Skype).

Marriage is the same way: I have to be intentional about taking care of it. Simply surviving here takes more time and energy, so it's tempting not to spend enough time on my marriage. But of course when I don't spend time on it, my marriage suffers. The less time I spend on my marriage, the farther I drift away from my husband, and the harder it is to bring us back to together again. Likewise, the more time and effort I pour into my marriage, the easier and more fulfilling it is. It becomes life-giving instead of life-draining, as it does when I'm not nurturing it enough.

In order to pour so much time and energy into my husband and my children, I have to be intentional about filling myself up. I have to be vigilant about taking care of my spirit by getting up early to spend time with God. I have to be diligent about taking care of my mind and body by eating at regular intervals throughout the day, exercising four or five days a week, and going to bed on time. If I don't do these things, I don't have enough emotional energy to pour into my husband and children, who need me so much.

In many ways marriage and parenting on the field is the same as it is in my home culture, but its intensity level is higher. Missionary life simply requires more of me, and in order to match its intensity, I have to be intentional about taking care of both myself and my family. I have to daily turn my heart toward them and toward God. When I don't, the consequences are great. But when I do, the reward is greater still.

# What Christians Can Learn from a *New York Times* Article about Sleeping with Married Men

BY *ELIZABETH*

THE *NEW YORK TIMES* RECENTLY PUBLISHED an article by Karin Jones entitled, "What Sleeping with Married Men Taught Me about Infidelity."[1] A friend shared it, and I read it. I found I had a lot to say about it, so I commented on my friend's Facebook share, where it received so much positive feedback that I thought I'd share it here. But my response will make more sense if you take the time to read the article first.

My worldview obviously differs from the author's—in fact I might say it diverges greatly—but I think she makes some important observations. My thoughts on this subject are influenced, of course, by eighteen years of marriage. But they are also greatly informed by my husband's research on relationships and sex.

Before you think that sounds too weird, let me explain why he reads extensively about these issues: he works with a lot of couples in his pastoral counseling ministry. For the record, I don't know who any of his clients are; I only know about the ideas in his books. (The only exception to this would be when a client of his walks up to me and announces, "Your husband is my counselor." This is not frequent, but has occasionally been known to happen.)

And now that I've finished all my caveats, we can move on to my thoughts about the *New York Times* article.

~~~~~~~~~~

1. Jones, "What Sleeping With Married Men."

I know it might sound crazy to say this, but I think a lot of Christian wisdom is not super helpful to marriage and that we can also learn from secular or research-based sources. First off, sex is more important to a marriage than we in Christian circles sometimes like to think. Dr. Barry McCarthy, author of the 2015 book *Sex Made Simple: Clinical Strategies for Sexual Issues in Therapy*,[2] claims that a counselor simply cannot afford to treat only the communication/relationship aspect of a marriage and assume good sex will follow.

Rather, McCarthy claims, sex must be addressed separately and intentionally, in addition to other relationship needs. Sex is too important to the marriage for a counselor to be silent on the issue. And it's highly complex and individual. This is part of the reason it needs purposeful addressing, though many counselors are uncomfortable talking about it.

The research shows that couples in America are having less and less sex, with a good percentage (around fifteen percent) being in what is considered a "sexless marriage" (sex ten times a year or less).[3] The research also shows that when a couple stops having sex, it's more often the husband's decision,[4] not the wife's (this information was also found in McCarthy's book, where he quotes H. Feldman's 1994 article in the *Journal of Urology*).[5]

The fact that sexlessness was primarily dependent on the man was news to me as women often get slandered in culture for being "frigid." This mischaracterization seems key to common Christian teaching that women want affection and connection, while men want sex. Research shows that this traditional approach is unhelpful in the sexual arena: women want good sex too. This is something the author of the *New York Times* article touched on and something proponents of the traditional view often neglect. God made us all sexual beings, and satisfying sex is important for both spouses in a marriage.

Another aspect of relationships that the article's author noted was that men do not just want sex. They want connection and affection as well. Maybe it's modern American culture, or maybe it's American Christian culture, or maybe it's both, but men are sometimes expected to be emotionless and connectionless in favor of more manly behavior.

2. McCarthy, *Sex Made Simple.*

3. McCarthy, *Sex Made Simple*, 53.

4. McCarthy, *Sex Made Simple*, 3.

5. Feldman, "Impotence."

If you want support for that claim, you can listen to this radio program[6] about the way men's human needs are marginalized in modern American culture. I think the church needs to push back against this aspect of mainstream culture and show a better way—one based in our foundational beliefs of a relational Godhead and of humans created in God's image. The Bible is actually good news for culture, even when culture accuses it of being otherwise.

This artificial differentiation between men's needs and women's needs is unhelpful for marriage and society in general. Men are images of God as well as women, and God is a relational God. Men and women both want loving, secure attachments, and men and women both want satisfying sex. I wish we didn't have some of these stereotypes, stereotypes I learned before marriage as important for maintaining a happy marriage: a man should give his wife the affection she so desires, so that she will be more willing to give him the sex he so desires.

The Bible does not even support this idea of "his needs, her needs" or "women give sex to get love and men give love to get sex." The woman in *Song of Solomon* showed strong sexual desire and initiation. Paul, often accused of being misogynistic (though I no longer think he was), told married couples that sex goes both ways—the wife's body belongs to her husband, and the husband's body belongs to his wife's. Meaning: the woman has desire too. Men aren't the only ones who want sex. It seems to me that sex is actually a place in marriage where our theology gets worked out, but we rarely think about it that way.

I do appreciate the author's note that even the urge to have an affair could be the beginning of an important conversation in marriage. Of course we as Christians believe this: temptation does not inevitably lead to sin. Temptation can be a wake-up moment and lead to increased marital intimacy, but only if we, like the author suggests, are willing to be honest with ourselves and with our spouses.

If we desire something we are not currently experiencing, we need to talk to our spouses about it, and not (if the Bible is our authority) seek out extramarital affairs. Research from the Gottman Institute indicates that being able to talk about sexual issues is essential to sexual satisfaction: "Only 9% of couples who can't comfortably talk about sex with one another say that they're satisfied sexually."[7]

---

6. Vedantam, "Guys, We Have A Problem."

7. Benson, "Couples That Talk About Sex," lines 2–3.

Meaning: if you can't talk about sex with each other, the likelihood that you're having mutually satisfying sex is pretty low. But, like Jones explains in her article, talking about sex can be risky. You might find out something about yourself that you don't want to know. You might feel rejected. And that was apparently too high a risk for the married men she was sleeping with.

Esther Perel, who is referenced in the *New York Times* article, has a fascinating TED talk on the interplay and tension between love and desire.[8] I've actually watched it several times as I believe its vocabulary is helpful. It may not be specifically Christian teaching, but there is nothing anti-biblical about it. It frames the monogamy conversation better than it has sometimes been framed, and I encourage you to watch it (TED talks are, after all, fairly short).

The Bible seems to indicate that the intimacy—including sexual intimacy—that we can experience in marriage is only a small picture of God's love for us and what he intends for us to experience with him for all eternity. So it only makes sense that Satan would attack our sexuality as it is intended to be lived out, both before marriage and in marriage.

Our cultures are obsessed with sex, but according to research, few people are actually having mutually emotionally and physically satisfying sex. So the ways we as a culture are seeking sexual fulfillment are not working. We're seeking it in all the wrong ways. Sometimes because terrible things have been done to us, sometimes because we have simply believed the culture's (Satan's) lies. There are a myriad of reasons our sexuality gets broken in this world.

If we care about our own marriages and the marriages of our children, if we care about the marriages in the future church, sex cannot be some taboo topic that we think will work itself out in silence. It won't. It needs specific cultivating and sometimes outside help (in the form of medication or therapy), and there is absolutely no shame in seeking help and wholeness for a part of our lives that is not thriving.

But if we feel ashamed of needing help, we won't seek it. So if this chapter can do any good in the world, I hope it can empower people in marriage whose sex life is less than they desire, to seek out help somewhere. I believe seeking healing is worth it.

---

8. Her TED Talk is titled, "The Secret to Desire in a Long-Term Relationship."

# Women Have Desire Too:
# The Thing We Overlook When We Talk
# about the Billy Graham Rule

*BY Elizabeth*

So I DECIDED TO weigh in on the Billy Graham Rule. Sounds risky, I know, but realize before you read this that I'm not attempting either to criticize a rule *or* to make new rules for people. I'm just reflecting on the atmosphere of sexual teaching I've personally encountered in Christian culture.

I'm not assuming that my interpretation of Christian sexual teaching is universal or even up-to-date. I speak only from my experience growing up in 1990s middle America. Church culture in various places and in various times will likely be different, as will each of our interpretations of said church culture.

Growing up in the church, I didn't get the sense that the power of a woman's sexual desire was really acknowledged. A woman's sexual attractiveness was certainly acknowledged; young men were taught how to fight their attraction to women, and women were taught how to cover their attractiveness. This led to an idea of women as temptresses, but only so far as their appearance goes. The temptation and attraction of the female wasn't at the soul-level. It was only skin deep.

We were taught that women didn't have the strong sexual desires or visual natures that men had. This of course meant that no one taught girls how to keep their sexuality under control in any way other than their clothing choices.

I think this does a grave disservice to both men and women. Men become dehumanized through this view: they are greedy creatures who must be sexually satisfied at all costs and who are incapable of looking beyond a woman's appearance to see her soul. It reduces sexual desire to physical appearance, while I believe sexual desire is very much rooted in the emotional and spiritual.

Women fall by the wayside when we see through this lens. Girls are not taught how powerful their desires can become. They are not taught that forming an intimate emotional relationship with a man could stoke their sexual desire in ways that are later difficult to manage. They're only taught that they must keep their bodies under wraps so that the men can manage their desires. But girls aren't taught that they themselves might need to control their desire, or given any practical ways to do so.

So the thing that concerns me about the Billy Graham Rule conversation is not whether it is wise to follow it, or whether it is legalistic to follow it. What concerns me is the way the conversation seems to reduce women to an object of desire and not a *source* of desire.

Perhaps I do not fully understand the conversation, but this is the way I see it: when we talk about women as temptations to men (because we tend to think more about the ways the Billy Graham Rule *protects men*), we are talking about the way women's *bodies* are tempting. The impression I receive, then, is that if a man is in a room alone with a woman, he won't be able to contain his sex drive, especially if that woman is considered societally "beautiful."

The way I hear it discussed seems to me almost to border on harassment or assault, the way a man wouldn't be able to control himself in a woman's presence. In this view, a woman tempts a man passively but not consensually. I think this is ludicrous. It means we don't think men have any self-control at all. It means we don't think of men as being fully human with a mind and a will that can make self-sacrificing choices.

I know, through both personal experience and years' worth of conversation and reading, that there is an abundance of bad men in this world. Many men are willing to take advantage of women's physical and social weaknesses. But I have also met an abundance of good men who respect women as fellow humans and would not dream of taking advantage of them.

I'm deeply bothered when I sense men and women being categorized so simplistically. Men are not merely dominators who, at the same time, are helpless in the face of a pretty woman. And women are not merely seductresses unaware of their overpowering attraction to men. People are more complex than that.

Whether couples or singles choose to follow the Billy Graham Rule should depend on their personal and shared histories. It should depend on their consciences and their circumstances. But it should not depend on a distorted view of male and female sexuality.

For myself, having lived nearly 37 years as a woman in a woman's body, I will say that if I were going to follow the Billy Graham Rule (but spoiler alert: we don't), the reason would not be because I don't trust men to control themselves. No, the reason would be because I don't trust *myself*.

I know how strong sexual desire can become. If my husband and I remained virgins before marriage, I have to credit *him* with the "no." I cannot possibly credit myself. The strength of desire surprised me—I think in large part because of the pervading idea that women aren't sexual beings in the same way men are. But perhaps my experience is singular. Perhaps other women did not grow up in an environment that minimized their sex drives.

It is for these reasons that I consider my own self as a potential source of desire. Even as someone enjoying a very happy marriage, I have to be honest and say that temptation or attraction can still occur. This statement is true for both of us (and yes, we talk about these things). Temptation happens simply because human desire is powerful—including the female desire that is too often neglected in these Billy Graham Rule conversations.

So what I wish for the world is not that we would universally follow the Billy Graham Rule or universally disregard it. What I wish is that we could have more and better conversations about temptation and about what it means to be a human made in the image of God.

I don't want us to treat other human beings as primarily sexual beings, thus reducing their humanity. Nor do I want us treat ourselves and others as immune to temptation, thus living in ignorance and arrogance. What I wish is that the world could be a place where both men and women truly see each other as the fellow humans that we are.

I want us to know ourselves and our spouses well enough that we know what kinds of boundaries to place around our marriages and our other relationships. I want us to pour into our marriages and live in love and trust with each other. I want men and women to be able to relate to each other in the church and in the workplace with interest, integrity, and respect.

I want us to understand so deeply who God created us to be that we won't waste time arguing over legalities but will work to build up the image of God in each other through thoughtful conversations, safe relationships, and a shared wonder and worship of the Maker of all things.

# I'm a Proverbs 31 Failure

## BY *ELIZABETH*

*"A wife of noble character, who can find" (Prov* 31:10 *NIV)?*

RECENTLY, AS MY HUSBAND read aloud from Proverbs 31 over the breakfast table, I wondered if maybe that was a rhetorical question. As in, "Can anyone find this woman?" She has an extensive list of accomplishments and abilities. She seems to be able to do it all with skill. Am I really supposed to be like her?

I have this vague notion that the modern Proverbs 31 woman stays at home with her (many!) children, educates them at home, makes all their (organic!) meals from scratch, enthusiastically serves her church community, and, after all that, is still (frequently!) romantically available to her husband. And while there is certainly nothing wrong with any of these endeavors individually, I personally cannot live up to all these expectations at once.

Thankfully, my husband has a firm belief that "nobody does it all." "Something always gets dropped," he often tells me. He believes this because he watched his mom choose not to do it all. He was never under the impression that one woman could—or should—do it all. His mom did stay at home with her eight children, and homeschool them, but she was not involved in church ministry, nor did she have a home business. The meals she prepared for her family were exceedingly simple. Sometimes it was cereal for supper. Other times it was baked potatoes, with nothing but cottage cheese as a topping. Her home, however, was a place of joy and peace that others felt drawn to.

(Incidentally, when my husband closed the Bible that morning, he sighed, "I don't think this woman exists. And if she did, I don't think I'd like her.")

I have never been one of those women who could juggle several responsibilities at once. In college, I took a mere twelve or thirteen hours each semester. With the remainder of my time, I tended to my marriage, and together we volunteered at our church. A couple of times I tried to extend my summer job into the school year. Each time the attempt ended with me quitting that job.

I recently had an opportunity to admit to myself yet again that I cannot do it all (and retain some semblance of sanity). I decided I should study Khmer (the local language) during my short summer break. It was so hard I about had a breakdown. Or maybe I did have a breakdown. Ask my husband. On second thought, don't ask him! It was he who suggested I quit studying, after noticing that I had absolutely no energy left over for the family. I was adamant that I continue—because a missionary wife should know the local language. It's, like, a requirement or something.

I know so many missionary wives who do speak Khmer well, and I thought I was such a failure not to be like them. But if I am to listen to my husband's wisdom, I must accept that I can't do it all. I must drop something. And at this point in my life, I am choosing to drop further language learning. I've got five people in my family who need me—to laugh at their jokes, to care for their troubles, and to be engaged with what's happening from day to day. I couldn't do that when I was studying language.

Truth be told, language learning is not the only thing I have dropped. I've also dropped ministry outside my home. I used to be active in ministry with my husband, and I loved it. Right now, though, the focus of my ministry is my home—my husband and children. But the truth of the matter is also that homeschooling all day pretty much takes everything I have to give. I need the help of a lady to do basic cleaning tasks each day, and to cook our noon meal. I have clearly failed in this whole womanhood thing. I mean, wives should cook and stuff, right?

But if I hadn't dropped the cooking and cleaning, I would have been forced to drop other things. Things I didn't want to drop. Like adequate school time for my children and adequate sleep for me (perhaps transforming me into the classic Proverbs 31 woman who wakens early and works late into the night?).

My husband doesn't want me *plus* language fluency. He just wants me. My children don't want me *plus* gourmet meals. They just want me. My friends don't want me *plus* a clean house. They just want me.

The best way for me to stay me is not to pretend I do it all and do it all well. Because I don't, and I can't. I very deliberately drop many things in my life, so that I may wholeheartedly embrace the things I haven't dropped.

I don't get it all done. I am a Proverbs 31 failure. But my family gets a happier me. A nicer me. A more likable me. If I didn't fail as a Proverbs 31 woman, I am convinced I would be far less successful at loving people. The greatest command of all.

# The Proverbs 32 Man

## BY *JONATHAN*

WOMEN HAVE HAD THEIR chapter long enough, and my wife's written about how she's pretty much failed at following it. I think it's time for the men.

It's time we define the ideal man to whom we should compare all men, henceforth and forevermore, regardless of context or culture, giftedness or calling, personality or preference. *This* is the perfect man.

Now, this isn't some sort of legalistic standard we're going to hold all men to. It's just sort of a guideline for men to aspire to. It's good for men to have goals and examples. If a guy feels bad because he isn't as awesome as the Proverbs 32 man, he shouldn't. He should be encouraged and challenged to try harder to honor God with his manhood. Proverbs 32 can provide a sort of prayer guide for the man who falls short, giving him something to lean into and press into and run hard toward. He should humbly allow this interpretation of perfection to take him deeper than his feet could ever wander.

Who can find the perfect man? A man who'll actually stop for a bathroom break, or ask for directions? Where is this man? Tell me if you know.

He's a businessman, survivor man, romantic man, warrior-poet man, and a soft man. He cries when he needs to and holds you when he's supposed to, and yet he can karate chop the tusks off of a hippo when necessary.

His wife can trust him to get the right kind of cheese at Target, and *not* stop at McDonald's on the way home. He will help the children to eat healthy and exercise regularly.

He is energetic and spunky, especially when accomplishing the honey-do list, but he calms down appropriately when inside.

His hands are busy paying bills and writing checks to pay for all the wool and flax his wife's hands are busily spinning.

He helps the poor and the needy, but he never lets them get the house dirty or interrupt date night.

He looks good in a suit, but is always modest.

He has no fear of winter, for his wardrobe includes plaid flannel for pseudo-adventuring in tightly controlled national forests and hip coffee spots. (Plaid is required in both places, as is facial hair, which he has plenty of.)

He quilts when he needs to, quoting Chesterton and Keller. He is Luke from *Gilmore Girls* and Mr. Darcy from *Pride and Prejudice*. He is also Aragorn and Thor.

His wife is well-known, but not too well-known.

He makes belted linen garments and sashes to sell to people, but only to married people, because, you know, purity.

He is clothed with strength and dignity and a strong sense of humor. When he speaks, he speaks with the wisdom of Solomon and the wit of either Jimmy.

His children stand up when he enters the room and he doesn't even have to ask them. His wife completely and totally adores him, boasting often about her "smokin' hot husband."

He serves on the deacon board, the mission board, the elder board, and he's even good with real boards. His hands are gentle but firm, and softly calloused.

Many men are awesome, but you are the awesomest. It's not a competition, but really, if it were, you would be winning.

There are tons of guys in the world, but you, Proverbs 32 man, with your ample character, charisma, and cash, surpass them all.

# TAKING CARE OF YOUR CHILDREN WELL

# Three Ways to Care for the Heart of Your Third Culture Kid

BY *JONATHAN*

JESUS LOVES THIRD CULTURE Kids (TCKs). He knows their needs and he hears their hearts' cries. He can tell the difference between normal teen angst and deep emotional pain. He feels their searching and longing for home, and he cares. Jesus knows the right thing to say at the right time, all the time. As parents, youth workers, family, and friends, we're not always so, um, Christlike.

Yet, in spite of our weaknesses, we have the great honor and privilege of parenting and loving TCKs. So may we, with great tenderness and sensitivity, care for the hearts of the kids we've taken with us.

If you're not raising kids abroad, please know that our TCKs need you too. They need extended families, peers, friends, team members, and churches who care.

So, with great deference to the TCKs who've shared their hearts with me, the experienced youth workers who've coached me, and the older parents who are busy providing such great examples, I want to consolidate a few ideas and share them here.

## 1. Allow ALL Emotions

One of the quickest ways to damage the heart of a TCK is to outlaw negative emotions (grief, anger, disappointment, etc.). Tell them they shouldn't feel something, or that they just need to suck it up, or that their feelings show a lack of gratefulness. Yup, that'll do it.

But, and this is the great part, allowing a TCK to experience the full range of emotions is one of the most caring things you can do. It's also one of the healthiest things you can do.

One TCK told me, "We were never allowed to show any sadness. Even when my siblings left the Lord, we still couldn't show any grief." She was hurting deeply, but her family had placed all negative emotions off limits. She locked her pain away and kept it private for years.

Another TCK said,

> "My parents were often busy, and would give me lines like, 'Living here is good for you! It's something few other people ever get to experience. When you get older and look back on this time, you'll be grateful for what you learned here.' Their comments were well meant, but they didn't know the depth of my pain."

After listening to TCKs and others dealing with loss, I've come to believe that Romans 8:28, although true, is often used as the perfect "anti-grief" verse. Please don't use it like that.

Often, a TCK who is not allowed the full range of emotions will cope by stuffing negative emotions (which is extremely unhealthy for their long-term emotional development). Alternatively, they may cope by removing whatever it is that outlawed their emotions; and if religion was the eraser used to remove emotion, religion may be the first thing they throw away.

Further Resources:

"Learning to Grieve," by Marilyn Gardner. https://communicatingacrossboundariesblog.com/2013/05/07/learning-to-grieve-well/

"God Can Heal Our Broken Potatoes," by Chris Bowman. http://www.alifeoverseas.com/god-can-heal-our-broken-potatoes/.

## 2. Ask Heart-focused Questions

Recognize that your TCK's experiences will be vastly different from yours, whether they are more positive or more negative. They may not identify with your host culture as much as you do. They may identify with it *more* than you. Are you okay with that?

When our family drives by the US Embassy and sees the flag flying, my kids feel nothing. When the President visited Phnom Penh and we saw Marine One (the President's helicopter) flying over the Mekong, I stood there and cried like a baby. My boys looked up at me and said, "OK, can we go eat now?"

If you really want to care for the heart of your TCK, you have to ask questions. And you have to care about their answers. But not just their answers, you have to care about the heart behind the answers.

Try asking questions like:

- What's something you like about this country?

- What's something you don't like about this country?

- What did you enjoy about our last visit to (insert passport country)?

- What was frustrating or annoying about our last visit to (insert passport country)?

- Where do you feel like your home is?

- Is there anything that scares you in this country?

- Is there anything that scares you in (insert passport country)?

- If you could change one thing about your life in this country, what would you change?

Here's an example of how this might pan out. Prior to our first trip back to the States, we asked our kids, "Where is home for you?" Two kids said, "Cambodia's home." One said "America's home" and one said, "I feel like I have two homes; one in America and one in Cambodia." We took their answers at face value, without trying to convince them that they should feel differently.

We also preemptively asked our friends and families in the States *not* to say things to our kids like "Welcome Home!" and "Isn't it great to be home?" Typically, it's very hard for a TCK to identify one place as home, so we gently requested that folks ask instead, "What do you like about America?" or "What are you looking forward to doing in America?"

It was a pleasure to see our kids allowed to identify Cambodia, America, or both as home. An older TCK once said, "The problem with Facebook is that you can only list one hometown."

Again, the goal is not just to complete a checklist; it's to see into the heart of your TCK. So be sure you're ready to really listen when they began answering. And again, if they say something you disagree with, or something that seems negative, so what? This is about *their* feelings, not about how your feelings are superior or more developed or how you see reality more clearly.

You want your TCK to feel heard, and that won't happen if you discount or disqualify their feelings. It doesn't mean you can't parent them or try to correct bad attitudes, it's just that first and foremost, you're aiming to hear their heart, not fix it.

Further Resources:

"Some Thoughts from Adult TCKs to Those Who Raise Them," by Marilyn Gardner. https://communicatingacrossboundariesblog.com /2014/05/22/some-thoughts-from-adult-tcks-to-those-who-raise-them/.

## 3. Study Your Family's Culture

I'm sort of a spy. (Not really, but we're toward the end of the chapter, and I wanted to make sure you were still paying attention.)

Shortly after arriving in Cambodia, with kids aged 8, 6, 3, and 1, I knew I needed help. So I called up the local expat youth pastor and started asking questions. I asked, "What are the main predictors of healthy TCKs in Cambodia? Have you seen any commonalties among the families who seem to have healthy teens? Any commonalities among the families who seem to *not* have healthy teens?"

And then I asked my real spy question, "What families seem to be doing really well?" She gave me her top three, and I've been collecting meta-data ever since.

"What it all boils down to," she told me, "is the family's culture." She said, "Generally, if the family culture is emotionally healthy, the TCK will be emotionally healthy." So, if you want to care for the heart of your TCK, consider your family culture as much as you consider your host country's culture. You live abroad, you study culture. So, what's your family's? What are your rituals and habits? How do you deal with grief and celebrations? Do you value saving face, or do you communicate very directly? Is there a lot of physical touch? Laughter? You get the idea.

Parts of all cultures are holy and reflect the wonder and beauty of God. Parts of all cultures should change when they come into contact with the gospel. What aspects of your family culture are awesome and wonderful? What parts need to be redeemed?

~~~~~~~~~~

May our TCKs be the most loved, most cared-for people on the planet. May they never doubt our love or the love of the Father. And in their search for home, may they find him.

# Three Ways to Care for the Heart of Your Missionary Kid

*BY JONATHAN*

I THOUGHT I WAS done with youth ministry. I thought I'd move to Cambodia, be a "real missionary" (whatever that is), and never attend another youth camp or weekend retreat. I thought I'd never smell junior high ever again, or play those stupid messy games created by someone who's never had clean-up duty. But I've never been so happy about being so wrong, because the missionary kids with whom I've had the privilege of interfacing over the past few years have encouraged and challenged and taught me so much.

They've also broken my heart:

As I've seen them say goodbye to home. Again.

As I've heard them describe the pain of being misunderstood.

As I've watched them hug good friends whom they know they will most likely never see again. Ever.

This chapter is dedicated to those students. To the ones who've let me in their lives, even just a little bit. To those who've laughed with me (and at me), to those who've answered my questions (even the stupid ones). Thank you.

And for the record, I tremble as I write these words, acutely aware of the multitudes of godly parents who are too busy caring for the hearts of their missionary kids to write a chapter about it. When I grow up, I want to be like them.

OK, here goes. . .

## 1. Don't Call them "Little Missionaries"

They're not. They're kids, with unique temperaments, callings, and gift-ings. If they've decided to follow Jesus, then of course they should be encouraged to do the things that Christians do (invite people to follow Jesus, love people, serve people, etc.). But God may not call them to the same cross-cultural work as you, or cross-cultural work at all. And. That. Is. OK. Let them follow God where he leads them, and please don't be offended if it's not into full-time ministry.

There's absolutely nothing wrong with sending our kids to local schools, or out with local friends, but if we have the idea that our kids are little "soldiers for Jesus," we're playing a dangerous game. Kids aren't soldiers, and they're not missionaries. They're children, and we should give them the space to develop as such.

My dad was a dentist, but I didn't grow up among whirring drills and nitrous oxide (bummer). But that's the point, isn't it? *I was allowed to grow up.* And although I'm sure my dad used the phrase, "You're going to feel some pressure," he didn't use it on me.

## 2. Be Purposeful and Strategic

In Missionary Land, there's a book/seminar/website for everything. We study how to cross cultures and what to do once we've crossed. We study how to help the poor without hurting them. We talk about planting churches without building them, developing disciples without depen-dence. We're purpose-driven, strategizing, apostolic, visionary, pioneer-ing, missional, culturally sensitive, community-developing, social justice flag-waving, chain-breaking, tired people.

But are we as purposeful and strategic in our God-given, God-or-dained role as parents? Do we ponder how to disciple other peoples' kids more than our own? We are the first representatives to our kids of what a Christ-follower looks like. It's an amazing privilege, and it is deserving of attention.

You've sacrificed a lot to be with the people in your host country. In loving them, listening to them, and serving among them, you are aiming to show Christ. Make sure you do the same with your kids.

## 3. Remember that your MK's good behavior does not validate your life or ministry, and his or her bad behavior does not invalidate it

This one's insidious and devastating, but tying your validation to your child's behavior (good or bad) is a socially acceptable form of idolatry. It has nothing to do with walking in obedience, and everything to do with looking outside of the Father for approval and validation.

All of us are on a spiritual journey. We mess up, find grace, keep walking. But this natural process often gets bypassed for MKs. They show up in churches and are expected to have it all together. No struggles, no sin, *definitely* no doubts. Maybe their parents expect this, afraid that a misbehaving or doubting child will threaten their support base. Maybe it's church people.

In many ways, MKs live publicly, whether they want to or not. I mean, how many families in your passport country send monthly or quarterly newsletters to each other? One missionary kid confessed, "I had to be perfect so I wouldn't mess up my dad's ministry." Another girl said, "Everyone thinks I'm better than them." I asked her to clarify. She said, "They think because I'm an MK I'm more spiritual than them. They also think that I'm arrogant because they think *I think* I'm better than them." It's confusing, I know.

The pressure to validate a parent's life choices is too heavy, and the risk of invalidating a parent's life choices or ministry is too damning. Missionary kids should not have to carry either burden.

~~~~~~~~~~

May our children know, beyond a shadow of a doubt, that our love for them is immense, never-ending, and flows straight from the heart of the Father. And when they feel our love, may they feel him.

# A Prayer for My Third Culture Kids

## BY *ELIZABETH*

I REMEMBER READING *The Witch of Blackbird Pond* together and feeling such a kinship with the main character, Kit. She'd lived a life of privilege with her wealthy English grandfather on the island of Barbados, but when he died, she discovered his large debts. In order to pay them all, she then sold all his belongings.

After that she didn't know what else to do, so she booked a passage to New England, where some of her Puritan relatives lived. Her cousins' conservative lifestyle and religious customs were completely alien to her. When the ship docked on the shores of Connecticut, Kit realized "There was something strange about this country of America, something that they all seemed to share and understand and she did not"[1]— a TCK moment if ever I saw one.

Kit suffers intense culture shock. She's already grieving the loss of her grandfather, and she now doesn't fit into Puritan culture. In some ways she's even rejected by the community. She doesn't understand their religion or their worldview, and friends are hard to find. Her uncle is particularly cold toward her, and she's never performed such difficult, backbreaking labor before. New England winters are brutally cold and long. She misses leisurely tropical island life in Barbados: the heat, the sunshine, swimming in the ocean, her grandfather's extensive secular library.

But she grows to love her extended family. She even grows to love the beautiful fields nearby. Toward the end of the book, Kit attends a wedding. She thinks about how she doesn't fit in in New England, even though she loves the people and the place: "An almost intolerable

---

1. Speare, *Witch of Blackbird Pond*, 14.

loneliness wrapped Kit away from the joyous crowd. She was filled with a restlessness she could not understand. What was it that plagued her with this longing to turn back?"[2]

She had previously decided to return to Barbados and search for work there, but as she continues reflecting on both her old life and her new life, she realizes she can't go back to the way life was with her wealthy grandfather. Her two cousins have both fallen in love, and she realizes that she has as well—only the man she loved wasn't a Puritan permanently rooted to the Connecticut soil. He was a sailor, a migratory man, a man of good character, a free spirit like herself. And he loved her back. "Home" for her would be anywhere he was. Marrying him would mean continually traveling between Barbados and Connecticut, always on the move, but always with him. Literally, and not just figuratively, she was going to live in the in-between.

Our homeschool curriculum chose this novel for its relation to the Salem Witch Trials in early American history, but for me it turned out to be a metaphor for the life of the TCK. Crossing cultures, never completely identifying with one culture, never fully belonging, always grieving a loss of some sort, but needing—so desperately needing—someone to love, care for, and understand her. So with that story in mind, I offer this prayer:

> My child, I'm well aware that in this life, not everyone gets married. But should you happen to marry, first and foremost I pray you will marry a fellow lover of Jesus. And then—oh then—I pray you will marry someone who feels at home in the in-between spaces, who knows how to live in the margins of life, who's comfortable crossing over and blending in, even if never quite fully. I pray you will marry someone with a wide view of the world, who doesn't think you're crazy for your wide view, either. I pray you will marry someone who looks to God for full identity and belonging, someone who will understand your need to do so as well. I pray you will marry someone who understands the pain of separation and of goodbyes, someone who shares your yearning for heaven. I pray you will marry someone who understands that love is the best kind of medicine for a hurting heart and who knows how to give it. That person doesn't have to be a TCK, though they might be. Your Papa isn't a TCK, but he understands loss and living in the fringe. He understands love and nuance. So I pray for you to experience what I have

2. Speare, *Witch of Blackbird Pond*, 232.

experienced myself: that your heart will be fully understood and accepted, fully loved and wanted, fully celebrated and cared for. I pray you will have many years of adventure together, tasting of a perfect heaven here on a very imperfect earth, each year growing ever closer to our God and to each other.

# Failing at Fatherhood (How Moving Abroad Ruined My Parenting)

*By Jonathan*

I SAT ON THE floor, weeping.

I was two whole days into living abroad, and I was already losing it.

Those tears portended more, and in our first year overseas, the thing that knocked me down the most, the thing that discouraged and distracted and depressed me the most, was the sense that I was failing at fatherhood.

I loved being a dad. It was a very core part of my identity, and something I really cherished. Moving to Cambodia, I had expected cross-cultural stress. I had expected transition tension and unmet expectations. I had even expected conflict with other missionaries and nationals. But I never thought I'd feel like my identity as a father was being shredded up and burned in the furnace of a cross-cultural move. That was a surprise.

Have you ever felt that? Like living abroad was changing your parenting in a not-so-positive way?

We moved overseas when our boys were six and seven and our girls were one and three. I suppose my fathering style could have been characterized as, um, BIG. I loved playing with our kids in wide open spaces, throwing things, kicking things, climbing things. We played loud and we took up a lot of space, and that's how we liked it.

And then we moved to a concrete box with bars on the windows in an urban capital of a developing country. No grass. No yard. No large spaces. For me, the shift from wide open spaces to urban jungle was rough. I had to adjust, but first I got depressed. Often, it'd happen on a Saturday; I'd wake up just wanting to go outside and throw a football with my kids.

And with the clarity of thought that overwhelms at times like this, I felt like I had moved from a garden to a prison. A prison that was 95 degrees and thick with humidity!

I had traded acres of green for walls of gray. En Gedi for Sheol. I watched my kids hang from metal bars on windows when they used to hang from giant limbs on oaks. They were happy, but I was dying.

I missed being able to step outside and kick a soccer ball. I missed our fire pit on cold autumn nights. I missed our porch swing. I missed our yard. I missed the way I used to father. But thank God the story doesn't end there, with a depressed dad missing what once was. No, the story definitely doesn't end there. . . .

## The Dawn

Slowly, I began to realize a few things. First, I still needed to play with my kids, and second, I *could* still play with my kids. That sounds silly, I know, but in the haze of transition, this realization wasn't a given.

I knew things had changed; I knew I had lost some stuff. I needed to grieve that loss well and figure out how to adjust and bend and change too. Basically, what I needed was some creativity, a little bit-o-crazy, and the willingness to spend cash.

And so it began. I penciled in a "man trip" to a national park an hour outside of the city. I took the boys and we hiked and wrestled and joked and ate junk food. It was glorious.

I was invited to speak in Beijing. The boys tagged along (thanks in part to the honorarium), and we walked Tiananmen Square and the Great Wall. We ate at McDonald's. A lot. The younger one navigated the subway system, and "a clear day" took on a whole new meaning.

I took the girls on a staycation. We got a hotel outside of town, stayed up late, and swam a lot. Of course, we also ate junk food. (Don't tell mom.)

We started Nerf wars, using multiple levels of our row house, with intense battles taking place over the "eagle's nest" position on the top floor. Best vantage point and all.

I bought a ping-pong table and crammed it in a corner. One side has two feet of clearance, so we use the walls and ceilings as extensions of the table. That table provides lots of play time that my kids enjoy and I need. Does that sound weird? It's true. I need to play with my kids.

Rainy season hit our town, flooding the streets up to our knees. I yelled at the kids to get on the moto and we plowed through the water, making a giant wake with our urban jet ski. Neighbors laughed at the crazy white guy with three little kids screeching with delight in monsoon rains. In America, we'd find a snow-filled parking lot and drift in our van. Here, we found a flooded street and pretended we were on a lake! Same Same (but different).

We play air hockey on the tile floors, using wooden blocks as pucks and plastic cups as the handheld hitter things. We use Lego men to play table football. We put a badminton set on the flat roof, supposing that a birdie falling from forty feet would do less damage than a volleyball.

We rent a soccer field for $7/hour to throw a Frisbee or a football. I don't feel guilty spending the money. In America, we didn't have to rent the park.

We go cliff jumping at the Olympic Stadium pool. My six-year-old actually chipped her tooth jumping from the five-meter platform. I was so proud of her. (Don't tell grandma.)

My youngest daughter loves motorcycles. She wraps her little five-year-old fingers around the handlebar and yells "Faster, Papa! Faster!"

We have disco lights in the bathroom. Long story.


## Practically Speaking[1]

So, here's what helped me through this particular parenting crisis. Maybe these will help you too.

- *Be Creative.* Early on in transition, creativity is very hard to come by. You're exhausted and on the edge already. So ask around. Ask other parents, "What do you do for family time here? Where?" Just remember, what works for one family might not work for your family. That's OK. Find the things that work for your family, and then do those things. Boldly.

- *Be Crazy.* The Cambodians think we're crazy, and maybe they're right. Maybe I am crazy, but I'm also not depressed. Are you willing to look a bit weird? (Wait, you're a missionary, what am I saying?) But seriously, are you? Your survival might depend on it.

---

1. This material is also discussed in the earlier chapter, "Living Well Abroad."

- *Spend Cash.* If you need to spend some money to share a fun experience with your family, spend it. And don't feel guilty about it. Now, if you feel like God doesn't want you to spend it, then don't. But if you're afraid of spending money because of what your donors might think, that's a pretty good reason to go ahead and spend it. Don't let your kids grow up thinking that the most important question when discussing a family activity is, "What will our supporters think?" That question has killed many missionaries, and their children.

## One Day

My kids still make fun of me for crying in those early days. Thing is, I don't think they realize I was crying for them; I thought I had lost them. I thought I had lost me. One day they'll know.

One day they'll grow up and read this, and when they do, I hope they know how very much I loved being their dad. In America, in Asia, and anywhere else in this whole wide world.

## A Prayer for Parents

*On this path of parenting abroad,*
*May the Father's grace be with you.*

*May he comfort you with his love,*
*Craft in you deep creativity, and*
*Fill your home with joy.*

*May the peace that flows from the*
*House of God flood yours,*
*Filling it with hope, intimacy,*
*And the occasional disco light.*

# What I Want to Give My Third Culture Kids

*BY Elizabeth*

I DIDN'T KNOW HOW hard it would be to parent Third Culture Kids. I assumed that my own TCK upbringing would make it easier; I was only partially correct. While it's true that we share common feelings and experiences, and that my kids enjoy hearing stories from my own TCKhood, I didn't foresee the way living overseas would duplicate the pain of my youth. The grief of constant goodbyes, the temporariness of our community, the missing of friends and family back "home"—all these things deplete me.

I didn't know I'd need to juggle my own complicated emotions at the same time as my children's. It's hard for me not to outlaw my own emotions or to give my kids the time and space they need to grieve and mourn their own losses. I want to find the silver lining too soon, to rush too fast to a happy ending. It's hard not to swoop in prematurely in an attempt to ease their pain.

So in times of emotional distress, I actually tell myself to shut up. Then I open my arms and give them space to cry. I open my ears and give them time to speak. I want to give them a safe place to express themselves and to process their own emotions. I don't do this perfectly by any means, but it is my heart's desire nonetheless.

There's something else I want to give my TCKs, and that's *privacy*. I've chosen a very public profession; my children, however, have not. They may go wherever I go and live wherever I live, but they didn't choose to live a public life the way I did. Perhaps when they're grown, they will. I don't know. I only know I want to give them the luxury of choosing it for themselves.

Not too long after moving to Cambodia, I decided to keep my children's lives and struggles offline. I pulled back from sharing things about them on social media, and I focused on telling my own stories, and not theirs, on my blog. I'm guided by my own mother's example in this. Some of you know I struggled with an eating disorder as a teenager. I'm open about it now, but I would have been mortified if my mom had shared it publicly *then*, and I'm thankful for the way she protected my privacy.

I'm absolutely in love with my TCKs. They're amazing—so amazing, in fact, that they deserve to grow up out of the public eye. They're public enough as it is. That doesn't mean I'll never tell a story about homeschooling or family life, or share photos from a vacation or outing. But it does mean that, especially as they grow older and barrel toward upper elementary and middle school, I try not to post private details about their lives. It means I think carefully before sharing about them, and that in any public discourse, you'll find me honoring them by accentuating the positive rather than the negative.

None of this means I don't have trusted real-life people to whom I turn for prayer and parenting advice, because I do. And it doesn't mean we don't have a sending organization and a sending church that are checking up on us and making sure that our whole family is thriving, because we're blessed to have both. And it most certainly doesn't mean we don't celebrate our children and their hilarious antics with our family and friends, because we do! That's one of my favorite parts of family life, in fact, and we have a private Facebook messaging group for our closest family and friends just so we can share their sweet words and funny stories across the continents.

I love these words from fellow blogger and overseas worker Lindsey Lautsbaugh:

> "If [people] want to share their good news on Facebook and bad news in person, what's it to you? That actually sounds pretty healthy to me. 'Keeping it real' does not need to be an occasional #hashtag. If I see only people's success and not their struggle, failure, and fights with their kids, then I assume someone else gets the privilege of seeing those glorious moments. Someone else gets to gently say, 'Let your children live to see another day, walls can be re-painted.' Someone else gets to say, 'Call the counselor, and I'll babysit for you and your husband tonight.'

Another friend gets to challenge our tendency to hide our weaknesses and struggles."[1]

In saying all this, I recognize that different families do things differently. Some families may be more comfortable sharing their kids' stories publicly—and I don't judge that. All I want to do today is share my own personal parenting philosophy: I respect your right to feel your feelings, and I respect your right to keep those feelings private. *Those* are the things I want to give my TCKs.

1. Lautsbaugh, "Let's Not Say That Anymore," lines 38–52.

# Particle Physics Finally Explains
# Third Culture Kids

*BY Elizabeth*

Some of you know I'm a science lover. Our friends back in the States know this too, and a couple times a year they send us a package with their old science magazines (along with other treats). I love Magazine Arrival Day.

Earlier this year I cracked open the September 2014 issue of *Discover* magazine and read about neutrinos—tiny, subatomic particles I don't even pretend to understand. I'm a chemist, for goodness sake, not a physicist. My scientific understanding only goes down as small as protons and electrons, and not a quark smaller. Neutrinos are smaller than that, and also, extremely secretive.

As I read (largely uncomprehendingly) through the article, one particular section caught my attention, and I paused. *Are we sure we're talking about tiny subatomic particles here?* Because to me, this paragraph sounded more like the description of a fellow Third Culture Kid than anything else. Or, to enlarge the conversation a bit, it sounded like a Cross-Cultural Kid (CCK) or Third Culture Adult (TCA)—terms I first read about in Lois Bushong's insanely helpful *Belonging Everywhere and Nowhere.*[1]

Check out what the magazine article had to say:

> Neutrinos are notorious shape-shifters. Each one is born as one of three types, or flavors—electron, muon, and tau—but they can change flavors in a few thousandths of a second as they travel, as if they can't make up their mind what to be. Neutrinos, like other subatomic particles, sometimes behave like waves.

---

1. Bushong, *Belonging Everywhere and Nowhere.*

But as the neutrino travels, the flavor waves combine in different ways. Sometimes the combination forms what is mostly an electron neutrino and sometimes mostly a muon neutrino. Because neutrinos are quantum particles, and by definition weird, they are not one single flavor at a time, but rather always a mixture of flavors. On the very, very rare occasion that a neutrino interacts with another particle, if the reaction appears to produce an electron, then the neutrino was an electron flavor in its final moments; if it produces a muon, the neutrino was muon-flavored. It's as if the shy neutrino's identity crisis can only be resolved when it finally interacts with another particle.[2]

So let's break that down a bit and see if we can find any similarities:

*Neutrinos are shape-shifters.* Or, as the TCK literature says, we are cultural chameleons who can shift between cultures and adapt to new ones more easily.

*Neutrinos can change flavors as they travel, as if they can't make up their mind what to be.* Again the chameleon quality is shining through. TCKs may have divided loyalties, and we might not want to choose one culture over another.

*Neutrinos are quantum particles, and by definition, weird.* TCKs often feel different from other people—"weird," if you will. (And for me, that differentness has sometimes left me feeling lonely.)

*Neutrinos are not one single flavor at a time, but rather always a mixture of flavors.* Likewise, TCKs aren't one single culture or flavor; we're a mixture.

*It's as if the neutrino's identity crisis can only be resolved when it interacts with another particle.* Not only do we often struggle with identity crises—*who am I?*—but TCKs can also be so good at adapting that we take on the culture of whatever people we most recently interacted with.

2. Setton, "Neutrinos: Ghosts Of The Universe," lines 93–112.

# Two Challenges Homeschooling Families Face on the Field

## BY *ELIZABETH*

IN 2016, MY FRIEND Tanya Crossman published her book *Misunderstood: The Impact of Growing Up Overseas in the 21st Century*. Tanya worked with Third Culture Kids in Beijing for over a decade before writing her book, and I greatly value her insight into the hearts of TCKs today.

I'm passionate about homeschooling my four TCKs, so as soon as I received my copy of her book, I skipped straight to the homeschool section. Here is what I found:

> The majority of homeschool families I know do an excellent job. Unfortunately, I have also mentored and interviewed TCKs who had less effective, and less pleasant homeschool experiences. Those who shared negative experiences always referred to at least one of two key issues: working alone, and lack of social interaction.[1]

As a parent, I want to be aware of these two important issues. I spoke about them at a conference earlier this year, and though not everyone homeschools (or even has children), I think these issues are pertinent enough to warrant discussion here. Youth workers, sending agencies, and others who care about the well-being of TCKs may also be interested in how to help parents approach these concerns.

---

1. Crossman, *Misunderstood*, 76.

## 1. Working Alone

When we talk about working alone, we mean that neither parent is teaching the child, *and also that no outside tutor or teacher has been engaged either*. This could include single-parent homes or situations where both parents work full time outside the home. On a practical level, the child has no teacher.

It's unrealistic to expect a child to teach himself or herself completely, even in high school. (In my opinion, it's especially important for high school students to have educational and emotional guidance from adults.) Every child needs a teacher, a tutor, a mentor, a guide. And while it's valuable to learn how to teach oneself through books and videos, and while we do want our children to become lifelong learners, students generally need someone of whom they can ask questions.

This is something to be aware of even with curricula designed for homeschooled students, curricula that are marketed to "teach the student." Our students still need someone to ask questions of when they get stuck. Even university students have this type of help: professors have office hours or other times set aside to answer questions and dialogue with their students.

If a parent cannot be available to help with schoolwork, remember that there are still many other options:

- Classes can be taken online, with online teachers who can teach and answer their questions. Some homeschool curricula are designed completely for online work. Others provide email support for textbook work.

- Tutors can be hired, either from the local or international community.

- Teaching times can be swapped with other homeschool parents in the area.

- Some families hire a tutor or teacher from their passport country to come live with them.

- Even when a parent is the main teacher, *we must be diligent about setting boundaries around school time and not letting ministry obligations crowd out our kids' study time on a regular basis*. This guideline goes especially for older students, who need larger amounts of uninterrupted study time to complete their high school course requirements. At times there will of course be exceptions to this. It's simply something to be aware of.

In any case, the message is the same: children should not be expected to teach themselves entirely. Neither we nor our children need to be world-class scholars; that's not the point of education. And we don't have to teach everything ourselves. We do, however, owe our children some care and attention to their schoolwork. Otherwise they may become discouraged with their lack of understanding or progress. They may also become lonely, which leads us to the second issue.

## 2. Isolation

When we talk about isolation, we mean not having enough friends or sufficient social interaction. Homeschooling is by nature less social than local, international, and boarding school options. At the same time, we remember that social needs vary from child to child. Some children need more social time than others. Other children are overwhelmed by too much social interaction.

But all children need friends, and teenagers especially need friends. The number of teenage TCKs in a community can tend to shrink as families with older children make the decision to move away (for many varied and valid reasons), while families with teenagers don't typically move to the field.

In addition, we as parents have social needs. The work of home education can be grueling. We need others to help us, to give us encouragement, to suggest fresh ideas, and simply to be friends. For parents and children both, community can be difficult to find on the field. This is especially true when families are geographically isolated.

Here are a few ideas for combating social isolation:

- Sometimes there are local co-ops or support groups we can join.

- Sometimes it's as simple as planning more times for our kids to hang out with their friends, or for families to spend time with other families.

- If you live far from other homeschooling families, this may even entail traveling an hour or more once a month.

- Online community can be helpful. Moms could join a Velvet Ashes community group. Your children could Skype with friends in your home country or other international kids your family has met through the years.

- Depending on their age, kids can text and message friends who live both far and near. This avenue of communication has become important to our family in the last year or so. It involves more technology than our kids may have used when they were younger, but we remember that it's for the vital purpose of human connection.

- Some families even move from rural areas to urban areas when their children reach the middle school or high school years.

Homeschooling families in general need a lot of support, but these workarounds are especially important if parents are homeschooling not by choice, but out of financial, geographical, or other necessities.

I've found personally that when our family started seeking out more consistent community (through a co-op in our case), my teaching, my confidence, and my peace of mind all improved, and my children's social lives improved. It turns out that they needed friends as badly as I did.

And we were in a good situation, where I had sufficient time to homeschool, I felt equipped to homeschool, and I wanted to homeschool. *We still needed more support than we had been receiving.* It's been about two years since we joined our homeschool community, and it's been key in helping our entire family thrive and be able to stay on the field happily.

It's probably going to take some sacrifices to meet these two needs. But we must remember that sacrifices are *always* made; we just have to decide what things we are going to sacrifice. Are we going to sacrifice our children's needs in favor of the ministry's needs, or are we going to try to find a healthier balance for the whole family?

Most families I know care about these issues and work hard to ensure their children are thriving both academically and socially. So this discussion is not a judgment, but rather a reminder to all of us to continue to be aware of the issues our children face and to keep finding ways for them to thrive in cross-cultural life.

# The Little Word That Frees Us
## (Lies, Part 1)

*BY ELIZABETH*

WE TALK A LOT about Missionary Kids (MKs) being Third Culture Kids (TCKs), but we talk less often about another aspect of their lives: the Preacher's Kid (PKs) aspect. These MKs of ours, these kids we love so fiercely, are both TCKs and PKs. They deal with both the cultural issues of TCKs and the potential religious baggage of PKs. It's the religious baggage that I want to talk about in this chapter.

Timothy L. Sanford, an adult MK and licensed professional counselor, wrote about some of the ramifications of growing up in ministry and missionary families in his book *I Have to be Perfect, and Other Parsonage Heresies*.[1] To give you a bit of context for this little-known book, Ruth Van Reken, co-author of the classic book *Third Culture Kids*, both endorsed it and helped to edit it.

I'm not a PK or an MK, and I can never presume to speak for them. This book was, however, surprisingly relatable for me, and at times rather painful. Perhaps it's because I entered ministry at age nineteen—not still a child, not quite a woman. Perhaps it's because I spent a few formative years in a highly legalistic church where everyone seemed to be on display. Whatever the reason, I found I was susceptible to the lies addressed in this book. If I, without growing up in a ministry home, resonate with these PK issues, then maybe other missionaries and church workers do, too. I also know that many MKs and PKs end up serving overseas, and I began wondering if the ideas presented in this book have broader applications for the body of Christ.

---

1. Sanford, *I Have to Be Perfect*.

While acknowledging the very special and unique lives PKs and MKs have lived, I also want to recognize that adults in ministry roles can absorb false ideas about themselves, about God, and about his people. And we all need truth and grace extended to us.

So this series is for all people in ministry contexts. Whether you grew up as a PK or an MK, whether you are currently or were formerly in overseas missions or local church ministry, or whether you're married to someone who is, this series is for you. It's also for the church at large. If you are someone who cares about the walking wounded among us, this series is for you, too.

I believe, along with William Paul Young, that "since most of our hurts come through relationships, so will our healing."[2] Sometimes the church gets stuck in damaging behavioral patterns, and we, as a collective people, perpetuate beliefs in the lives of ministry families that simply aren't true. Lies seep into our souls, and as a community we need to acknowledge them, wrestle with them, and ultimately reject them for there is a religious culture at work here that needs destroying.

I love the church, and I believe one of the glorious reasons God places us in a local body is so that we can "love each other deeply, from the heart" (1 Pet 1:22 NIV), and by so doing, participate in the healing of each other's hearts. That is what these chapters are about. Sharing our stories, and finding healing and wholeness together.

It is not about blaming parents or making anyone feel guilty. Rather, it is about mobilizing the church to dismantle some of our harmful systems. It is about calling on Christians to change the way we do life together. Ministers, missionaries, and their families are the most notable casualties here, but the body as a whole suffers when any member suffers. I believe we can be part of the healing.

But we need to do something first: we need to give ourselves permission to be honest. Before moving on to the lies PKs tend to believe, Timothy Sanford gives us permission to say the little word "and." Saying "and" enables us to tell the rest of our story; it enables us to tell all our story.

This is where he caught my attention—because I had not given myself permission to say "and." I had only been saying "but." "And" is not the same as "but." "But" tries to nullify, where "and" respects and includes. "But" attempts to cancel out the bad in our lives by focusing on the good,

2. Young, *Shack*, 11.

or to cancel out the good in our lives by focusing on the bad. The problem is, this doesn't work. The negatives don't nullify the positives in anyone's life, and the positives don't nullify the negatives. Ever.

For some reason this concept was even more freeing than the yays and yucks I learned about in mission training. The good doesn't mean the bad didn't happen, but neither does the bad mean the good didn't happen. They both happened. The question is: Can I hold them both together at the same time?

For a long time, I couldn't hold them both together. I had thought it was disloyal to admit that my parents' choices could ever cause me pain. But as a TCK in a military family, there was pain associated with our various relocations. There was good and there was bad in our life, just as there is good and there is bad in everyone's lives. I needed permission to say so. I needed permission to say, "I had an idyllic childhood, *and* all the goodbyes and hellos were painful."

And perhaps you do too. Perhaps you need to know it is equally valid to talk about the negatives as well as the positives. Perhaps you need permission to break the silence you've been holding. Perhaps you need permission to say:

> "My parents were good people, *and* they did some bad things, too."

> "Our church (or agency) leadership loved us, *and* they made decisions that hurt us, too."

> "I had some really neat experiences because of my parents' jobs, *and* there were some pretty awful experiences, too."

Sometimes we just need permission to say these things.

Furthermore, when I read this book, I realized that I must also give that permission to my kids. The life my kids live because of my choices, it's not all bad. And it's not all good. (But neither would their lives be all good or all bad had I not gone into ministry or not chosen to live overseas.)

Oh how I want to see life in black and white, as purely good or purely bad. But life is never black and white, and I learned I can't take offense at the various things my kids might say were good or bad. I need to let them hold their own "ands."

"But" is insufficient. We need to say "and." This little word opens up a whole new life for us. And. Just breathe. In, and out. And then, tell the rest of the story, the rest of *your* story. Tell all of it together. Tell the entire thing, the parts that make you feel broken, and the parts that make you feel whole. Tell your ands.

Wherever you are in the world, it is my prayer that you will find people who can handle all the ands of your life.

What are the "ands" of your life? Are you being honest about them with yourself and with others? Or is there something you need to say that you're not saying?

Perhaps the situation is reversed, and you need to hear someone else's "and." Are you willing to listen, even if it brings you pain?

Are our communities safe enough to tell the whole story of our lives? Are our communities safe enough for the "and?" Are we brave enough to listen to each other's "ands?"

# "I'm Not Supposed to Have Needs"
## (Lies, Part 2)

BY *ELIZABETH*

IN THE LAST CHAPTER I began a series on life in ministry families and the thinking patterns we absorb along the way. As I mentioned then, this conversation is for everyone—whether you grew up as a Pastor's Kid (PK) or Missionary Kid (MK), whether you entered ministry as an adult, or whether you love people who are.

In this chapter we'll continue by discussing three of the lies Timothy Sanford writes about in his book, *I Have to be Perfect, and Other Parsonage Heresies*. As we process these statements, keep in mind that everybody experiences life differently. You might react to some of these ideas and not to others, and that's okay.

### "I'm here for others" and "Other people's needs are more important than my own"

*Ouch*. These two lies hit close to home for me. They're so intertwined that they're hard to separate, and I've believed them both as a ministry wife. I've assumed people can walk all over me. All over my time, and all over my feelings. I've allowed people to trash my home, believing I must silently endure it as service to Christ. I've bought into the lie that I exist only to serve others, and that I can't have needs of my own. Furthermore, I thought if I didn't let other people do those things to me—and even more specifically, if I weren't joyful about it—then I wasn't a good Christian or a good ministry wife.

I required these things of myself. Did God require them of me? Must I only ever serve others? Philippians 2:4 (ESV) tells us to "look not only to our own interests, but also to the interests of others." That's an intriguing grammatical construction, the "not only, but also." The apostle Paul, arguably the greatest missionary of all time, seems to be assuming that we have needs of our own and simply encourages us to care for others in addition to ourselves.

Galatians 6:2 (ESV) instructs us to "Bear one another's burdens." Other versions say to "share" or "carry" one another's burdens. I have a hard time deciding which verb I like best, so let's use all of them: we are to bear, share, and carry one another's burdens. The words "one another" imply a reciprocal relationship: I help to carry your burdens, and you help to carry mine.

We're accustomed to carrying other people through *their* difficult times. We're not "supposed" to have troubles of our own. We're not supposed to need someone to carry us; instead we need to keep carrying other people. But what about those times when we can no longer carry someone else? What about the times we can't even carry ourselves? Can we let someone carry us for a change?

Being in ministry or missions doesn't mean we'll never need to be carried. It doesn't mean we'll never have needs. Sometimes we get comfortable stuffing our needs down and ignoring what our souls are saying to us. Sometimes we get accustomed to giving when we have nothing left to give. And sometimes we model those behaviors in our families.

Maybe we can start to acknowledge that we have needs of our own. Maybe we can allow others to pour into us for a time. Maybe we can give ourselves a little bit of the grace we offer so freely to others. (The flip side of this, of course, is that other people have to be willing to care for us, too.)

What does it take to create a community characterized by Galatians 6:2, a community of mutual burden-bearers who help each other through the troubles of life? It takes an acceptance, *by all of us,* that we don't always have to be strong. It's okay to be weak. It's okay to depend on others, even if we're in ministry—perhaps *especially* if we're in ministry.

The idea that "other people's needs are more important than my own" sounds very spiritual. It sounds very sacrificial and giving. But we are all of us humans, created and finite beings with limited resources. Our lives are powered by the Holy Spirit, true, but none of us can survive if we think we are *only* here for others, or if others' needs are always more important than our own.

There's a deeper, more insidious lie at work here, too. When we believe the lie that the only purpose of our life is to serve other people, we buy into the falsehood that we earn our worth, that our performance justifies our existence, that what we do, the service we yield for others, is what makes us valuable in both God's eyes and other people's eyes.

We need to remember the truth. We need to know, in the core of our being, down in the cellar of our souls, that God's love and approval do not depend on anything we do. The same God who made us from dust knows we are dust, and he redeemed us himself. We are caught in his arms, caught in his gaze, and there is nothing left for us to prove. There is only God's love, and the cross has already proved it.

## "I should already know"

This lie claims that I should already be farther along in my spiritual journey than I am right now. That whatever I know, I *should* know more. That wherever I am, I *should* be farther along. That whatever my faith is, it *should* be stronger. That however my relationship with God is faring, it *should* be better.

And of course my own personal favorite, oft-uttered in frustration: "Arg!! I should be a better person by now!!"

So. Many. Shoulds.

Saying and believing "should" entraps us. I *should* be nicer to that person. I *should* forgive those people. What happened back then *shouldn't* still hurt. I *shouldn't* be so angry at God. I *should* be less selfish and more generous. I *should* be more mature. I *shouldn't* struggle with this sin anymore. I *shouldn't* struggle with the "little" hardships in my life. I *should* be happier.

There's nowhere to go but down to the depths of despair if I don't do what I should do. If I'm not living life the way I should, then I'm a bad person. If I'm not as good as I should be, I've failed in my faith. If I'm not as dedicated as I should be, I've failed in my Bible study, failed in my prayer life, failed in my service to others.

*Should* looks to a past full of failures.

*Should* judges us as insufficient! Inadequate! Unworthy!

*Should*. This one single word oppresses us.

What can we do about the crushing shoulds in our life? Timothy Sanford suggests replacing them with coulds. Where *should* condemns,

*could* gives hope. Where *should* breeds anxiety and fear, *could* sees opportunity for growth. Where *should* paralyzes, *could* expands. I *could* talk
to God more. I *could* read his word more. I *could* forgive that person. I
*could* love that person more fully. A life of *coulds* is full of possibilities.

I want to give you permission to dump the shoulds in your life. I'd
love to simply say the words and be confident that you're no longer cap-
tive to your own shoulds, but I know better—I know it takes more than
just saying the words. I'm going to say them anyway: you don't need to do
more or be better than you are right now. You are already enough.

Wherever you are in your walk is acceptable for today. You're right
where you're supposed to be. Every day you'll grow. Every day you'll be
farther along than you were the day before, even if you don't feel the
change. Every day you'll receive another dose of grace, the medicine settling deeper into your soul.

The beauty, the mystery of it all, is that grace happens without any
shoulds at all. So let us release ourselves from the tyranny of the shoulds.
Let us release our pastors from the shoulds. Let us release our missionaries. And for goodness sake, let us release their children. As people loved
by a holy God and saved by grace alone, let us rid ourselves of these lies
before they imprint themselves onto the DNA of our souls.

~~~~~~~~~~~

Have you ever felt your needs didn't matter, or that you should already
know or be a certain something?

In your life, do you think those beliefs came from within yourself,
or externally from family culture or church culture, or some combination
of the three?

Do you need to take some time to detox from these unspoken beliefs, to give yourself a time of solitude and silence in order to relinquish
these pressures into the Father's hands?

# "I Can't Trust Anyone" (Lies, Part 3)

## BY *ELIZABETH*

THE LAST TWO CHAPTERS have been exploring the ideas in Timothy Sanford's book *I Have to be Perfect, and Other Parsonage Heresies*. I hope this exploration is as healing for you as it has been for me.

So far, we've given ourselves permission to say "and." Then we began to exchange our "shoulds" for "coulds." If you're new to the conversation, you might want to go back and read those first two chapters.

### "I'm different"

Before we dive into this lie, I need to clarify something. Sanford, himself an MK, says this belief has nothing to do with the legitimate "different-ness" of being an MK and having a blended-culture worldview. That's the TCK part of being an MK, and is a different discussion.

Rather, the belief that "I'm different" comes from being treated differently. It comes from living under different expectations and being required to abide by different rules. Sanford says this is not imaginary: though church members try to deny it, they often *do* judge PKs and MKs differently. People apply standards to them that they don't apply to regular people. Likewise, we ministers and missionaries often apply standards to ourselves that we wouldn't think of applying to nonministry people.

We need to pause here and acknowledge the truth inside the lie: adults and children in ministry contexts *do* have different experiences, and those experiences can be quite exotic. More travel, more exposure to other cultures, more opportunities to attend events and meet well-known Christian leaders.

Other times our experiences are darker. We (along with our children) see the underbelly of church and missionary culture. We know all about problem people and problem finances. We know who is against us, and at times we even know who is responsible for eliminating our positions and reducing our influence, *all in the name of Christ*. These are the secrets we must keep and the burdens we must bear—and that too, makes us feel different.

If we think we're different, however, we may keep ourselves from pursuing deep relationships. We may push people away and close our hearts to them. We may become lonely and even depressed. Alternatively, we may slide from believing we're different into believing we're better. We may like our positions of influence and authority: they boost our ego and pad our sense of pride. Although it's uncomfortable to admit sometimes, we are a tribe who likes to set ourselves not merely apart, but also *above*.

Neither of these reactions is right or healthy. We may lead very different-looking lives, but we bear the same image of God. We may shoulder different responsibilities, but we share the same human need for unconditional love and acceptance. I don't believe God's desire for those in ministry is any different than for anyone else. I believe he wants all of us to experience authentic, life-giving community. But if we believe we're different, we may cut ourselves off from the fellowship we so desperately need. If we believe we're different, we may deprive ourselves of the deep relationships our souls crave.

We need to delete the "missionaries are better" mindset from our vocabularies. We need to stop isolating and elevating people in ministry and start embracing each other as equals, no matter which labels we personally claim. We need to take responsibility for the pedestals we've placed certain people on—even if we placed *ourselves* on those pedestals.

We need to level our hierarchies. Missionaries sin, ministers sin, and our children sin—just the same as everyone else. We all need a Savior. Honesty, openness, and acceptance are for *all* members of the body. They're for the ones preaching from the pulpits, and for the ones sitting in the back row. They're for the ones sending monthly newsletters across the ocean, and for the ones sending monthly checks in the mail. They're for everyone.

## "I can't trust anyone"

"I can't trust anyone" closely follows "I'm different." Many of the same experiences that lead us to believe we're different also lead us to believe we can't trust anyone, and it can be hard to tease out the differences.

At first glance, "I can't trust anyone" might not seem like a lie. If church people have let us down, if they've mercilessly judged our struggles, if they've betrayed our confidences and broadcast our private stories to the world, this statement might seem true. And we might have decided we're better off on our own. We might have decided we don't need anyone after all.

Truth be told, I had trouble writing this section. Unlike some of the other lies in this series, I don't have significant personal experience with this one. I've certainly considered myself "different," and at times "better," but I haven't personally struggled with trusting people. I've always had a small circle of people I could trust, and I have a feeling this is because I didn't grow up in a ministry home.

My story is not everyone's story, however, and I've spoken with enough pastor's kids and pastor's kids' spouses to know this trust issue is a big deal. It plays out in loneliness, arrogance, and a lack of close relationships.

While I've generally had safe people in my life, I know this much is true: some people *cannot* be trusted. Some people are *not* safe. There is truth inside this lie. Sometimes unsafe people in the church hurt us deeply. Sometimes religious people wound us so severely that it almost seems irreparable, and we decide never to trust church people again.

While it is most definitely true that some people can't be trusted, it is also true that some people *can* be trusted. Trustworthy people may be hard to find, but they do exist. And without that elusive trust, we can't have meaningful relationships. When we choose not to trust people, we cut ourselves off from the relationships that can buoy us in times of trouble. When we tuck our weaknesses away where no one can find them or use them against us, we may think we are safe, but in reality we are alone.

If there truly is "neither Jew nor Gentile, neither slave nor free, nor is there male and female, for you are all one in Christ Jesus" (Gal 3:28 NIV), then perhaps there should be no pastor or member either, no missionary or sender. Not that there aren't differing roles and responsibilities in the church—because there are—but because we are all one in Christ, and all equal in his church. So let's accept each other's weaknesses and respect each other's stories. Let's push back against the prevailing church culture that ranks us over and under each other, and love each other as equals.

I'm not saying we can't be friends with people who've had similar life experiences. Those people instinctively understand us, and they can be a refuge for us. What I am saying is that we can be friends with people outside our circles, too. Others in the body of Christ can love us well, too. There are people "outside the tribe" who can accept our entire story, with all its complications and paradoxes. And we can love them in all their glorious complexity, too. Reaching out to people who aren't exactly like us is what the church was designed for.

## "I can ruin my parents' ministry"

Of all the lies listed in the *Parsonage Heresies* book, this one strikes me as the most tragic. It tells children they make their parents credible—or not. It tells children they prove their parents' worth—or not. It tells children their behavior makes an adult's ministry successful—or destroys it.

This lie places the burden of an adult's employment squarely on the shoulders of a child. This is unfair in any profession, and completely out of place among God's people. Children—loved by God, sought by God, cared for by God—should never feel the pressure to ensure their parents' wage-earning ability.

Although this statement upset me more than any other lie in this book, I don't have actual experience with it—probably because I didn't grow up in a ministry home. But I can imagine it doesn't feel like a lie. I can imagine having social, emotional, or educational difficulties and being afraid to express them, because taking care of those issues might take my family off the field.

While I've never met any parents who held their children responsible for their ministry career, adult PKs and MKs probably have painful stories to back up this belief, and for those stories, I am truly sorry. Whether this pressure came from within your family or externally from church members, or some deadly combination of the two, I am so, so sorry. That's a heavy burden to carry.

I'd also like to consider the corollary of "I can ruin my parent's ministry": "I can ruin my husband's ministry." I am much more familiar with this fear. I didn't originally want to move overseas, but I thought if I refused to go, I'd ruin my husband's missionary dreams. I am not the only wife who's ever felt this. Kay Bruner writes in *As Soon as I Fell*, "All through our training, I had heard how important it was for the wife to 'be involved in the project.' People said that if the wife wasn't involved in the project, the whole thing would go down in flames. I didn't want to be the reason our project failed."[1]

That's a *lot* of pressure, and I've spoken with other wives who feel the same way. We're afraid we can ruin everything for our husbands. Sometimes that idea is even planted by well-meaning organizations and leaders. Sometimes it comes from inside us. And honestly, I don't know what to do about this issue.

I don't even think this pressure is relegated to children and spouses. I think as adults in missions, we fear that our own sin or poor choices might cause us to fail, so we silence our own struggles. Other times we have medical issues that need tending, and we're faced with the choice to hide or deny them, or to seek help off the field if needed.

To be honest, I'm not sure how to separate the truth from the untruth in these beliefs. I'm not sure how we as the body of Christ can deconstruct these harmful lies. I hope and pray this pressure to perform for the sake of your parents or spouse is becoming a relic of the past, but I have a feeling this is something we need to do more work on.

---

1. Bruner, *As Soon as I Fell*, 62.

# "God Is Disappointed with Me" (Lies, Part 4)

BY *ELIZABETH*

## "I have to be perfect"

I GREW UP HEARING sermons about the goodness and severity of God, and about God not hearing the prayer of the sinner. Girls' Bible study times were filled with questions like, "If women are to remain silent in church, is it a sin to whisper in church to ask someone the song number if I didn't hear it announced?" and "How long should my shorts be?" So by the time I entered ministry at the age of nineteen, no one had to tell me I needed to be perfect; I already knew I needed to be perfect. And not only did I know I needed to be perfect, I knew everyone else needed to be perfect as well.

At the same time, I knew everyone wasn't perfect. As a teenager, I knew my church friends were being physically and sexually abused at home, but no one would ever dare talk about that at church where their dads were leaders. This taught me that the families around me weren't perfect; it also taught me that they needed to appear that way. Furthermore, it taught me that the rest of us needed to treat them as though they were perfect. The appearance of perfection mattered more than actual righteousness.

Those are my stories; your stories will be different. Yet our collective stories may have taught us something dark and devious: that ministry and missionary families are (or should be) holier than everyone else. Our stories may have taught us that in order to serve God, we need to be super human. At the very least, our stories may have taught us that we need to project an image of perfection. Sometimes we extend this expectation to others and become judgmental of their nonperfection; other times we require it only of ourselves.

Of course, none of us is perfect. We all know this very well, because we all wrestle with our own sin natures. So we can become discouraged when we fail to meet our self-imposed (or church-imposed) "shoulds" over and over and over. The pressures placed on missionaries, ministers, and their wives and children are often unattainable, and put them at risk for depression. The painful irony here is that since they're supposed to be perfect and not have any major problems, there's shame both in the depression (or other mental health issues) and its appropriate treatment.

To illustrate this, Sanford once took an informal survey at a PK conference, asking for a show of hands of people who had been diagnosed with depression, placed on anti-depressant medicine, or hospitalized for depression. Eighty percent of attendants raised their hands, at which point a woman in the back piped up with "But we're not allowed to be!"

James says in his letter that "We all stumble in many ways" (Jas 3:2 NIV), and John's first letter tells us, "If we claim we have no sin, we are only fooling ourselves and not living in the truth" (1 John 1:8 NLT). So the truth is, we can't be perfect, and we don't have to be. Yes, some of us are better than others at appearing perfect, but nobody actually is perfect. We sin, we mess up, we fail. Regularly. I repeat: we don't have to be perfect. We don't even have to give the impression.

Now this is much easier to say than it is to live. All those things I'd learned in church? Well, they had impacted my conception of God and who I was in relation to him. I hadn't realized it before, but I had zero theology of grace. I thought I needed to prove my worth and earn my salvation. It was only about eight years ago that I began deconstructing these harmful beliefs. For about four months that year, I met with a counselor once a week. I spent lots of time in prayer with my Bible study group, and I read lots of Paul: Ephesians, Galatians, Romans. (I'm unabashed about my love for Paul.) Over and over again I listened and cried and danced to Chris Tomlin's cover of Matt Maher's song "Your Grace is Enough." These things transformed my thinking about sin and grace.

That year was a turning point in my walk with God and my understanding of grace. I relinquished the old ways of thinking, though I confess they still creep back to haunt me from time to time. In those times, I have to return to God and ask him to renew my mind yet again. (And yes, when I forget grace, I still sometimes beat myself up by thinking, "I should understand this better by now!")

Our attempts to be perfect cripple our experience of Christ. His perfection, and his perfection alone, undergirds the entire gospel. And the gospel is completely counter-cultural, in every culture. This is why we sometimes struggle to accept it: it seems quite literally too good to be true. Except that it is true! Grace, full and free, releases us from the requirements we feel from church members and supporters (and ourselves) to meet some impossible standard of perfection that Jesus already met. In Christ alone our hope is found.

Grace isn't necessarily easy medicine to swallow for us perfectionists. I would often cry my eyes out in a counseling session and then be so exhausted I could sleep for the rest of the day. A single chapter cannot easily dismantle our beliefs surrounding God's approval and our efforts. Unraveling our thinking is, frustratingly, not an overnight process. I do believe, however, that it's a process he is faithful to fulfill.

## "I'm damned if I do and damned if I don't"

This phrase reflects the either/or mindset that has plagued me for so much of my life. It's this kind of black-and-white thinking that has gotten me into so much inner turmoil: If I make one mistake, then I must be a total failure. And depression ensues. The "damned if I do and damned if I don't" attitude also gives way to futility: If I can't do something perfectly, then I won't do it at all. This goes for spiritual things like Bible reading and also seemingly less spiritual things like interpersonal conflict and offering apologies.

The tragedy of either/or thinking is that it doesn't acknowledge paradox or complexity. It doesn't acknowledge that sanctification is a process. It doesn't acknowledge that we are not fully regenerate yet and that no, we are not there yet. These are truths my beloved apostle Paul acknowledged. (Romans 7 and Philippians 3, anyone?)

Brennan Manning said, "When I get honest, I admit that I am a bundle of paradoxes. I believe and I doubt, I hope and I get discouraged, I love and I hate, I feel bad about feeling good, I feel guilty about not feeling guilty. I am trusting and suspicious. I am honest and I still play games. To live by grace means to acknowledge my whole life's story, the light side and the dark."[1] According to Manning, living by grace means embracing all the *ands* of our lives. (Don't you just love Brennan Manning?)

1. Manning, *Reflections for Ragamuffins*, 29.

When *and* isn't a part of our collective vocabulary, we tend to believe we are judged as either one hundred percent good or one hundred percent bad, with no middle ground. We feel stuck. We know everything is not all right, both in our own personal lives and in our families' lives, but since image is more important than reality (as we discussed earlier), we don't feel the freedom to tell the whole truth. In a way, this is a consequence of believing we have to be perfect—and if we're not, we just better keep our mouths shut about it.

I still don't know why I didn't feel free to tell anybody about my friends being abused. I wasn't being abused at home; so why should I have been scared to tell anyone about my friends, whom I loved? Perhaps I had picked up on the idea that the church is "supposed" to keep silent about these things. Just let the leaders lead; the abuse they perpetrate against their children at home has nothing to do with their reasonable service at church. Just let the teachers teach; the pain they inflict on their children at home has nothing to do with their reasonable service at church. The unspoken rule becomes: Keep these things secret. Don't ever tell the truth. Speak up, and you'll be punished. Speak out, and you'll be judged as rebellious.

It's hard to keep the ugly truth bottled up all the time, and it tends to leak out in one way or another. One way it leaks out is by escaping into another world. In particular, Sanford says people use food (either binging and purging, or restricting) and sex (mostly porn) as escapes, as some of these can be hidden, at least for a time. He says the truth also tends to slip out in sarcasm, which sometimes seems bitter and angry. However, sarcasm and escapes may not be our main problem: they may only be the mechanism we're using to tell our stories.

So what is the cure for "Damned if I do, damned if I don't"? I believe it's to allow ourselves to say *and*. It's to allow ourselves, as Brennan Manning said, to be honest and admit we are a bundle of paradoxes, and to allow each other to say it as well. It's when we acknowledge our whole life's story, the light side and the dark side, that we can begin to live by grace alone.

## "God is disappointed with me"

The lies in this series are all somewhat related, and this last one closely follows "I have to be perfect." It represents the fear that if I'm not perfect, then God will be mad at me, that if I make a mistake (or several), he'll disapprove of me. We can spend our whole lives trying to make God happy with our behavior. Working, working, working, trying so very hard to please him.

This one is listed last in the book because it's what Sanford calls a "holy heresy about God." The other lies are about myself and others, but this one goes straight to the heart of God. Sometimes when we grow up in church, we get the idea that God is just waiting for us to make a mistake so he can bring down his wrath, and punish us once and for all. We get the idea that we don't deserve his love and aren't good enough to earn his forgiveness, and not that he delights in us and sings over us, not that he loves us with an everlasting love and has saved us by his own hand.

If that's the kind of angry, vengeful God we know, we might end up walking away from him.

I won't even pretend to have all the answers here for how to deal with this lie. It goes really deep and takes a lot of time to shed. What I hope to do is to give you some resources that have helped me deal with this lie. I pray they can deepen your intimacy with God and strengthen your trust in his love.

Beginning to walk in the assurance of God's unconditional love for us is an intensely personal journey. We walk part of it together, in safe community. We must also walk some of it alone, in the secret places of our hearts. It's when I close the metaphorical door of my prayer closet and meet with God one on one that he touches me most personally and most deeply. I pray God will grant more and more of those sweet times of fellowship to all of us.

## Resources for Encountering God

### Brennan Manning

I mentioned Brennan Manning earlier in the chapter. The summer after I finished that four-month stint of counseling was my first introduction to Brennan Manning. My husband led our youth group through the *Ragamuffin Gospel, Visual Edition*. It's an abridged version of his original work, with art. It was a balm to my soul and cemented in my mind the things I'd been learning that year.

I also recommend Manning's *Reflections for Ragamuffins*. Each day has a Scripture and a selection from his other writings.

## Henri Nouwen

I'd never read anything from Henri Nouwen before this Lenten season, when a friend of mine in Phnom Penh gave me a copy of *Show Me the Way*.[2] It's a collection of excerpts from his many books, and it's profoundly affected my relationship with God.

## The Bible

I know I've recommended Paul's letters already, but I'll say it again—I love Paul so much, especially Ephesians, Galatians, and Romans. Hebrews is also helpful, but then, we don't know who wrote that.

The book of First John. Also helpful is Beth Moore's explanation of the life of John and his relationship with Jesus. Moore's *Beloved Disciple*[3] Bible study rewrote my understanding of the apostle John.

The Psalms. I've often felt God's love through the Psalms. (And I'm betting you probably have too.)

First Corinthians 13, viewed as a letter to you from God. We know that God is love, and I Corinthians 13 is one of our best descriptions of what love looks like practically. First Corinthians 13 therefore gives us a glimpse into how God sees and treats us. This is an exercise Sanford recommends that made a big impact on me when I first read it a year and a half ago. Write the entire chapter out in your own handwriting, use your own name, and ask God to show you his great big heart for you.

2. Nouwen, *Show Me the Way*.
3. Moore, *Beloved Disciple*.

# I Was Sexually Abused: Here's What I Want All Parents to Do if Their Child Tells Them That They Were Abused Too

## BY *JONATHAN*

I THOUGHT I HAD AIDS.

I thought I was going to die.

That's why I told my dad about the abuse. That's why I crawled out of bed late one evening, approached him as he was paying bills with a checkbook in the kitchen, and spilled my guts.

I told him I had done terrible things. I told him I was a horrible sinner. I told him I wasn't a virgin.

It was the late '80s, and all I knew was that people who did bad things got AIDS. I had done bad things, therefore I had AIDS and was going to die.

Perhaps that sounds ludicrous, but that's how my kid-brain interpreted the data, and that's why I told my dad.

What my dad did next is what he should have done. It's what any parent *should do* when a child says they've been abused. It's what any church leader *should do* when someone says they've been abused. But terribly, it's not what many parents and leaders actually do.

He believed me.

That's it. That's the main thing: Believe your child.

## "Innocent Until Proven Guilty"

As an attorney, I'm tremendously thankful for our legal system. It's got issues, for sure, but the general principle that a defendant is innocent until proven guilty is absolute bedrock. It's vital to the just operation of a courtroom.

But we're *not* talking about courtrooms. We're talking about living rooms and bedrooms and kitchens. And in those places, you should always, always, always start off believing your child. Or friend. Or parishioner.

Somehow we've got this false idea that false accusations are the norm. They are not. Allegations that turn out to be fabricated do happen, and we should be aware of the possibility, but our default should be to believe the person who's talking about being abused.

Because sexual abuse is far more common than made-up stories about sexual abuse.

Now, believing the child in front of you does not mean you automatically believe the accused is guilty. I'm not saying you jump to conclusions and throw the accused under the bus. I'm just saying that you have to start off listening and hearing and giving space to the person in front of you. Start off believing.

## Know That It's Often Unbelievable

Sexual abuse often happens in the context of a known relationship. You and the child will likely know the abuser, and *that is typical.* For me, it was a neighbor, and the majority of the abuse happened in my house.

You will probably know the abuser. You might even be related to the abuser, and again, that's what will make the allegation so unbelievable.

If your child tells you about being abused, it will certainly be something you don't want to hear about, and the thing is, it will likely involve someone you don't want to think about. But listen to me, please. Don't rush to defend the accused. Rush to hear the child.

I've heard enough stories from teenagers and clients and patients to say, with all the fire in my bones: if your child tells you about being sexually abused by someone you don't want to think could do it, *believe your child.*

My dad believed me. He told me I wasn't going to die. He told me I hadn't done anything wrong. He hugged me.

And honestly, I don't remember what happened next. I don't know if they talked to the neighbors. I know I didn't see that neighbor anymore. I wish I could ask my parents what that was like. What did they think?

What did they feel? Unfortunately, that conversation will never happen; both of my parents died many years ago.

I don't remember many of the facts. But I do remember the feelings.

I felt loved.

I felt heard.

I felt protected.

I felt valued.

I did *not* feel silenced.

My dad was not incredulous or doubtful or skeptical. He started off believing me, and he kept on believing me. He hugged me. And that's exactly what I needed.

# WORKING WELL (WITH YOURSELF AND OTHERS)

# Dealing with Conflict on the Field, or Not

BY *JONATHAN*

LET'S TALK ABOUT CONFLICT, 'cause *that's* fun. I mean, hypothetically, at some point in the (distant) future, you may or may not experience an uncomfortable disagreement with someone. Maybe.

In this imagined scenario, the ensuing discussion could arise between you and your spouse or kids or co-workers. When conflict comes, what will you do? Will you run away scared? Hunker down? Gear up? Lock and load?

Whether your natural tendency is to ostrich or explode, these two principles must be remembered:

1. Conflict always has context
2. Conflict always precedes closeness

How many of you have ever experienced conflict? Go ahead, raise your hands. Do you see all those hands raised? Yeah, me neither, but I'm guessing that all over the world people are raising hands. It's a pretty shared thing, this interpersonal junk.

Conflict is not something "out there" that other people deal with. This is us. This is our story.

## Oh, Conflict!

I used to work in an Emergency Room, so I've had people try to cut me, spit on me, and in other ways break me. I've helped security guards and police officers wrestle dangerous patients to the ground. By the way, did you know they make "spit hoods"? It's a mesh net that covers a patient's head to keep the spit from getting from their mouth onto your face. Pretty cool, eh?

I've also worked in churches with church people. I served as a youth pastor, working with peoples' kids. Sometimes there was too much pizza, other times, not enough. Sometimes parents thought we weren't doing enough cool stuff, while other parents thought we were doing too much cool stuff.

I served as a worship pastor. Corporate worship, now there's an area where everyone has ideas and they're not afraid to share them. It was an a cappella church (i.e., no instruments), and you would think that might reduce disagreements. *Not so.*

I served as a camp director. I listened to staff complaints, teen complaints, parent complaints, caretaker complaints. Once, a camp manager was angry with me because I wouldn't tell the teenagers to *stop splashing in the pool.* Apparently, by playing in the pool, too much water was splashing out of the pool. Duly noted. And ignored.

We've all experienced conflict, and we'll all experience conflict again. So here's the first thing we must remember.

## Conflict Always Has Context

Conflict is very rarely *just* about the facts, and it never happens in a vacuum. All parties bring their unique historical issues to the table even if they're not aware of it. That's what makes this all so interesting.

Much of conflict's context exists just under the surface:

- Fears (of losing love, or support, or respect, or safety)
- Past experiences with conflict (positive or negative)
- Goals that might be thwarted
- The family's approach to conflict
- The culture's general approach to conflict

If we don't want to fly blind (or be blindsided), we must seek to understand the context. In addition to considering underlying fears and goals (yours and theirs), ask yourself these questions:

- What is the typical approach to conflict in my passport culture?
- Growing up, how did my family handle conflict?

- Do I pretty much handle conflict the same as #1 and #2, or have I changed?

- What words come to mind when I hear the word "conflict"?

Consider talking through this list at your next team meeting.

Now, when we're looking at the cultural component, it's important to remember that the gospel is countercultural in every culture. There are parts of your culture that are really bad and unhealthy and need to change, just like mine! And there are parts that are great and wonderful, just like mine!

I was speaking at a regional missions conference last month and I asked the participants to tell me what words came to mind when I said "conflict." Many of the attendees said things like "scary," "shame," "anger," "rage," "dangerous," "yelling," and a whole slew of negative words. One lady stood up and said, "Opportunity!"

She was from Switzerland.

Our background and culture will greatly influence how we deal with conflict, for good or bad. Do we run away and hide or prepare to fight? Do we get louder or quieter? Do we think conflict is mainly about peace or justice?

Painful experiences from our past also provide context for our current conflict. If a current situation triggers painful memories or associations from times past, that matters. It's possible the current situation is solely because someone's a jerk, but most likely, there's also underlying pain and fear that is historical. It's worth your time to see it and address it.

## Conflict Always Precedes Closeness

Many people treat conflict as if it's radioactive. They avoid it at all costs and only touch it with protective suits, Geiger counters drawn.

That makes sense if you see conflict as a direct threat to closeness or intimacy. However, I believe that conflict is necessary for intimacy. Put another way, intimacy requires a tremendous level of honesty, and you cannot be honest with another human being for very long without conflict.

Conflict does not necessarily lead to intimacy, but you cannot have intimacy without honesty. And you cannot have honesty for very long without conflict.

## Conflict and Christ—Changing the Paradigm

Conflict is scary. It's also normal, and it can be healthy and actually really good. Just ask Jesus. There's the famous "Get behind me, Satan!" passage. And the incident with the tables. There's the conversation with Peter about feeding sheep that left Peter feeling hurt. There's the whole white-washed tombs fiasco, and the time Jesus just ignored the Pharisees.

Jesus once abandoned a crowd that had plans he didn't like. Another time he allowed the crowds to worship him, which was something the ruling elite didn't like. Jesus surprised Pilate with his silence. And he taught the disciples to ignore some of the most respected people. At least once, Jesus didn't like his Father's plans and told him so.

Can you think of some more examples?

## The Way of Jesus

He didn't do conflict the same way every time. He occasionally used conflict as a doorway to deeper intimacy and commitment. Sometimes he was very passionate and active, while other times he ran away or was silent. He stated his opinion clearly, but remained aware of authority lines and obeyed. He was *always* aware of the context.

How does Jesus' approach differ from yours? Do you need to more actively engage in necessary conflict, or do you need to pursue holiness for a bit and shut up? Jesus' approach varied. Does yours?

## Conflict and the Love of God

Now we come to it. The best advice I can give you for dealing with conflict: Become more and more aware of the magnificent love of God.

> I pray that from his glorious, unlimited resources he will empower you with inner strength through his Spirit. Then Christ will make his home in your hearts as you trust in him. Your roots will grow down into God's love and keep you strong. And may you have the power to understand, as all God's people should, how wide, how long, how high, and how deep his love is. May you experience the love of Christ, though it is too great to understand fully. Then you will be made complete with all the fullness of life and power that comes from God. (Eph 3:16–19 NLT)

You want to get better at dealing with conflict? Wrap your heart around the love of God. Dive deep into the love of the Father. Ponder the intensity with which the Father loves the Son, and see how the Son loves the Father.

Consider the mystery that the eternal Creator loves humans, and meditate on the miracle of the incarnation. Invite the Holy Spirit to show you what he thinks of your teammate or spouse or child.

## Remember How Loved You are

Do you really believe that God loves you regardless of your work product? Do you believe that even if you never accomplished anything else, he would still love you the same?

He loves you just as much now as he did before you were a missionary. You cannot earn more of God's heart. It is not divisible. It is turned toward you, just as it has been since the dawn of creation.

The father did not kick the prodigal son out. The son left, and the father let him. But, as soon as that son came back within sight, *the father ran.* And he still runs for you, for your heart.

And whether you return to him from a life of workaholism or whores, ministry or mud, when you return to him, *he still runs*, because the Father loves you, and he entered into great conflict to make a way for you to come back. Don't ever forget that.

## To Recap:

The next time you meet conflict, remember that it's got context.

Remember that it precedes closeness.

And remember the crazy love of God.

May God richly bless you all.

~~~~~~~~~~

Further resources on conflict:

*Necessary Endings,* by Dr. Henry Cloud
*Crucial Conversations,* by Kerry Patterson, Ron McMillan, and Al Switzer

# Run Away! Run Away!
# (and Other Conflict Styles)

BY *Elizabeth*

I DON'T LIKE CONFLICT. I'm scared of it. I don't want people to be upset with me; I don't want people to think I'm upset with them. Conflict is stressful and instills in me a strong desire to *run away*. I shut down both physically and emotionally, and I fail to deal with the issue at hand.

I want everyone to be happy. I want this to happen *without actually having to talk about the things that make me and other people unhappy*. But I can't avoid unhappy situations indefinitely. With more than 7 billion people on this planet, and no two of us alike, conflict is unavoidable. I can't hide away forever from my emotions and the emotions of others.

In mission training I learned that my approach to conflict has a name: I am an avoider, or turtle. Turtles believe that any conflict, regardless of what it is or how it is handled, will inevitably harm relationships. We thus avoid conflict at all costs. We hide in our turtle shells and refuse to come out to talk. However, when cornered or forced into conflict we aren't ready to deal with, some turtles (like me) might lash out in anger. The typically conflict-avoidant turtle has now morphed into a snapping turtle. Ouch!

Perhaps you also dislike conflict, but instead of running away from it, you simply give in to everyone else's wishes, never voicing your own. If you want everyone to be happy and are willing to give up your own wants and desires in order to maintain harmonious relationships, then you might be an accommodator, or teddy bear. Teddy bears, like turtles, wish to preserve relationships. Instead of outright escapism, though, teddy bears ensure that in any given situation, everybody except themselves is satisfied. They try to make everyone happy, but they are in danger of never feeling heard by others.

Or maybe you're not afraid of conflict at all. Maybe you're so confident that your solution is correct that you won't even consider other people's ideas. If so, you might be a shark, or competitor. (And you might be interested to know that turtles and teddy bears are petrified of you.) When a decision must be made quickly, you have the ability to lead a group and make that decision both quickly and confidently. However, in slower situations, people may feel you do not value them or their contributions. People want you to listen to them and take their perspective into account when making a decision, something that is not easy for you to do.

There are a couple other conflict styles. A compromiser, or fox, wants everyone in a given situation to give up something they want, with the assurance that they will receive something else they want. Everyone wins a little, and everyone loses a little. Ideally, everyone receives something they want, but each person is also missing something they want. That's because compromisers are looking for a good enough solution in the quickest time possible—and this is especially helpful in a time crunch. However, compromisers can sometimes be seen as acting too quickly to reach a solution, making people feel unheard.

The last style is the collaborator, or owl. A collaborator is similar to a compromiser, and it is sometimes difficult to distinguish between the two. But where a compromiser wants everyone to win a little and lose a little, a collaborator wants everyone to feel one hundred percent satisfied with the outcome, and they are willing to work as long as it takes to find that perfect solution. Although they care about everyone's happiness level, coworkers can be frustrated by the slowness of the collaboration process. The collaborator, likewise, can become frustrated when people aren't willing to work on a problem as long as he or she is willing. Incidentally, in mission training, we learned that collaborators are often the most frustrated people on the mission field. They want a perfect solution every time, and that's just not possible.

So what happens when all these conflict styles try to interact?

1. Turtles run away from important discussions. The turtle is scared, and hiding meets the turtle's need to avoid conflict. Other styles want to discuss the problem at hand, but they become frustrated by the turtle's refusal.

2. Teddy bears make everyone happy, right? But nobody can help them, because nobody knows what they want. Compromisers and collaborators often *want* to know how teddy bears (and turtles) feel. They value every person's input and want to make a decision that incorporates everyone's needs. When they can't coax the turtles and teddy bears to share their needs, collaborators and compromisers become frustrated.

3. Competitive sharks may get things done quickly, but they risk alienating people while doing it. And they don't just alienate turtles and teddy bears—they can also alienate compromisers and collaborators, who want everyone's input to be valued, including theirs.

4. What about when a shark meets another shark? Sounds scary to my turtle self. Let's not even go there.

5. A compromiser may try to get to a solution too fast and fail to listen closely enough to people. Compromisers might convince people to give up too much too soon when making a decision, and they might not realize that's hurting people.

6. Collaborators want to find a perfect solution, and they don't care how long it takes to get there. If you're a collaborator and people don't want to talk to you, it might be because they know the discussion will be L-O-N-G. A solution that makes one hundred percent of the people one hundred percent happy may not be feasible. So you might need to settle for less-than-perfect and learn a few things from the compromiser.

Knowing I'm a turtle has helped me understand why I react the way I do to certain people's conflict styles. It explains past relationship patterns, and it illuminates current relational issues.

As a turtle, I've often felt a sense of pride in the fact that I preserve relationships by avoiding conflict. But pride is bad news, and the supposed relationship preservation is only partly true anyway. Sometimes relationships are preserved by actually talking about sensitive subjects instead of avoiding them.

I'm learning that if I avoid all difficult conversations, I risk growing bitter about an issue. I'm learning that I can't just think about myself and my own personal need to avoid conflict. I'm learning that sometimes I need to love someone enough to broach difficult subjects.

I'm learning that I can have calm, rational conversations about sticky subjects. I'm learning that these conversations can be gracious and kind instead of the violent explosions I expect them to be. And I'm finding that these kinds of conversations can lead to solutions I had never even thought of.

In short, I'm learning that I can and must grow in conflict resolution—and that it's not as scary as I had always thought.

# Conflict and Our Dustlikeness

### BY ELIZABETH

CONFLICT. IF YOU'VE BEEN IN church work for long, you know what it's like. People abound, and conflict happens. Then there's the big blow-up or the cold exit or, even scarier, the explosive exit. I've been in church work for a decade and a half now, and big blow-ups and bad exits seem to be the default setting for church conflict. I don't like this kind of conflict. I run away from it—and from the scary people who cause it.

Kay Bruner likes to say that there are difficult people on the field. I say yes. Yes, there are difficult people on the field, and sometimes, they are *me*. Sometimes I'm difficult, and sometimes conflict comes *because* I am difficult. Not because I mean to be, of course—but my good intentions don't remove my propensity to offend.

I have a hard time fessing up when I offend, and my reasons for this are twofold. First, I don't really like the fact that I'm still not perfect and that I still sin against others. This acknowledgment is still so cumbersome to me. But secondly (and perhaps more importantly), I fear I won't be forgiven. Oh, I know God forgives me; I have full assurance of that. But I still don't trust *God's people* to forgive me. I've been in too many relationships where people said they would forgive, but they never really did.

Lately, however, I've had ample opportunity to seek forgiveness, and God's people are proving me wrong. They are forgiving me and showing me the love of Christ in tangible ways. Receiving their forgiveness and their assurance of committed love is an almost sacramental experience. It's a direct connection with my Savior: someone is sticking with me. Someone is forgiving me, giving me a second chance. *That* is Jesus in bodily form.

Receiving compassion for our dustlikeness helps us to be more compassionate toward ourselves—and toward others. It helps us to forgive ourselves, and in turn, to forgive others. Unmerited forgiveness is a gift we believers give each other. It points other people to Jesus and is *because* of Jesus. And while the usual take on conflict and reconciliation is usually humility, I think if we focus on that we are missing the point. The point is God can forgive, and God's people can forgive, and wherever you find restoration and reconciliation happening, the Spirit of God is moving among his people.

In this way, conflict can be a conduit for grace. The only catch (yes there is a catch) is that the forgiveness, reconciliation, and move of God that I'm talking about only happen in community. And I'm convinced that one of the bravest things we can do is to *stay* in that community. When it gets hard, when it gets uncomfortable, when conflict starts to escalate, can we stay in relationship with others? Not in pathological or dangerous relationships, but in regular, everyday, fallen relationships?

All of our relationships will have a degree of unhealthiness, because all of our relationships have people. Our relationships are not going to be perfect, and our community will disappoint us. And sometimes our community will be unhealthy because *we* are unhealthy. Other times we will make allowances for other people's issues because they—and God—make allowances for ours. Let's not make a cold or explosive exit too soon, for unconditional love is only proved unconditional when we stay.

So the next time you're in conflict with someone on the field, think of me, the difficult one, and be kind. Be kind to your difficult person. Show them Christ's love, and give them another chance. Or a second or a third or a seventy-seventh. If they prove to you that they intend to be difficult or abusive, then by all means draw some boundaries and don't give them limitless chances to harm you. But maybe by giving them a second chance, you'll prove to them what God's love looks like, and they, like me, will recognize grace and be grateful—and you will have won a brother or a sister over.

# A Letter to Singles

*BY JONATHAN*

YOU ARE LOVED. CHERISHED, even.

Not because you were brave enough to move overseas "alone." Not because you ignored the caring relatives who asked, "How in the world will you find a husband over there?"

You are loved. Adored, even.
Not because you're an independent thinker or a strong person.
Not because you've sacrificed.
You are loved. Anticipated, even.
Because of him.

You are loved by the eternal God, your harbor.
You are loved by a dad who wraps you up in his everlasting arms.
You are loved by the One who knows the true depths of loneliness and the rich intimacy of friendships.

Indeed, you are loved.
You are valuable.
And you are needed. Our churches, our teams, and our families need you.

You probably know that already. You probably feel that already. But just in case you don't, as a brother, father, husband, team leader, pastor, and friend, let me remind you how much we value you and need you.

We don't need you to be a wonderful Christian woman. We need you to be a wonderful Christian human, unique because of your personhood, not just because of your womanhood. We need you to love people uniquely, heartily, and with passion.

You see the woman caught in adultery differently. We need your eyes. You are more aware of the emotional needs behind the physical needs. We need your awareness. We need your heart.

We need you to lead. Your perspective is valuable, your needs valid, your abilities real. You see problems and solutions differently. We need your intellect.

We need you to support us. Not like a cook supports the troops, but like a soldier supports a comrade. We serve side by side in this thing.

My kids need you, and not as a babysitter. My sons need you to show them what a strong woman looks like. Teach them that a woman's value does not come from the fact that she's got a body, or a husband, or kids.

My daughters need you. They need to see a woman who's willing to follow God's call regardless of who joins her. They need to see a woman who pursues God on her own, enjoying her own relationship with him.

You are not half a unit. Some stray ingredient that I guess we'll mix in with the real ingredients of teams and churches and potlucks. You are not leftovers.

Without single women serving abroad, there would be a gaping hole in the church and in the history of modern missions. And in my own life.

Growing up, the names (and books) of Amy Carmichael, Gladys Aylward, Corrie ten Boom, and Elisabeth Elliot taught and inspired and coached me. I read their books, listened to their stories, and learned from their faith.

Single women still teach, inspire, and coach me. I am grateful for ladies like Amy, Sara, Yvonne, Tanya, Christina, Rhoda, Ann, Jenny, Sue, Sarah, Mary, Sovannara, Emma, and so many more. I listen to them speak, I read what they write, I watch them love people, I observe their journey through Facebook status updates, and I am grateful.

I need them. The church needs them. And Jesus loves them, and he loves you too—not because you're awesome or beautiful or perfect, and not because you're really good with Instagram filters, but because you are part of his Bride, his people. You are immensely valuable.

Every day, Elisabeth Elliot began her radio program with this reminder, "You are loved with an everlasting love—that's what the Bible says—and underneath are the everlasting arms."

May you remember his everlasting love,

May you rest in his everlasting arms,

Today, tomorrow, and every day.

With deep appreciation and gratitude, your friend,
*Jonathan Trotter*

# Making Friends with Short-Term Workers

## BY *ELIZABETH*

EACH YEAR AT THE end of summer, the interns head back home. Short-term teams taper off, and kids go back to school. The time when life on the field supposedly returns to normal. Summer winds down. I want to take some time in this chapter to honor the short-term workers who have touched my life over the years.

I didn't know my life would intersect with so many short-term workers when I first moved overseas. It all started when we'd lived in Cambodia for six months, and we met a girl volunteering at the orphanage next door to us. She'd been surprised most of the volunteers weren't believers and was desperate for some Christian fellowship. So we took her to church with us.

When we hugged her goodbye at the end of the summer, she connected us with a friend of hers. Her friend had a roommate, and both of them introduced us to another girl. They were all working short-term for NGOs, and over a period of about six months, they all came to church with us on Sunday mornings.

They managed to squeeze into our mini-van with our four rambunctious kids. We ate donuts for breakfast, and after church we often ate lunch together. We laughed over homeschool jokes—my husband and one of the girls had been homeschooled. And we introduced *Anne of Green Gables* to one of the girls, who had never had the pleasure of meeting Miss Anne Shirley.

God kept giving us opportunities to host more people in our home. One girl's work kept her very culturally immersed. After she finished her work commitment, she stayed in our guest room a short while. She needed a chance to rest, and our daughters had a blast doing cooking projects with her.

When it came time for those girls to leave on a jet plane, I cried. I didn't know I could get so attached to someone who was only here for a short time. I didn't know it would be that hard to bid farewell to someone I knew wasn't staying long. But we had spent time together, made memories, forged friendships.

Another year we had our own intern. She'd been part of our family life for over three months, and we sent her on her way with our blessing. God was doing some neat stuff in her life, and we had a front-row ticket to watch. We pondered life together, shared countless meals, and laughed hysterically over nothing . . . and everything.

Each of these girls became part of our family. They left a part of themselves with us when they left, and they went with our love. I still miss each of them. I'm so thankful I can follow their continuing journeys on Facebook—when they start grad school, when they finish grad school, when they get engaged, when they get married, when they have children. Being able to see these things unfold in their lives brings me joy.

They were real-life friends for a season, but friends-at-heart forever. These short-term workers have enriched my life as I have learned their stories, enjoyed their senses of humor, and discovered what brought them to Cambodia in the first place. It all seemed to be an accident, this habit of taking girls to church, but I sometimes wonder if the reason we were willing to open our home to new people is because older Christians opened their homes to us when we were younger, teaching us by example what hospitality looks and feels like.

When I was a lonely, young college student, church ladies took care of me. One let me do laundry at her house, another let me cry to her when I was stressed. Both let me hang out at their houses on my eighteenth birthday. And incidentally, these ladies took *me* to church when I was without a car.

Later, when we were freshly married and still in college, church families continued to welcome my new husband and me into their lives. They included us at Christmas dinners and birthday parties. They invited us over to build campfires and watch meteor showers.

One family in particular shared their life with us. Nearly every Saturday found us driving to their house in the country, where we ate homemade bread and kielbasa soup, played board games, and sang songs with the guitar. Their family was our family, and I felt like I had a mom and a dad nearby. I believe it was out of these good experiences that we were willing to offer our own family to other people.

I've talked before about how goodbyes are hard for me. Sometimes goodbyes can make us reluctant to form new relationships, but if we're reluctant to reach out to new people, we may be missing out on what they have to offer us: new perspectives, unique senses of humor, and life stories that can illuminate ours.

We're missing out on the global nature of the body of Christ—and so are the new workers. They're missing out on what we have to offer them—a home away from home, someone to sit next to in church, someone to debrief with over coffee.

Short-term workers are a gift to us. They are only given to us for a short time, but we can make the most of that time. We can invite them into our homes and into our lives, we can make a place for them in our hearts. And they, in turn, can make a place for us in their hearts. We can remember forever the sojourners who were with us in body only a short time, but are with us in spirit always.

So don't be afraid to welcome new people into your life, whether they're with you for ten weeks or ten years. And remember that the love you show a college student today might be passed on to a missionary tomorrow.

# On Not Being the Casserole Lady

## BY ELIZABETH

MANY A CASSEROLE LADY has cared for me. The Casserole Lady brings food to the hurting, nourishment to the weary, comfort to the downcast. She's first on your doorstep with home-baked bread and brownies, with meatloaf and soup, and of course, with casseroles galore. She ensures you don't need to plan and prepare meals when you're grieving a loss, are freshly postpartum, or find yourself in any other time of need.

I love the Casserole Ladies, but I am not one of them.

Sometimes I think about people with the gift of hospitality and get this gnawing, guilty feeling. Why can't I be more like them? I wish I could, for hospitality seems like the real spiritual gift. Delivering meals to doorsteps, inviting large groups into your home for meals, hosting people long-term as part of your family—this all sounds so very first-century Christian. I sigh and start to think I must not measure up.

But I think my accounting system is off when I calculate this way. Maybe I shouldn't be tallying things up like this. It shouldn't be about me, me, me. It shouldn't be about how valuable or useful my gifts are. We shouldn't have a usefulness hierarchy—that's a joy-stealer if ever I heard one. Instead, I've come to believe that it's about the love behind my actions. It's about my offering of love to the Lord's Beloved, for I speak a language of love to the church that is no less than those gifted in hospitality.

This idea of speaking a language of love originated in Gary Chapman's book, *The 5 Love Languages*,[1] where he specifies these five love languages:

- Words of Affirmation

---

1. Chapman, *5 Love Languages*.

- Physical Touch

- Acts of Service

- Gifts

- Quality Time

I've mostly heard the idea of love languages applied to individual relationships, and to marriage in particular. It generally seems to be discussed in the context of getting your own needs met, explaining why you're disappointed when they aren't, and of course making sure you meet your spouse's needs in return. (Note: I'm not saying that's how it's discussed in the book. I'm just saying that's how I've usually heard it discussed amongst others.)

That approach just doesn't satisfy me anymore. I want to reframe the gifts discussion, and I want to reframe the love language discussion. I want to stop talking about the gifts we receive from God and start talking about the love we offer back to him. I want to move beyond just determining how I prefer to receive love, and start embracing the way I most wholeheartedly give love.

Some people, like the Casserole Ladies, love through their acts of service. (And we're all grateful for them!)

Some people love through monetary gifts. (And building funds and charities everywhere are grateful for them, not to mention those of us in support-based ministry who rely on gifts for our daily bread.)

Some people love through physical touch. (And we're all grateful for the huggers and the greeters and, let's not forget, the tireless nursery workers and stay-at-home moms.)

Some people love through quality time. (And we're all grateful for the preachers, teachers, and small group leaders who painstakingly prepare lessons week after week, and for those who sit with people, whether sick or well, whether discouraged or not, and give their time to them.)

Obviously this is not an exhaustive treatise on all the ways members of the body might speak these five different love languages! I just want to ask this question today: How do you speak love, out of an overflow of your own heart, to the church? Not what you think you should be doing to serve, not what you see someone else doing, not what you've always done, but how do you speak love in such a way that brings you joy?

For me, the way I most wholeheartedly give love to the body of Christ is through words of affirmation. I use words with the hope of blessing people, not for my sake, but for theirs. I offer words, and not just in books or blog posts—though they're here too. I also pour all my love into emails and private messages, just because I want to, and because it brings me joy. It is through words that I give gladly and love fully.

I take my counsel from Peter, who says "Do you have the gift of speaking? Then speak as though God himself were speaking through you" (1 Pet 4:11), and from Paul, who says, "If your gift is to encourage others, be encouraging" (Rom 12:8). I hear their commission to speak and encourage not through the lens of gift or skill or talent, but through the lens of love.

I want the discussion of love languages to be about what we give, *for the pure joy of it*, and not what we need from others. I want to approach service from the vantage point of love, and not of giftings. Not from a focus on me and what God has given me, but from a focus on offering my love to others. Not in order to pigeonhole myself into speaking only one language, but to embrace the way I show love and to give my whole soul to it.

I want our love languages to be an outpouring of love, a breaking open of our alabaster boxes.

~~~~~~~~~~

What is your offering of love to the church? What language do you speak to her?

Check out Julie Meyer's song "Alabaster Box," in which she talks about pouring out all her love for Jesus. And we cannot end without a quote from Henri Nouwen who, in his book *The Return of the Prodigal Son*, expresses my feelings and experiences so well:

> "When I first saw Rembrandt's painting, I was not as familiar with the home of God within me as I am now. Nevertheless, my intense response to the father's embrace of his son told me that I was desperately searching for that inner place where I too could be held as safely as the young man in the painting . . .
>
> I have a new vocation now. It is the vocation to speak and write from that place back into the many places of my own and other people's restless lives. I have to kneel before the Father, put my ear against his chest and listen, without interruption, to the heartbeat of God. Then, and only then, can I say carefully and very gently what I hear.

I know now that I have to speak from eternity into time, from the lasting joy into the passing realities of our short existence in this world, from the house of love into the houses of fear, from God's abode into the dwellings of human beings. I am well aware of the enormity of this vocation. Still, I am confident that it is the only way for me."[2]

---

2. Nouwen, *Return of the Prodigal Son*, 17.

# That Time Paul Talked about Breastfeeding

BY *ELIZABETH*

MY HUSBAND AND I worked in local church ministry for over ten years before moving abroad to serve for the last seven. There's something I want you to know about this life: you're going to need a lot of fortitude for the journey. Working with people, in any time and any place, is hard. It doesn't matter if it's in your home country or a host country. Working with people is heart-wrenching and soul-filling, and you need endurance.

This is something else I want you to know: in the years ahead, never hesitate to serve out of your feminine strength. A lot of teaching models are filled with masculine metaphors. There's battle this, and army that. There's fighting here and soldiering on there. The Bible itself is filled with battle-speak. We are to put on the full armor of God so that we can take our stand against the devil's schemes. But the same Paul who told us in Ephesians 6 that our battle is not against flesh and blood and that we were to arm ourselves and stay alert and be persistent and stand firm, that very same Paul was not ashamed in his first letter to the Thessalonians to compare himself to a woman.

In I Thessalonians 2:7, Paul, Silas, and Timothy jointly describe their conduct among the believers there: "We were gentle among you, like a nursing mother taking care of her own children" (ESV). I was in a training session last year when I first truly took hold of this verse. We had studied the great faith and love of the Thessalonian church in chapter 1, and now we were in chapter 2 studying the attributes of the men who'd told them the good news. When we got to the verse about these three men acting like a mother, some of the men seemed to want to brush it off and focus instead on verse 11, where the letter writers compare themselves to good fathers.

But I couldn't brush Paul's words off. I remembered how physically demanding it was to be a nursing mother. I had to speak out:

> "We have this idea of a mother with her nursing baby that's all sweetness and light. But it's not. It's really hard work. You have to feed yourself well, so you can feed your baby. You have to get up at all hours of the night to care for a crying child, and you have to try not to be cranky about all that lost sleep."

As I spoke, women all around me nodded their heads in agreement, and several told me afterward how glad they were that I had said that. They had lived it, too, and they knew the challenges of mothering. You need a lot of stamina. You don't sleep through the night for months on end. Sometimes you get painful mastitis or yeast infections. You have to keep up your water and calorie intake. To your embarrassment, you leak milk everywhere. Or you have to work hard to make *enough* milk. Sometimes you can't figure out for the life of you how to make this child stop crying, but somehow you have to stay calm while you do it. On top of that, you're basically tethered to your child because you don't know when they'll need to eat again. You sacrifice many things for this child, this child whom you love so tenderly and so fiercely.

Somehow this was something the apostle Paul understood. When we serve people, we have to make sure we're getting our spiritual nourishment first, before we can pass anything of value on to them. Living and working among the continual, desperate needs of other people can physically and emotionally deplete us. And sometimes other people's needs interrupt our planned and preferred schedules. Paul knew all this. He lived all this. At the same time, Paul felt incredible affection for the Thessalonians. Paul, Silas, and Timothy loved them so much that they shared not only the good news with them, but their own lives as well (v. 8). And they'd spent plenty of time praising them in the chapter before.

Over the past few months I have been unable to let verse 7 go. I've learned that in the Greek the noun was unmistakably feminine. It was *trophos*: a caregiver, a person sustaining someone else by nourishing and offering the tender care of a nurse. I've learned that it had the connotation of mother's care, of holding a child close, wrapped in her arms. There is familiarity here. Affection. Tenderness. The verb was *thalpo*: to cherish, nourish, foster, comfort, nurture, or keep warm. There is action here, decision, deliberate investment. And the phrase "her own children" (*heautou teknon*) indicates belonging, an inclusion, a turning toward.

All of these feminine-sounding words can illuminate our own roles, wherever God has placed us. They are not weakness. They are not unnecessary or irrelevant or dispensable. They are strength and they are resiliency and they are *essential*. Whether or not you've ever been a nursing mother, you have a yearning for relationship that can solidify your ministry, not undermine it. Whether or not you've ever been a nursing mother, you have an instinct to care for people sacrificially. Whether or not you've ever been a nursing mother, you have the capacity to lead with endurance.

Paul wasn't ashamed of these qualities, and neither should we be. It is good and healthy to identify as a woman and serve out of our God-given identity. Of course, men can be nurturers too—just see verse 11—and women can be warriors—just see Deborah—but when I read these verses, I feel so much validation. Validation of my work and validation of my worth. All those years living and ministering as a woman, they weren't wasted. And as someone who has had a fraught relationship with the apostle Paul over the years, these verses are yet one more reason I can love both him and his letters, for he wasn't afraid to lean into the feminine for the sake of the people he was serving. It is something we needn't be afraid of either.

# Missionary Mommy Wars

BY *JONATHAN*

I JUST WANT TO come out and say it; I'm not a mommy. Shoot, I'm not even a woman. (OK, those were some of the weirdest sentences I've ever written.) But despite my obvious shortcomings, I'm still writing this chapter. Here's why:

I look around and see young moms and experienced moms who are serving cross-culturally, and they're under siege. I see them, battle-weary and bleary-eyed, burdened by expectations that would crush the strongest. I see them wrangle toddlers *and* tonal languages. I watch them brave open-air markets with raw meat hanging on hooks *and* open-air homes with neighbors peering in through windows.

Missionary moms are exposed on all fronts, and they feel it. Every-one's watching them. The local people watch every move, confused by the foreigner and her progeny; when she returns "home" for a visit, she feels watched just the same. (And for the record, jet lag does strange things to children, so any misbehavior can and should be blamed on jet lag, for at least the first two months.)

The mom on the foreign mission field is stretched thin. She must take care of her household, figuring out how to do all the stuff she used to know how to do. She must learn the local language and culture, edu-cate her children, save the world, communicate with senders, support her husband, and convert everyone through her calm spirit and mild demeanor.

I'm speaking with slight hyperbole, sort of, but if you pause and observe, you too will see that missionary moms, especially the newbies, have a whole lot on their plate, and it's stressing them out big time.

Missionary dads are expected to do the work. Period. They are judged, for better or worse, on their work product: How is the ministry going? Not so with moms. The missionary mom is judged by how well her kids behave, how well her kids transition, how well her kids are educated, how healthy her marriage is, how well she knows the local language, *in addition* to how well the ministry is going.

It's not fair, and I'm calling it. We need to pause and care for the women among us who are being crushed by unrealistic expectations. So can we call a cease-fire? Can we stop taking aim at missionary moms, expecting them to be *everything,* and then criticizing them when they fail to accomplish the impossible?

And can you, missionary mom, stop taking aim at yourself? You can't do it all, but that doesn't make you weak; it makes you human.

Paul says in Ephesians 4:16, "He makes the whole body fit together perfectly. *As each part does its own special work*, it helps the other parts grow, so that the whole body is healthy and growing and full of love." No part does *all* the work. Each part does its own work, and that work is special. What is the special work to which God is calling you?

Maybe, right now, your primary task on the mission field is taking care of your own little people. That is special work that helps the whole body to be healthy, growing, and full of love. It's not less than. Maybe it's leading an entire mission. That too is special work that helps the whole body to be healthy, growing, and full of love. It's not less than.

When missionary moms, due to external pressure or internal in-securities, try to do *everything*, the whole body ends up being hurt, not helped. The most important thing for you to do is the work God has called you to do.

I'll say it again: a healthy mission field does not depend on you do-ing it all. Health and growth and love come when each person does the work that God is asking *her* to do. No comparisons allowed.

The mirage of the perfect missionary mom is alluring and dan-gerous. If you try to follow her, you will be perpetually discouraged, depressed, and exhausted. On the flip side, if you feel like you *are* the perfect missionary mom, you will be perpetually arrogant, haughty, and annoying.

What would change if you forgot the mirage of the perfect mission-ary mom and started remembering the Perfect One instead?

Remember, his burden is light.
He is the Lord of rest, the Bridegroom, longing for his Bride.
He is not a taskmaster, demanding more widgets.

He is a loving Husband, pursuing his favorite girl.
He is a tender Father, splashing in the ocean with his children.
He is a Warrior, protecting his people.
He is a Comforter who really sees.
He knows you are human, and he's glad about it.
He knows you can't do it all, and he's okay with it.
He is jealous for you, longing for your whole heart.
He wants your gaze fixed on him, not the mirage.

The next time you're tempted to criticize another mom, lay down your weapon and state what she *is* doing instead of what she's not doing?

Before you criticize yourself, identify and declare what you *are* doing instead of what you're not doing.

Are you doing what you feel like God has led you to do? Wonderful! The body of Christ needs you to do that. The mission field need you to do that. Your family needs you to do that.

*So here's to the missionary mom, the one in the trenches with the toddlers.*
*The one who raises kids abroad and then sends them "home."*
*Here's to the missionary mom, far away from pediatricians and emergency*
*services, who lives with constant awareness that help might not be coming.*
*Here's to the missionary mom who lives in a glass bowl,*
*aware of the stares.*
*The one who liked shopping when shopping was simple.*
*The one who would really like a Starbucks coffee. Like, right now.*
*Here's to the missionary mom whose children experience*
*more goodbyes than most.*
*The one whose kitchen looks more like Bear Grylls than Martha Stewart.*
*Here's to the mom on mission, the one who rocks the cradle*
*and changes the world.*

# What to Do about Women's Roles

BY *ELIZABETH*

I'VE SAT AROUND THE table and been told—on more than one occasion and on both sides of the ocean—that what I'm doing is not enough. That I am not working hard enough. That what I'm doing with my children is too small. That I'm not properly serving the needs around me. And all the while, I'd been following, to the best of my ability, what I thought God had for me in that season of my life.

There have been times I've been beyond frustrated at the state of church culture. A culture that seems to honor and esteem men above women. A culture that grants men more options in where and how to serve God than it grants women. A culture that judges women for the few options they *do* have, no matter which ones they choose. You stay at home with your children? You should be working all day. You work all day? You should be staying at home with your children.

Sometimes I wonder why men are privileged to choose their ministry emphasis, but wives are pigeonholed into their husband's jobs. Is there no difference between the way God fashioned the two parts of a couple, that they might possibly be able to serve in different capacities?

I have cried so many tears over this.

I'd love to see a Christian culture that places fewer unattainable expectations on women. I'd love to see a Christian culture that ties up fewer heavy burdens on women's shoulders. I'd love to see a Christian culture that lifts a finger—or five—to ease those unbearable demands.

The reality is, we may not be able to bring cultural change across all of Christendom. We may not be able to exert organization- or church-wide influence, but we can attend to the one thing we do have influence over: our relationship with God.

When we tune our hearts to the heart of God, when we commune with him, when we feel his pleasure, the displeasure of people feels much less intimidating and much less invalidating. This I know: the deeper I go into God's love, and the more consistently I spend time with him, the less the voices of inadequacy clamor for my attention. It might sound cliché, but it's been my experience.

Spending time with God won't magically make stressful relationships disappear. It won't miraculously change people's expectations of us, and it won't change a church culture that seemingly judges women more harshly than men. It will, however, modulate some of the disapproving looks and comments.

The time we spend soaking up God's love and grace will inoculate us against some of the disapproval of men and women. The confidence we have in being his daughter *that comes through spending time with him* makes the criticisms of how we're not correctly filling our role pack a smaller punch. And when God's love and affirmation burn in our hearts, that fire spreads to other women.

I'm not saying it isn't important to discern our roles. It's very important to humbly determine our giftings and prayerfully decide how we're going to serve God practically and wholeheartedly in this season of our lives. I'm not saying we won't ever need to have discussions with our husbands, teammates, and organizations about our roles in our marriages, teams, and host cultures. And I'm most certainly not saying that a daily devotional time will immunize us against ever receiving criticism (warranted or not), or feeling its sting.

What I *am* saying is that the shackles of expectations we feel both externally from others and internally from ourselves are too heavy. What I *am* saying is that Jesus wants to free us from the burdensome expectations of people and that the yoke he offers us is light, much lighter than the yoke others would place upon us. What I *am* saying is. . .

I believe we are children of the King first and foremost.
I believe our various roles in the Kingdom have got to flow out of that.
I believe it is for freedom that Christ set us free.
I believe that if the Son sets us free, we will be free indeed.
I believe that freed people free people.
I believe that healed people heal people.
I believe if all we ever do is bring our freed selves to the table, then that is worth it.

# Misogyny in Missions

## BY *JONATHAN*

"LADIES WHO LUNCH—WITH MEN"[1]

That's the name of an article I shared on Facebook recently, not knowing it would unleash a torrent of opinion. How should men and women interact? If they work together, what sorts of rules should we put around their interaction? How do we safeguard marriages while treating women with respect? Do our rules surrounding male-female interaction demean women?

It was an interesting discussion, and one that I think our community needs to have.

## Women as Traps

Are men and women who aren't married to each other allowed to meet together? Ride in cars together? Be in the office alone together? If we allow those types of things, is an affair inevitable?

The author of "Ladies Who Lunch" references The Billy Graham Rule. She says,

> "The 'rule' goes something like this: to avoid temptation, or the appearance thereof, it has been said that Billy Graham never meets with a woman alone. Graham has done his best to avoid solo encounters with females—whether over lunch, prayer, dinner, a meeting, or any other occasion."[2]

---

1. Bianchi, "Ladies Who Lunch—with Men."
2. Bianchi, "Ladies Who Lunch—with Men," lines 18–23.

Many churches and missions agencies have similar rules and policies, and I believe they've typically been enacted with good intentions and without malevolence. However, I believe there are problems with strict enforcement, least of which is that it misses the heart of the matter entirely, treating women as traps.

These types of rules, broadly applied, end up sexualizing every woman I meet, dehumanizing her, and turning her into an existential threat to my marriage, an illicit liaison waiting to happen. That, to me, is simply untenable.

Bill Gothard, Doug Phillips, and Josh Duggar all had *very strict* rules surrounding their interactions with women, or at least that's what it looked like. The thing is, moral purity cannot be created through rules, and frankly, rules provide much less protection than we think while objectifying women more than we think.

These rules have been made by men for men, and typically, the conversations are filled with male voices. I'd love to hear from the women. I'd love to hear your thoughts on the matter.

## Culturally Sensitive?

Perhaps some of these policies are the result of cultural sensitivity. Great. There's certainly a place for that. Perhaps the driving force is our fear of false accusations. OK, we can talk about that. Or perhaps the rules exist because deep down, to the core, we believe that women are scary. Well, I'm not really okay with that.

Protecting marriages is a great thing, and recognizing the great risk of moral failure is wise, but when that slips into discouraging men from having normal and healthy friendships with women, we're in dangerous territory, and we end up robbing our communities of something both the men and the women need: healthy relationships with one another!

The difference is subtle, but just because something is hard to see doesn't mean it's not there.

## Objectification Much?

Do our rules actually end up objectifying women? Often, I think the answer is *yes*. Now, if you're a guy and you don't like what I'm saying, can I ask you a question? Do you watch porn? Do you watch movies or shows that objectify women?

Using women in private and then piously protecting yourself from them in public seems a bit disingenuous. Don't punish women in public for your sin in private. Deal with your own stuff.

My wife experienced this in a local church before we met. Despite strict rules being in place, and with high levels of outward purity being evident, a respected leader abused girls. He's still a leader.

I experienced it too. Charismatic leader, courtship culture, very restrictive purity rules, and a leader who's now been accused of sexually molesting scores of young women. He's still a leader.

I'm *not* saying that every guy that disagrees with me on this has a porn problem or is an abuser. It's just that I've come across too many men with "high standards" in public who hurt women in private. I'm not okay with that, and I'm pretty sure Jesus isn't either.

## Should We Have Rules?

Yeah! In Proverbs 5, the young man is warned about the immoral woman. (And I will certainly teach my daughters to take heed and avoid the immoral man!) This is the woman whose lips are "as sweet as honey, and her mouth is smoother than oil" (Prov 5:3 NLT). This is the woman who "cares nothing about the path to life" (Prov 5:6 NLT).

He is warned: "Stay away from her! Don't go near the door of her house" (Prov 5:8 NLT). The caution is to stay away from her door, not all doors. He's not told to avoid walking by the houses of all women all the time. Just her house. She is dangerous. She's looking for an affair and she cares nothing about the path to life. This does not mean that all women are dangerous to him. Or me.

We shouldn't check our brains at the door and avoid all women. We also shouldn't check our brains at the door and embrace all women.

## False Accusations

Strict rules on male-female interaction probably do provide some protection against false accusations, and there's some value to that. Even so, we seem to be way more concerned with false accusations than Jesus ever was. He let women do stuff to him that *really* caused a stir and ignited the burning glares of the religious elite.

He didn't stop her and say "This looks bad. The important men are going to judge me." No, he saw *her* instead of the others. He saw what *she* needed instead of what he needed. She needed love more than he needed respect.

There are lessons here for us.

## Our Story

Early on in our marriage, I had to come to terms with the fact that my wife was in a male-dominated university studying engineering with a bunch of guys. She had male lab partners, she studied late on projects with guys; frankly, she was with guys alone a whole lot. I think my thoughts on this are greatly flavored by that experience.

And then, of course, I started studying nursing, which meant I was in a female-dominated world, with female lab partners, studying late on projects, etc. And then I worked as a nurse with a bunch of ladies. And then, as now, we talked about it. There were no secrets, but there was trust. And it was totally cool.

Nowadays, I do a lot of member care and pastoral counseling, and since women seek out pastoral care too, I often meet with women. If I'm going to have a meeting with a woman, Elizabeth knows about it. While protecting client confidentiality, I still tell Elizabeth when I'm meeting and where I'm meeting. There's still trust.

## Honesty as Protection

If I begin to feel any attraction, even slightly, for another woman, I tell Elizabeth. I name it and say it and steal temptation's power. The light defuses the darkness.

When I do this, I'm not telling my wife that I've fallen in love with another woman; I'm telling her that I don't want to. I'm acknowledging that there's some attraction there, but I'm affirming our relationship, and I'm recognizing that in the telling, the temptation's power is stripped and the threat greatly reduced.

Honesty. Trust.

We had conversations like this when I worked in a local church in America, when I was in nursing school, when I worked at a hospital, and now, when I'm working as a pastoral counselor. Not talking about it doesn't make it not exist. It just makes it a secret.

Women are not scary. Secrets are.

Talking about it brings it out into the open, and it also shows Elizabeth that I'm turning my heart toward her. And if I'm constantly turning my heart toward my wife, it'll be much less likely to turn toward another woman. It's locked on Elizabeth.

## Conclusion

Rules are easy to make. Rules make us feel safe. Rules are simple to follow. And rules are terrible at creating emotionally healthy, intimately connected human beings.

What if we spent more time growing intimacy on the inside of our marriages and less time trying to kill the threats on the outside? What if we worked to develop trust and honesty within more than we fretted about the dangers without? Sure, it might be scary, and it might be complicated.

But I think it'd also be really, really good.

# Four Tools of Spiritual Manipulators

BY *JONATHAN*

I GREW UP IN a very conservative subculture of an already conservative homeschool culture, in a pretty conservative stream of the Christian faith. Though I learned much from these experiences and am grateful for them, they laid the foundation for spiritual manipulation later in life. The manipulators used words and phrases that I had heard before. They seemed biblical and very right, but they were not.

I had been groomed for this. My family of origin was very loving, but that did not prevent me from absorbing patterns of interaction that left me wide open to spiritual manipulation. A foundation had been laid that gave the manipulators their tools—tools that inflicted deep pain. Tools that I'm just now beginning to recognize.

My hope is that this chapter will expose these tools and show how manipulators wield them. Many spiritual manipulators follow a pattern. They use the same key words, the same accusations, the same tactics. Their weapons can leave the target breathless, alone, and without recourse. There is no safe place to hide. If you've ever been targeted, you'll know the pain and confusion these four tools can inflict.

In brief, spiritual manipulators tend to use four tools: they accuse the target of disrespect, gossip, pride, and having a blind spot. Manipulators love using these four accusations, regardless of their truth. They are easy to drop on people, and usually the purpose is not to bring the target back to Jesus, but to manipulate the target and/or protect the manipulator.

If you are accused of these things, examine the accusations carefully. Seek God's counsel and the wisdom of trusted friends. It took years for me to recover from some of these accusations, and that only happened after many mature church leaders and friends (and a good therapist) countered and defused them.

## Tool #1: Disrespect

When the manipulator senses any sort of disagreement or eroding influence, he or she will accuse the target of disrespect. Manipulators will often start with the accusation of disrespect, hoping the target will apologize quickly and stop whatever action is "disrespectful."

Be very, very careful when you hear the word "respect" being thrown around, especially in conflict. In controlling religious circles, it is a magical tool used to shut people up. It is often used by manipulators to protect those in power, believing that if everyone would just be quiet and respectful, it would all be okay. But the trouble is, the minute you have to start demanding respect, you've lost it. Yes, of course, we are told to respect those in authority, the government, church leaders, etc. However, that truth is not a prohibition on kindly disagreeing and respectfully bringing up things you see as inconsistencies or flaws.

If you're accused of disrespect, check your motives, check with some trusted counselors outside the situation, and watch out for tool number two.

## Tool #2: Gossip

Manipulators will use a w i d e definition of gossip—and apply it liberally. They love labeling any negative talk "gossip," even if it's not. They will preach about it, talk about it, and elevate the sin of gossip to the level of blasphemy. By labeling all talk of this sort as gossip, they magically remove their own responsibility to deal with the truth.

Be aware that despite all the preaching and teaching on gossip, a concrete definition will be absent. For example, if reporting a possible crime to the authorities is gossip, it's time to reexamine the definitions.

I heard some really bad stuff about a person once, so I went to the person directly and asked if any of it was true. Their incredulous response: "You're asking me to verify gossip!" Well, I guess, but that's not gossip. I wasn't spreading false information, and I wasn't lying about anyone; I was simply going to the person who was the object of the gossip and asking about some things that very much pertained to my life. I thought that's what I was supposed to do. However, the manipulator accused me of gossiping.

When being accused of gossip, don't be surprised if the manipulator also blames you for taking up another's offense. Feel free to remind him, respectfully, that sometimes the Bible actually commands us to take up another's offense, especially when the other person is powerless to defend him or herself.

If you're accused of gossip, review the biblical definition, check your heart, and watch out for tool number three.

## Tool #3: Pride

If the first two tools don't work, manipulators will often accuse the target of pride. Manipulators seem to love the blanket accusation of pride. If the target disagrees or has her own opinion (of events or ideas), she is arrogant and prideful. A more humble person would see the correctness and rightness of the manipulator.

This type of accusation puts the target in an awkward position. The target can't really argue back, because that just reinforces the manipulator's point. The target is left with no alternative but to accept this accusation, and thus this is a very useful tool for manipulators. Furthermore, since we are taught from a very early age that pride is one of the worst sins ever, this accusation carries a lot of weight. We know it's serious business.

This accusation in particular rocked my world. I now realize that it was not made in good faith. It was not made to help me get closer to Jesus; the accusation was made to control me—to control my behavior. And control me it did. For years, I questioned everything I did, everything I said. "Am I being prideful? Does this look arrogant?" It was a life without freedom, a life without grace.

Fortunately, through wise encouragement from older Christians and a good counselor, I was able to see the damage done by the manipulator. The fear of coming across as prideful or arrogant is still there. The voice of the manipulator still rings loud and clear. However, I don't listen to that voice as much as I used to. I've realized that some of the things about me that were labeled "arrogant" and "prideful" are in fact gifts from God, gifts to serve the church, not sins to confess. I have found freedom.

## Tool #4: The Blind Spot

Manipulators tend to save this one for last. If they've tried everything else and are unable to manipulate the target, they may simply accuse the target of having blind spots, and if the target denies the existence of a particular blind spot, that's taken as proof of its existence.

This is the manipulator's perfect tool.

Do we have blind spots, spiritually? Yup, probably. And could God use a manipulator to reveal those blind spots? Maybe. But it seems that confronting blind spots is better done by a caring friend or a close confidant—not a manipulator who uses the "doctrine" of blind spots as a last resort, with the end goal being control.

Spiritual manipulators are angered and annoyed by people who aren't easily manipulated. And although anger can be holy, it is one of the surest signs of a spiritual manipulator who's out of a job. A spiritual manipulator who can't manipulate is like a gun with a knot in the barrel. So be careful!

Spiritual manipulation hurts and wounds—deeply. If you've been targeted, may God in his infinite mercy restore the damage done. May he provide deep peace and a safe shelter. May you see the character of his heart, washed clean of the manipulators who used God's words to damage and control rather than to heal and set free.

Grace to you all.

# What Jesus Has to Say
## about Dealing with Rejection

*BY ELIZABETH*

REJECTION. I HATE IT. I hate the feeling, and I was feeling it again in a major way, so I searched through my journals till I found the entry I was looking for. It was the notes from a sermon Tim Krenz preached to the graduating seniors at our church. The ideas helped me so much that I recopied my notes into my current journal, and now I'm going to share them with you. It's based on the words of Jesus in Luke 10:5–11:

> "Whenever you enter someone's home, first say, 'May God's peace be on this house.' If those who live there are peaceful, the blessing will stand; if they are not, the blessing will return to you. Don't move around from home to home. Stay in one place, eating and drinking what they provide. Don't hesitate to accept hospitality, because those who work deserve their pay.
>
> "If you enter a town and it welcomes you, eat whatever is set before you. heal the sick, and tell them, 'The Kingdom of God is near you now.' But if a town refuses to welcome you, go out into its streets and say, 'We wipe even the dust of your town from our feet to show that we have abandoned you to your fate. And know this—the Kingdom of God is near!'"

Tim offered the graduates a handy little acronym for dealing with rejection: GRAD. It stands for:

- GO

- REMEMBER

- ANTICIPATE

- DETERMINE

Here's how we can deal with the rejection we so much long to forget: We GO out into the world like the disciples of long ago. We REMEMBER who we are (God's children) and what we have (God's word and God's Spirit). We ANTICIPATE rejection—whether it's unfounded or not, we cannot avoid it. Lastly, we DETERMINE ahead of time how we will respond: by shaking even the dust of that rejection off our feet.

Down to the last bit of dust, we will not carry it around with us, because we remember that even when man rejects us, God has not rejected us. We don't call down fire from heaven on our rejectors like the Sons of Thunder wanted to do in the previous chapter (Luke 9:54). No, we do not take that rejection up: we shake if off, shake it off, and shake it off again.

# How Buddhism Taught Me to Love My Neighbors Better

## BY *ELIZABETH*

A FEW YEARS AGO I didn't like my neighbors very much. We had new neighbors, and they played their music loud, blasting it out of their apartment with the door open. Sometimes for hours at a time.

This caused problems for me. I teach my children at home, and we need an environment conducive to learning. But sometimes this month the music was so loud it prevented their little brains (and mine!) from functioning.

Now we are no strangers to noise during the school day. There's loud traffic—always—and we've endured months on end of the pounding of homemade pile drivers while new buildings are being constructed. Once it was next door, and the other time it was across the street.

The metal shop two houses down from us sometimes starts screeching by 6 a.m. And then there's the demolition of old tile and brick in the walls, floors, and bathrooms that accompanies new neighbors. They want to (understandably) clear out the old (possibly moldy) tile and personalize their new homes.

Once the drilling got loud enough that we had to leave the house and go to a coffee shop to study—a decision which was rather cumbersome with four children and their books, but my kids were sitting right next to me, and I was shouting at them, and they *still* could not hear what I was trying to teach them.

Music or karaoke, however, is different from these things. It's not about people settling in to a new house or building a new house or even, as in the case of the metal shop, providing employment and incomes for people. It's just some guy listening to his music *way too loud*.

It's loudness on purpose, for no discernible economic purpose. I was annoyed. Angry, too. The noise interfered with my job as a home-school teacher. It interfered with my mental stability. And thanks to the anger and irritation issuing forth from my mouth and from my heart, it interfered with my self-perceived holiness.

As in most cases when we don't quite know how to handle neighbor issues in a culturally appropriate way, we asked our landlord what we should do. His answer was most enlightening.

He told us that maybe our neighbor was working through something hard, and that we could build up merit by being patient with him and letting him blast his music. But, if the music really was too long and too loud, then our neighbor could gain merit by being more sensitive to everyone around him and turning the volume down. (For context, our neighbors generally don't blast their music.)

Our landlord was speaking from his own Buddhist background, a background and belief system I don't share, but he had something to teach me.

The first thing he taught me is that I need to be more patient and long-suffering—gracious if you will. If Christ lives in me, then I can certainly offer patience and mercy to a neighbor. I can refrain from getting angry at him. The life of the neighborhood doesn't revolve around me, anyway.

The second thing my landlord taught me—or rather, reminded me—is that there's a kernel of truth in every belief system. Like my Buddhist neighbors, I also believe I should show patience to people who behave in (what seem to me to be) annoying ways.

Certainly, our motivations aren't the same: I show patience not to build up good merit, but because Jesus has shown me such great mercy. In showing patience, I am merely passing on the patience I have already received. I am giving grace because I have been given grace, not, as in the dominant belief system in my country, giving grace in order to *earn* grace.

But all grace comes from God, and grace was present in our recent conversations. I found a divine thread running through a very works-oriented system. Do I believe in karma, merit, and reincarnation the way many Cambodian Buddhists do? No. Did I need and appreciate the reminder to treat others with kindness? Yes.

My landlord's Buddhist teaching was a mirror for my soul, and that soul had some nasty stuff in it. It was unloving, unreasonable, and un-Christlike. If my landlord can offer grace in an uncomfortable situation, how much more can I, who claim to follow Christ, offer grace to the people next door?

Later I would sit with God in the not-so-quiet and let him remind me of his great love for all people—annoying neighbors included—and I would remember that God's great love for my neighbor is the same great love he has for me. I would remember that, truly, I am no less annoying than my neighbor. I would realize that I hadn't been obeying the Jesus I say I love and believe in, because I wasn't loving my neighbor as myself.

So did my neighbor still play loud music with the door open? Yes. Did it still disrupt our concentration? Yes. And was it still annoying? Yes. But do I offer more grace and love in my heart than I did before? Also yes. And does the same angry, anxious feeling rise in my chest like before? A resounding no.

I may not believe Buddhism holds absolute truth, but there are slivers of truth to be found here, slivers of truth thick enough to instruct a stubborn, self-centered Christ-follower like me.

# ANTICIPATING WELL (RECOGNIZING SOME OF THE COMMON PITFALLS)

# The Idolatry of Missions

*BY JONATHAN*

MISSIONARIES ARE LIKE THE church's Special Forces, right? They go into enemy territory, sometimes covertly, tearing down walls for Jesus. They have special training, preparing them to serve in the darkest places around the globe. Missionaries are on the front lines of the kingdom of heaven, right? I'm sorry, but no.

Wherever the gospel is advancing, there is the front line. Wherever lives are being transformed by the love of Jesus, there is the leading edge of the kingdom. But aren't missionaries the cream of the crop? Um, yeah, no. Turns out, we're just people. We may travel more than most, and maybe we speak more languages than some, but the idea that missionaries are somehow set apart is dangerous. I'd like to begin a discussion about this. Care to join?

Whether these false ideas come from the missionaries themselves or those who send them, the consequence is the same: damage. Damage to the missionaries and damage to the churches who send them.

## How These Lies Damage Missionaries

If a missionary believes these lies (cream of the crop, Special Forces, etc.), and if churches reinforce them, one of two things will happen.

*Option 1:* When the missionary realizes he isn't Superman (or supermissionary), confusion, discouragement, and maybe even depression will set in. He may be forced into secrecy, covering up and hiding the fact that he is, in fact, human. He may feel like a failure because he now realizes he's not the best of the best, like all the "real" missionaries. He may create a thin veneer of perfection and hide behind it for a Very.

Long.Time. Obviously, this is not healthy, but it does make sense to the missionary who's comparing himself to a false notion of perfection. And when a whole community of missionaries builds walls and covers up, the fallacy is reinforced: everyone looks super on the outside, and no one can see the inside. And the damage continues.

*Option 2:* If a missionary believes these lies, and continues to believe them, she may become extremely arrogant, judgmental, and condemning. The judgment and condemnation will be aimed at other missionaries who just can't hack it, as well as all the lesser people back home who never even tried. After all, she's the top of the class, the one called and equipped for greater works. Again, these attitudes make sense if she starts with the basic assumption that missionaries are better. Now, it's true, most people will never talk like this, but I bet you've met people who act like it.

## How These Lies Damage Sending Churches

We'll address this more in a bit, but for now, let me just say that when a church believes these lies, it effectively keeps missions *out there*. Missions becomes something missionaries do "somewhere over there." The great call of God becomes disconnected from the church of God, and that's really, really sad.

Furthermore, it minimizes and marginalizes the godly saints in the local body. The old lady who just put her last few dollars in the plate may have sacrificed more than the family who moved abroad. The arithmetic of the Almighty includes variables we can't see.

One of the kindest, godliest men I've ever known worked on an assembly line for most of his life. You know what he did during his shifts? He talked with God and he memorized the Word. And so, when this blue-collar shift-worker of an old man looked you in the eye and shook your hand, you felt like you knew Jesus a little better. He was faithful to his Lord for decades longer than I've been alive. And whatever reward I get in heaven, I'm pretty sure it won't be any grander than this faithful, Spirit-filled saint's.

When the church idolizes young missionaries, it runs the great risk of forgetting the faith-filled old people. The plodders who've loved well and remained faithful for a lifetime. And when the church neglects those people, the church misses out big time.

It's not just the faithful old that tend to get marginalized. What about the faithful young? Is the work I do abroad more important than the local pastor in my home country who loves God with all his heart, and loves his people with sacrificial and compassionate love?

Is my job more important or more holy than my friend who's a doctor in an inner-city emergency room? He loves and treats folks most people wouldn't even touch. And he does it with kindness, giving strong witness to the Spirit of Christ who lives in him.

My job—loving and serving people across cultures—is what I'm called to do. I really believe that. But as I've said elsewhere (see *Missionary Mommy Wars*), I sure hope some people are called and equipped to do work other than this. And I sure hope they realize their work isn't second-class.

## The Risk of Idolatry

Why do churches put missionaries on a pedestal? Why do missionaries put themselves there? I'm not sure, but what I do know is that they, and we, do. And it's dangerous.

I grew up in a culture that idolized missionaries. By the time I was a teenager, I had read the biographies of Adoniram Judson, Gladys Aylward, Jim Elliot, Nate Saint, Elisabeth Elliot, Hudson Taylor, Amy Carmichael, Brother Andrew, David Livingston, and others. We revered these people. My parents even made sure I got to meet Elisabeth Elliot when she came to town, and we had a handwritten note from her on our fridge!

These people were great and faithful and followed God in amazing ways, and I'm so grateful I was exposed to their stories; I in no way want to dishonor them. The error was mine, not theirs, because somewhere in all those stories I got the idea that really good Christians became overseas missionaries. If I wanted to sort-of serve God, I could become a pastor, but if I *really* wanted to serve God, I'd become a missionary. And if I didn't care about serving God at all, I could become a lawyer (which I did, by the way, but that's a story for another time).

The truly faithful, the truly holy, the ones most loved by God and most in love with God, would obviously serve him overseas. No one said it out loud, but I internalized the message nonetheless. I doubt you've heard these things spoken out loud, but have you ever felt them?

For too long, we have idolized overseas missions. We need to stop now.

I'm afraid that in our desire to be good followers of God, we've lost intimacy with him. Intimacy is personalized and requires time and a willingness to pay attention to subtle cues; we've preferred the one-size-fits-all, task-driven, widget-producing faith that measures success not by love, but by product.

Have we cared more about the work our hands do than the love our heart does?

Have we challenged people to obey the call instead of the Christ?

Have we sent and honored missionaries who are filled more with ambition than adoration?

Again, these things make sense if overseas missions is the end-all, but it's not. Serving cross-culturally is definitely a valid response to the gospel, but it is not the only valid response to the gospel.

In fact, if traveling a long ways is how we serve God, then Jonah was doing a great job even *before* the whole fish incident. Remember, serving Jesus isn't about traveling the right distance as much as it's about traveling the right direction.

We've called moving to a foreign land the pinnacle of obedience, but in some cases, moving to a foreign land might be more like running away—disobedience in its most spiritual form.

## A Caveat

Please don't hear what I'm not saying. I'm not saying cross-cultural missions is bad. I am a missionary serving outside of my passport country, and I love it. I really do. I hope to stay here for a long time. I've recruited people to serve overseas, I've preached to teenagers about serving overseas, I've passionately extolled service abroad (See *Remember the Ten Reasons You Should Be a Missionary*). And I plan to continue!

But here's the problem. Early on, I internalized the idea that this job, this ministry, was in fact the best. It's what the best Christians do. It's what the holiest Christians do. It's what people who don't have problems do. But you know what, that's crazy talk. I'm not setting out to discourage folks from cross-cultural missions. I am trying to say, if you're going to follow God across cultures, do it because he called you. Do it because you love people. Don't do it because you think it's what good Christians do.

## Conclusion

Before we moved overseas, I wrote a song that had these lyrics, "To the ends of the earth, or down the street, where you send I will go, I will go." I sang it with gusto and enthusiasm. I now realize it's ridiculous; it's based on the false dichotomy that some are called to go to cool places (the ends of the earth), and others are just called down the street.

We are *all* called down the street, it's just that some of us have to travel a bit to find our street.

God didn't want to send me to the ends of the earth *or* down the street. He wanted to send me to Cambodia *and* down the street. Why? Because the call of God is local. It's right here, with the people in front of me.

He may call you to change streets (and that's totally his prerogative), but once you get to your new street, you still have to love and serve the person in front of you. He may send you to a street that looks (and smells) nothing like the streets you're used to. Great! But you know what, once you get there and learn their language, you still have to love and serve the person in front of you. It's not rocket science.

So, whether your street is paved and filled with luxury cars, or it's a collection of muddy ruts and filled with wildebeests, the call of God is the same. Love well. Serve well. Live your life in such a way that when people look at your eyes, they see our Father's compassion; when they see you create, they marvel at our King's genius; when they watch you sacrifice, they know our Savior's kindness.

No matter what street you live on, may you truly experience life on the front lines of the kingdom; not because you live on a special or super-holy street, but because on your street, "the blind see, the lame walk, the lepers are cured, the deaf hear, the dead are raised to life, and the good news is being preached to the poor" (Matt 11:5 NLT).

# "God Bless America!"
# and Other Dangerous Prayers

BY *JONATHAN*

I LOVE AMERICA. I love her mountains and her national parks. I love her North Atlantic coastline and her national anthem. I love her freedom of speech and her universities. As an attorney, I especially love her Constitution and her history of Law.

God bless America!

But that's a dangerous prayer, because often, with the same tongue that we mouth "God bless America!" we spit "God destroy Iran!" Or North Korea. Or China. Or whatever. We want to bless America and curse our enemies. And while that kind of talk is certainly in the Bible, it's not very biblical. It is not the way of Jesus.

As believers in America, we're taught, often accidentally, that to be a Christian is to be American, or at least to look Western. But Jesus, the guy from the Middle East, would disagree. We're taught that the prototypical American is a salt-of-the-earth, hard-working, white Christian. Thomas Jefferson would disagree. Benjamin Franklin probably would too.

## Patriotism vs. Nationalism

When nationalism starts parading as patriotism, you end up with a riot.

The patriot says, "I love my country, my homeland, my people!" And that's great and not necessarily inconsistent with the way of Jesus. The nationalist on the other hand says, "I love my country, my homeland, my people! And I think our culture and our values are better than everyone else's!"

The patriot says "God bless America!" but would be thrilled if God blessed Algeria and Russia too. The nationalist says "God bless America!" but would be thrilled if God absolutely destroyed all the "bad people," convincing the world that we really are superior. Obviously.

Now, there is nothing particularly surprising (or wrong) about a country wanting to make itself great again—several countries are predictably trying to do that very thing right now—but while the desire for national greatness is not necessarily evil, it is necessarily secular, and when the line between patriotism and nationalism gets blurred, we must speak up. As followers of a refugee who grew up in occupied territory where public executions and infanticide happened, we must speak up and call patriotism good and nationalism evil.

## Under His Banner

As followers of Christ, our great desire is that he would be made great. We desire that his greatness would be known everywhere, not our country's. We want the banner of our God to be raised up, that his love would be seen, and that all those who see it will run to him and be saved.

As citizens of America, we should celebrate and honor and cherish the United States. She remains a fantastical experiment in human government, bought with blood and sacrifice. (She is far from perfect, of course, and some of her story is violent and abusive and should be labeled as such. But that is a chapter for another book.)

As citizens of the Kingdom, we should celebrate and cherish and love the global Church, the Bride, wherever she may be found. Her flag is our flag. And she is not just in America. She's in Algeria and Russia and Brazil. There are millions in the kingdom who speak Arabic and Urdu and Mandarin. Our fellow citizens live in the jungles of the Congo and the Amazon.

And everyone who's not already a part of the Kingdom of God? Well, we want them to know they're invited!

So may God bless Algeria and Afghanistan and Argentina, and may God bless America!

We should pray for God's will to be done on earth as it is in heaven. We should pray for justice to run down like a mighty river. And we should pray for a heart like his that wants no one to perish, not even ISIS soldiers. Is it un-American to talk like this? I hope not, but maybe.

Our first allegiance is not to Rome, or Washington. It certainly must not be to elephants, donkeys, or three-lettered news agencies. This was settled long ago; our first allegiance, our deepest love, is toward the King.

~~~~~~~~~~

I do hope God blesses America. I pray that he blesses America with peace. I pray that we would learn to love one another, and perhaps even our enemies.

I pray that more and more people would meet Christ, and be changed.

I pray for the *religionists* like Paul, that they would meet Christ and be forever changed.

I pray for the *government contractors* like Zacchaeus, that they would meet Christ and be forever changed.

I pray for the *militant nationalists* like Simon, that they would meet Christ and be forever changed.

I pray for the *white-collars* like Nicodemus and the *blue-collars* like Peter.

I pray for the *rich women* like Joanna, and the *used women* who show up at the well at noon.

I pray that they would all meet Christ and be forever changed.

Will you join me?

~~~~~~~~~~

*"After this I saw a vast crowd, too great to count, from every nation and tribe and people and language, standing in front of the throne and before the Lamb. They were clothed in white robes and held palm branches in their hands. And they were shouting with a great roar, 'Salvation comes from our God who sits on the throne and from the Lamb'" (Rev 7:9–10)!*

# Before You Cry "Demon!"

## BY JONATHAN

*"A mighty fortress is our God, a bulwark never failing;*
*Our helper he amid the flood of mortal ills prevailing.*
*For still our ancient foe doth seek to work us woe;*
*his craft and power are great, and armed with cruel hate,*
*On earth is not his equal."*[1]

I BELIEVE THE ENEMY is real. I believe he still seeks to kill and destroy. He still deceives. He still lies. He still wars against the King. I also believe we blame him for way too much.

We talk about how we're under attack or how our ministry team is receiving a whole lot of opposition. And sometimes, we really believe there's spiritual warfare going on, but often those words and phrases are simply code for "my life's falling apart right now and I need help" or "our team members are all really angry with each other." It's easier to say "we're under attack" than it is to say "we're really drowning."

A conversation on Facebook illustrates the problem. After a missionary described a bunch of really hard stuff that was happening in their life and ministry, a friend left the following comment: "That kind of opposition makes me think that you're doing something powerful."

Do we really believe that? Play that logic out a bit: "Oh, bad things are happening to you, you must be doing something right." Or reverse it, "Oh, things are going well for you, you must be doing something wrong." That's crazy talk, really, but we do it all the time.

---

1. Luther, "Mighty Fortress Is Our God," in Howard, *Songs of Faith and Praise*, Hymn #10.

Do we really believe that the only reason difficult stuff happens to Christians is because we're doing something right and the hounds of hell are now opposing us? It's possible, of course, but we make the assumption automatically and apply it liberally. Is it possible that Satan and his demons are wreaking havoc on a specific missionary or ministry? Absolutely. But just because it's a possibility doesn't mean it's the only possibility.

*"Did we in our own strength confide, our striving would be losing,*
*Were not the right man on our side, the man of God's own choosing.*
*Dost ask who that may be? Christ Jesus, it is he;*
*Lord Sabaoth, his name, from age to age the same,*
*And he must win the battle."*[2]

This is not an exhaustive treatise on spiritual warfare in missions. I'm not trying to outline how demons work in unreached areas, or in an animist who's invited spirits to manifest through him. I am trying to talk about how we talk about spiritual warfare in our families and in our ministries. I'm not so sure it's healthy.

## Biblical Precedent

Defaulting to "demon" has some biblical precedent: unfortunately, it's the Pharisees, a group we typically avoid emulating. Remember, they cried "Demon!" and it was actually Jesus. Oops.

David didn't blame the demonic for his troubles; he blamed God (and his own sins): "Your arrows have struck deep, and your blows are crushing me. Because of your anger, my whole body is sick; my health is broken because of my sins" (Ps 38:2–3).

Job might have been justified in crying "Demon!" when his world came crashing down, but he didn't. He easily could have said, "The devil's out to get me because I'm a good guy doing good things!" But he didn't. He went the other direction, blaming God for taking everything away from him. (And God didn't really deny it, although he certainly added a few theological clarifications to Job's understanding.)

Jesus himself could have cried "Demon!" in the garden, but he didn't. He cried "Father!" Again, I'm not saying we can't call out and

2. Luther, "Mighty Fortress Is Our God," in Howard, *Songs of Faith and Praise,* Hymn #10.

identify enemy activity; I'm just saying that we should be aware that there may be other actors, other parameters. Blaming the devil shouldn't be our default.

## Why We Need to Stop Crying "Demon!"

### 1. It's not biblical

It could be spiritual warfare. It could be demonic. But often, we don't really know for sure. We need to remember that what we call "oppression" or "spiritual warfare" might just be the result of foolish choices. It could be the result of disobedience or God's discipline. It could be providential protection. Often, we just don't know. Better to cautiously say what it is that we don't know, than to boldly say what we think we know but don't.

Imagine a person's car runs out of gas on the way to church. You could say, "Wow, Satan must really be against you being at church today." Or maybe they just forgot to fill up on the way home from work on Friday.

Imagine a preacher's printer malfunctions an hour before church, preventing him from printing out his notes. It could be a malevolent plot against him and the Word, or perhaps he's a procrastinator and God's trying to teach him to plan ahead. I don't know, and that's precisely my point. We certainly shouldn't jump on the judge's bench and condemn the guy, but neither should we excuse any potential character flaws by blaming demons.

### 2. It's not helpful

I often hear people cry "Demon!" when they're trying to encourage someone who's having a rough go of it. They're trying to support a friend. Or they're trying to make sense of their own suffering. There are better ways. When something bad happens, human nature loves to blame someone or something. But when we do this we're playing a hyperspiritual form of the blame game. And what scares me is that once we assign responsibility to Satan, the analysis ends. No more responsibility. No more accountability. No more discernment required. Boom, it's Satan. End of discussion. We really need to stop the automatic jump to demon blame.

### *3. It can block us from finding and treating the real problem*

Citing "warfare" can be a wonderful excuse. Blaming demons has a magical way of putting the attention "out there." It keeps the locus of control outside of me. Maybe it's a spiritual attack, or maybe it's depression. Maybe it's both. Maybe demons are messing with your ministry, or maybe your team just needs some training in conflict resolution.

Maybe you need to attack the enemy and take back ground, or maybe you need to see a counselor. I don't know. What I do know is that when we're quick to blame demons, the sort of analysis and prayerful discernment that could lead us to the root never happens, and that hurts our churches, our families, and our souls.

Peter Scazzero, author of *The Emotionally Healthy Church* and pastor/planter of a large, multiethnic, multilingual church in New York City, makes some interesting observations about a difficult season in ministry. He says,

> "Pausing and reflecting on the state of my soul were both frightening and liberating. At the time I thought all my problems stemmed from the stress and complexity of New York City. I blamed Queens, my profession, our four small children, Geri, spiritual warfare, other leaders, a lack of prayer covering, even our car (it had been broken into seven times in three months). Each time I was certain I had identified the root issue. I hadn't. The root issues were inside me. But I couldn't—or wouldn't—admit that yet."[3]

### Tort Law & Toyotas

There's an area of American law that can help us here. It comes from tort law (which unfortunately has nothing to do with cake) and deals with liability and negligence.

Basically, proving that someone was negligent requires showing that the events that happened would have been "reasonably foreseeable to the average person." This "reasonably foreseeable" test could help us pause for a second before defaulting to demonic.

If something bad happens, take a breath and ask, "Was it reasonably foreseeable that this might happen?" For example, your car breaks down

---

3. Scazzero, *Emotionally Healthy Church*, 29.

after twenty years and 210,000 miles. Yeah, it could be demonic oppression; it could be Satan messing with you and your Toyota. Or, it could just be a really old radiator. It's reasonably foreseeable that old cars will occasionally act old. Even Toyotas.

On the field, you get a stomach bug. Yes, it could be a spiritual attack, or it could be that you were trying to be polite and ate some food from a street vendor. In your country, street vendors don't wash their hands or their food. So, was giardia reasonably foreseeable? If so, pause a bit before you cry "Demon!" and take some Flagyl.

To sum up, if the thing that happened would have been reasonably foreseeable, there's a good chance you're not dealing with spiritual warfare. It might be, of course, but it's probably not.

> *"And though this world, with devils filled, should threaten to undo us,*
> *We will not fear, for God hath willed his truth to triumph through us.*
> *The Prince of Darkness grim, we tremble not for him;*
> *His rage we can endure, for lo, his doom is sure;*
> *One little word shall fell him."*[4]

## And Finally

Does your theology of spiritual warfare make you afraid? Does it scare your kids? Do you talk more about demons than Jesus? Do your conversations focus more on the power of the devil than the power of the cross? If so, you might need to recalibrate. Remember his victory. Remember his presence. Remember his coming.

There is darkness, yes, but darkness dies when the Son rises.

> *"That word above all earthly powers, no thanks to them, abideth;*
> *The Spirit and the gifts are ours, thru him who with us sideth.*
> *Let goods and kindred go, this mortal life also;*
> *The body they may kill; God's truth abideth still;*
> *His kingdom is forever."*[5]

4. Luther, "Mighty Fortress Is Our God," in Howard, *Songs of Faith and Praise,* Hymn #10.

5. Luther, "Mighty Fortress Is Our God," in Howard, *Songs of Faith and Praise,* Hymn #10.

# It's Not All about War:
# Balancing Our Kingdom Rhetoric

BY *JONATHAN*

HOW WE MOTIVATE PEOPLE to care about cross-cultural missions matters. But should we even try to motivate people to care about cross-cultural missions? Should we try to motivate people to do cross-cultural missions? Yes, I think so, but when our talk of kingdom and mission skews too much to an emphasis on war and doing battle, people pay the price and we all suffer in the long run. I've done it before, and I was wrong.

It's a classic motivation strategy, really. Focus on the danger and the risk and the glory. Highlight the adventure and the cost. Appeal to our desire to make a big splash in a book-worthy, mic-dropping, eternity-altering manner. If you can make sure the danger seems enormous and foreign and somewhere exotic, even better. If you can talk with passion about the millions who will die without Christ *unless people go*, good on you. The gospel calls us to go and sacrifice and burn and bleed for the eternal destiny of souls.

But when we overemphasize some of those intense facets of radical obedience and overlook the more mundane ones (like "a long obedience in the same direction,"[1] faithful plodding, and deep friendships that span years), we set people up to fail and burn out. We set them up for idolatry. When the magnificent doesn't happen when they thought it would, or when they realize that "failure" is a word they're beginning to apply to themselves, the results can be destructive.

---

1. Peterson, *Long Obedience*.

## Scorched Earth or Green Grass?

Jesus didn't talk war very much, actually. Some, but not a lot. A military commander would have talked like that, for sure, but a military commander he explicitly was not. That's what people wanted him to be, but he just wasn't, or at least not the type of commander they imagined.

People wanted epic. (People always want epic.) They wanted a strong fighter and warrior. They wanted munitions, and he didn't provide them. Or, at least he didn't take aim at the folks his listeners wanted destroyed (Rome).

People always want epic. They want to see power and a flood of victory and they use big and overwhelming words that sweep us away with their immensity and majesty. But the Scriptures also talk about green grass and a Shepherd. They speak of the Father's house, of peace, safety, and comfort. They speak of calm and Shalom.

## Mobilization vs. Member Care

I see this illustrated in the differences between mobilizers and member care folk. Is a healthy tension between the two necessary? I think perhaps.

One wants to send everyone, packing luggage in coffins if need be, for the glory of the cross. These people love John Piper and David Platt and stats about how many people die every minute. Paul is their patron saint.

The other wants to keep people healthy and whole, preferring writers like Ruth Van Reken and Pete Scazzero. They probably spend an inordinate amount of time in the Psalms.

One is all about sacrifice. The other is all about Shalom. One says, "Go and die for the King!" The other says, "Come and find rest for your soul."

One's like the battle-hardened soldier who runs headlong into the fight. The other is like the medic who's trying to keep people healthy, and then when that doesn't work, cleans, bandages, and packs up the results.

Both are emphatically *for* Jesus.

## We Need Both

As a young man, I jumped into the battle-talk-saves-the-world camp. It motivated me. Nate Saint the martyr was my hero, and John Piper was my soundtrack.

Now, I am much more medic than fighter, and I sometimes feel the tension. The truth is, we need both. We need to be overwhelmed by God's intense love for the nations and the certain truth that God desires *all* people to know him and love him, and that he calls his church to participate in taking the gospel to the ends of the earth.

We need to remember that the Bible supports both the mobilizer and the medic, the call to arms and the call to his arms, and we need to make sure that our churches and organizations do too.

## This Is Our God

May we remember the fire in his eyes *and* the tenderness of his touch. May we remember that he spoke hard truth harshly sometimes, *and* he spoke comforting truth softly sometimes.

May we remember that we are in a battle and that we have an enemy, *and* may we remember that we are in a royal procession, en route to the greatest victory celebration the cosmos has ever seen.

May we remember that our Warrior is gentle, refusing to break the bruised reed or snuff the smoldering wick, *and* he remains capable of destroying the armies of darkness and death itself.

*May we remember the full character of our God.*
*The Lord of Hosts is his name.*
*The Lord strong in battle.*
*The King of Glory.*

*May we remember the full character of our God.*
*The Wounded Healer.*
*The Great Physician.*
*The Lamb who takes away the sin of the world.*

May the magnificent love of our jealous God propel us to obedient service, far and wide. And may the intimate love of our Father God sustain us once we get there.

# Why I Can't Care about Every Crisis
## (the Challenge of Living in Two Worlds)

### BY ELIZABETH

"WHAT ARE PEOPLE THERE *saying about Syria?*"

This question was posed to me during a Skype conversation with a friend back in the States. My answer? "I'm not talking to anyone about Syria. I've got things to deal with in my own personal ministry, and I've got things to deal with in my team ministry. I've got the daily work of homeschooling—a career unto itself—and your basic 'how do I get food on the table?' questions. I'm also living in a culture that has its own political and safety issues. So finding out what other people in my life think about Syria is pretty much not going to happen."

I ended my rather lengthy explanation by saying, "I just can't care about everything."

While my statement might sound a bit cruel, I think it also sums up the struggle of overseas missionaries and expatriate Christians in general. How can we stay connected to our world back home while also embedding ourselves in our lives here? How can we tend to relationships in our host culture and relationships in our sending culture? How can we care about global politics *and* local politics *and* politics in our passport country? (And just to be clear here, that actually makes three worlds we're expected to live in, not two.)

Here's how I deal with these challenges.

## 1. I don't try to keep up on everything

Something I learned a few years back was that I couldn't care about every single crisis in American evangelical Christianity. It was too much to keep up with. These days I don't keep close tabs on that scene. I've also found it's not helpful for me to know every single detail about the political scene back "home." It distracts me from the person right in front of me (that's my own personal limitation and may not be the case for other people).

Politics in my host culture can be confusing, and keeping current can be discouraging at times, so I depend on my husband—who enjoys staying updated on global current events—to update me on news items relevant to Cambodia, America, and the rest of the world.

This is how I personally cope with the overabundance of information in our technological age. Others may keep up on global politics differently, and that's fine.

## 2. I do try to stay connected to my life here

I'm an introvert, but relationships are still important to me. I try to stay connected to my friends here, whether that's having them to dinner at our house or going out for coffee with a particular friend. I've never been a huge telephone conversationalist, but I've Skype-called friends in-country who live too far away for us to get together with easily. (I have relatively good internet access.)

I plan separate times for my kids to hang out with their friends here. (They're getting old enough that we don't call them play dates anymore.) I've found that friends have become more and more important to my kids as they've gotten older. It takes work on my part to arrange these times, but it pays dividends in their happiness.

Of course when we talk about relationships on the field, the revolving door of friends immediately comes up. That's not the focus of this chapter but is addressed in other chapters.

## 3. I do try to stay connected to friends and family "back home"

This part is tricky because I know missionaries and other expats tend to disconnect more and more from "home" the longer they are gone. That is still a temptation for me, but in recent years I've tried to be more pro-active in planning Skype and Facetime sessions with close friends and family. We did a lot of Skyping our first couple of years overseas, but then we let the habit slip.

In some ways that's good; we really settled into *this* place.[1] But we still need those relationships; those people were rocks for us and our kids before we left. And although our lives have all changed in the last five-plus years, those relationships are still supportive and life-giving. We don't want to throw away that gift.

Parents and grandparents won't always be around either, and we want to take advantage of the time we do have. We also keep in mind that most people don't stay on the field forever; we need to stay in touch with our "home team" because they are the ones who will be welcoming us back one day. We just have to be flexible when planning across time zones (this action point also presumes adequate internet access).

---

1. Of course we don't want to be so connected to our old homes that we aren't rooted in our current place, but neither do we want to neglect the people and places of our past, which is why I encourage this point.

# Sometimes Missionaries Get Sick

### BY ELIZABETH

Sickness in a third-world country can be scary. One September I watched my husband battle a 103-degree fever and a pain level of 10 on a scale of 1 to 10 (meaning the worst pain he had ever experienced). He was sick for about two weeks, and I was scared. I remember just standing there in the room, staring at him, with no thoughts whatsoever. I hated watching his temperature rise and his pain increase to unbearable levels, regardless of the medicine I had given him. I felt so helpless.

I wondered what happens when your head pain gets to the level of a 10. Can it get worse than 10? Does your brain explode and you die? (Yes, a little bit of overreactivity still wheedles its way into practically every health issue I face.)

We had asked all our prayer supporters to pray for us, and it's a good thing we did, because most of the time I had absolutely no words to pray. Sometimes I could get out a feeble, "God, help!" But for the most part, I had to depend on the body of Christ to pray for us, because I literally couldn't pray myself.

We never really knew what caused his severe illness. At the time, the most likely diagnosis we received from doctors was viral meningitis. He was sick again the next month with a freakishly painful ear infection and then went the entire next year without being sick. Not even once.

But when September rolled around again, he became very sick. Again. What started as slight discomfort on a Tuesday night degraded into a full-blown fever, headache, and nausea by Wednesday morning. Those were the exact same symptoms he had experienced the previous year. I dreaded repeating last year's ordeal. Another high fever, more worrisome head pain, another lengthy recovery time.

Those are the times I'm especially thankful others are praying for us, because I can't possibly think of anything to say to God. Not that I am angry at him or blame him for the illness. I do, after all, live in a developing tropical country, which means we can contract rare tropical diseases that place a strain on our bodies. It also means that conditions aren't exactly hygienic anywhere we go. Open sewers anyone? Men peeing on the side of the road? Children defecating on their front porches during potty training? All common sights here.

On the second day of illness, Jonathan went to the doctor for blood tests. Often a blood test is the only way to differentiate among the many diseases that can happen here, as the initial symptoms of malaria, dengue, and typhoid can be similar. The next day we received a diagnosis of typhoid fever and immediately put Jonathan on the antibiotics he needed. His fever and pain improved relatively quickly, but his fatigue lingered.

When my husband is sick, I get discouraged. In the middle of it, it feels as though he will never get better. I'm worn out, taking care of all the children and the house by myself. I don't sleep much at night because I'm awake worrying about him. I don't sleep much at night because I wake up every two hours, when he does, to give him more medication. Sometimes I feel like I need a vacation to recover from *him* getting sick.

I freely admit that tropical diseases are one of the yucks of missionary life.

This is something I didn't truly understand about missionary life before I came here. I didn't realize that no matter how hard we scrub the house, that no matter how often we wash our hands, that no matter how well we cook our food, that we will still get sick. I didn't realize all sorts of strange un-American illnesses happen here. Or at least, I didn't realize they would happen to *me* (perhaps by virtue of the fact that I didn't want it to happen to me?). I didn't realize how scary some of the symptoms could be.

I don't think the prospect of this kind of sickness would have stopped me from coming, but I'm sure I would have been more nervous about moving (as if I hadn't already been nervous!). Now that I've settled into my life here, it doesn't matter that I didn't know. I would still have come. And I would still come today.

But I know now that missionaries can't make it through illness without help. We need doctors' help. We need God's help. And we need his people's help. I'm thankful for all three.

# Revolving Door, Revolving Heart

BY *ELIZABETH*

MISSIONARY CULTURE IS VERY transient. People are always arriving; people are always departing. Arrivals and departures are never on the same schedule. The fluidity and inconsistency of this relational landscape reminds me of the military culture in which I grew up. And although I knew coming in about the mobile nature of expat workers, at the one-year point I was still surprised by what it did to me on the inside.

In that year I met plenty of people who moved here after me. I met other people to whom I'd already had to say goodbye. People I had just barely started to get to know, people I had started to pour my heart into. People with whom I had hoped to build a relationship. Poof! And one day, they're gone.

And that was only in one year. I dread this happening to me over and over again, for years on end. I say this because I do *not* like goodbyes.

And in addition to my excessive fears and worries, my dislike of goodbyes was actually one of the reasons I didn't want to move to Cambodia. I didn't want to *move*, period. Growing up, I moved a lot. Moves (nearly) always entailed traumatic goodbyes, and they always entailed traumatic hellos. So now I just like to stay in one place. After we moved to the parsonage in 2006, I told Jonathan, "I am never moving again!" *That* didn't exactly pan out for me.

I lost a best friend once, during an Army move. I didn't have another best friend for three years. And for reasons totally unrelated to being a TCK, reasons I'm still not quite sure I understand, I eventually lost that best friend too. The loss shook my world—a double whammy in the middle of my Year of Anorexia.

When I was heartbroken over this friend—and I mean *heartbro-ken* —my parents assured me that high school friends generally aren't life-long friends, but college friends can be. I must have internalized that pretty well, because I didn't have another best friend until college, five long years later. It was then that I was finally able to form a lasting fe-male friendship. (Hooray! We're still friends.) When she got married and moved away, my new husband learned just how unexpectedly unstable I can be when faced with a goodbye.

During some of our missions training, an adult TCK shared that there was such a revolving door of people in his childhood that he even-tually closed his heart to new people. He just flipped a switch, and turned it off.

I have not yet closed my heart to new people because I really *like* peo-ple, but when you really like people, saying goodbye is something you re-ally *don't* like. And in this transient missionary community, no goodbye is ever your last.

I have a remedy for goodbyes. It includes copious amounts of cry-ing, hugging, and hand-waving. There is a prescription for getting lost in Jane Austen. On occasion, a secondary prescription for *Anne of Avon-lea* or *Jane Eyre* might be filled (as there is a hierarchy of needs which takes into account the depth of sorrow, time available for mourning, and whether or not the husband is out of town).

You may have a more effective remedy for goodbyes; this is mine.

For all of us, though, friendships are seasonal. And as we edge ever closer to the date of our death, we must all say more goodbyes than hel-los. For military and missionary wives and their husbands and third cul-ture kids, those goodbyes are simply accelerated and multiplied. In other words, we bid farewell early and often.

The task of the human heart, then, should any of us choose to accept it, is to open ourselves fully to new people with the certainty that we will, at some time in this earthly life, have to say goodbye.

# "But I've Done All These Good Things"

## BY *ELIZABETH*

THE QUESTION CAME AS Jesus was beginning his last journey to Jerusalem. It came as he was heading toward his most heart-rending task, as he was starting the long descent toward death: "Good teacher, what must I do to inherit eternal life?"[1]

We all know the story. A young, rich, religious man calls Jesus good and then asks him how to achieve eternal life. Jesus first scolds him for calling anyone good but God. Then, feeling genuine love for the man, Jesus tells him to follow the commandments and proceeds to list several of them.

The man defends himself. "I've obeyed all these commandments since I was young," he says. But Jesus informs him that there is still something he hasn't done—namely, to sell all his possessions, give the money to the poor, and follow Jesus. The man's face falls when he hears this, and he goes away sad, for he is a very wealthy man.

I'd always glossed over this incident, thinking it might not apply to me. (I'd also neglected to notice until now that it occurred just before Jesus enters Jerusalem for the last time.) But one spring as I again worked my way through the end of Jesus' earthly ministry, it suddenly struck me: the story of the rich young ruler is *my* story.

"I've obeyed all these commandments since I was young"—once upon a time I said those words out loud, too. I'd just been confronted by my own sin, and I was shocked. I remember protesting, "But I've spent my whole life trying to follow God!" My statement was just another version of the rich young man's statement; it was just another version of pride.

---

1. The story is found in Luke 18.

320

And like the man, my face fell too. When I saw my attitude for what it was—sin—I did an abrupt U-turn. I interpreted my sin as the *worst* of all sins and became very depressed. My sin wasn't a sin that could be forgiven, you see. A sin like mine didn't deserve God's grace and forgiveness. Whereas before I had thought I was better than others, I now thought I was worse.

I rolled around in my sorrow and self-pity until a friend gently pointed out that I was exhibiting *reverse pride*: the kind of pride that says my sins are so bad they can't be forgiven. I had flipped from the regular old pride of thinking I was a good person, to the insidious, upside-down version of pride that said I could never deserve God's forgiveness.

But my goodness was never good enough anyway, and reverse pride is a sin to repent of, too. So Jesus basically said the same thing to me that he said to the young man: "There is something you still lack." That something was a humble awareness of grace. Because in the end, Jesus didn't ask me to give up all my possessions. (Moving to Asia isn't the same thing.)

What Jesus *has* asked me to give up is the idea of myself as someone who has done good things. He's asked me to give up the idea that I've followed the commands well. Because I haven't. And he's asked me to give up the idea that any sin is beyond his reach, including the prideful belief that I have no (or very small) sins.

As Jesus watched the man in this story walk away, he explained to his disciples how difficult it is for a rich person to enter the kingdom of heaven. His announcement left the disciples wondering who in the world *could* be saved—because to a certain extent, we all trust in both riches and our own good works.

But here is where the story gets good, because Jesus told his disciples that "What is impossible for people is possible with God" (Luke 18:27). And he kept walking toward Jerusalem to make the impossible possible. He kept walking toward Jerusalem to make the man's question irrelevant. He kept walking toward Jerusalem to demonstrate his genuine love for us and to give a very bad humanity the goodness that belongs to God alone, whether we've done "all these things" since our youth or not.

# Three Spheres of Offense: What We Get Terribly Wrong in Our Response to Abuse and How to Make it Better

*BY JONATHAN*

SOMEONE ALLEGES ABUSE. SOMEONE in power rushes to hush or silence the accuser, sometimes even using Scriptures or "biblical principles" as the gag. And it's so wrong. It's poison, offered as cure, both to the victim and those close by.

But there's an idea I've been developing that just might be an antidote. At least it has been for some, inoculating them and giving them words. And words are powerful.

I call it The Three Spheres of Offense, and when a church or organization forgets about these three spheres, it's nearly impossible to respond to allegations of abuse in a healthy way.

Originally, two things made me nervous about writing this chapter: 1) these issues deal with very painful realities, both mine and others, and 2) the ideas in The Three Spheres seem so simplistic.

But here we are.

Last year, I made a Facebook Live video[1] on this topic, and whatever uncertainty I had about the importance of this message vanished. The responses and private messages I received were real, they were honest, and they were empowering. So here it is:

---

1. https://www.facebook.com/jonathan.trotter/videos/10159880381065621/.

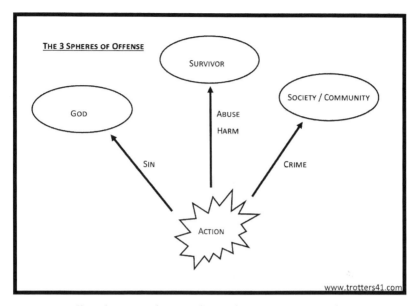

Basically, whenever there is abuse, there is one action (or one series of actions), but there are three impacts. In other words, for every offense, there are three distinct entities that endure the offense. Those entities occupy the three spheres.

When a church or an organization forgets these three distinct spheres, it can't respond to the accuser/survivor correctly.

You see, the entity within each sphere has a God-given right to respond to the perpetrator. The *offense against God* is sin, and God retains the right to respond to that offense. The *offense against the victim* is abuse or harm, and the victim has a God-given right to respond. The *offense against the community or society* is a crime, and society has a God-given right to prosecute and adjudicate. This is the oft-forgotten sphere.

We believe, as a community, that some behavior is wrong. As a society, we've decided that this type of action is harmful to us collectively, and that regardless of what the victim wants, the prosecutor gets to choose to prosecute, and if he or she so chooses, they are a representative of the offended society. That's how we get "The People of the State of Illinois vs. John Doe," or "The United States of America vs. John Doe."

## Stop the Robbing

When a church or ministry forgets that the society at large has a right to respond, or when an organization hides information from authorities, or shelters abusers, we slap our communities in the face. We rob them of their right to respond.

Maybe God's forgiven the perpetrator and they're now doing fantastic ministry. Great. Maybe the survivor's forgiven the perpetrator and has been totally healed of all damage and never even thinks about it. Okay, fine.

But that's not the end of the story: society still gets to respond. No matter what the church leadership thinks, no matter how "rehabilitated" the abuser seems, no matter how repentant and contrite, society still gets to respond.

And when a community finds out that we've hidden abuse, they rightfully despise us, and we look like fools because we are fools.

When a church or ministry forgets the third sphere, hiding and forgiving unilaterally, it does massive damage to society, which is not a "loving your neighbor" thing to do at all.

## Cross-cultural Considerations

What if you're living abroad, where reporting abuse is often more complicated? What if the offender might face harsher punishment than he or she would in their passport country? What if you don't think your host country has an adequate justice system? These are crucial things to consider.

But we must be very careful here. What are we saying if we hide an American's crimes from the local government when the crimes were committed in our host country? What if the victims are citizens of our host country?

Are we saying that we believe in following the law so long as we agree with it? Are we denying the local government the right to adjudicate their own way?

We are in danger here of sending a damning and very disrespectful message: "our people" deserve better than "their people." Would we report similar behavior to local authorities if it were committed by a national? If we're not careful, our hubris will show, with damaging results. And once again we must ask: Are we acting in a loving, Christ-like manner?

## While You're Here

I've written some about how my parents responded when I told them that I had been abused. Here are some of the main points:

1. *The idea that a person is innocent until proven guilty is great and helpful and very important in a court of law. It is not so great in churches or organizations.*

   If the gut response of the church or organization is to defend the accused, if that's the default setting, there's a very real risk that the least powerful, most marginalized, most hurting people will be ignored. Again, "innocent until proven guilty" is a solid principle for criminal courtrooms, but it really sucks in living rooms and board rooms.

2. *False accusations are much less common than true allegations. If you think that the majority of abuse allegations are concocted, you're wrong.*

3. *Allegations are often unbelievable.*

   Abusers are often known and usually respected. Unfortunately, that's how the abuse goes on for so long. It's not typically the outlying weirdo that everyone avoids, it's a person with authority and power that people want to love and protect. It's someone who, if he or she falls, would leave a hole in the organization or ministry.

## More Like Christ

Too often, in a rush to defend the accused, we're not much like Christ. We need to listen to the accusers, the victims, the survivors. That does not mean that we throw the accused under the bus. It just means that our posture toward the victim is one of listening and hearing and believing, not disbelief, distance, and doubt.

I pray that our posture would be Christ-like, standing in between the powerful and the abused. Too often, we flip that on its head, landing on the side of the powerful person who already has a voice, who already has the stage. We need to bend down, to be next to the person who is saying, "I'm hurting."

This is my prayer.

# RECALCULATING WELL
# (WHEN THINGS DON'T GO
# AS PLANNED)

# When the Straight and Narrow Isn't

*BY JONATHAN*

MY PARENTS HAD THEIR life all mapped out, and then their baby was born with chromosomal abnormalities and died at home, surrounded by tubes and oxygen tanks, only a month old.

As a teenager, I had my life pretty well planned out (get my pilot's license, be Nate Saint), but then my mom got cancer and died, and the path of God darkened. The "plan of God for my life," the path I was following with full confidence and youthful arrogance, disappeared, because sometimes the straight and narrow *isn't*.

God doesn't always lead in straight lines. He is the God of fractals, making beauty and order out of lines that look like a drunk man was drawing during an earthquake, left-handed.

> *"God moves in a mysterious way*
> *His wonders to perform.*
> *He plants his footsteps in the sea*
> *And rides upon the storm."*[1]

The paths of God meander, but somewhere along the way we got this idea that we should be able to sit down, especially in January, and map out THE SPECIFIC WILL OF GOD FOR OUR LIFE AND MINISTRY FROM NOW UNTIL FOREVERMORE. I'm sorry, but my life's just not working out like that. But if yours is, then hey, more power to you.

Don't mind me, I'll just be hanging out back here with all the folks who are a wee bit confused by God sometimes.

---

1. Cowper, "God Moves In a Mysterious Way," in Howard, *Songs of Faith and Praise*, hymn #26.

*"Deep in unfathomable mines*
*Of never-failing skill,*
*He treasures up his bright designs*
*And works his sovereign will."[2]*

I'm a fan of vision and purpose and alignment. I've read tons of books on leadership and vision. Really. My personal "Vision & Mission" statement is taped to the tile on my office wall and I read it several times a week. However, I'm beginning to wonder if these ideas are more suited for a corporation than my life.

Perhaps God has a higher purpose than us coming up with a goal and then perfectly implementing it. It really seems to me that few people, even the heroes of the faith, saw the whole plan of God for their lives and then developed perfect action steps that they then enacted flawlessly. Mission accomplished.

Perhaps the Kingdom of God advances less militaristically and more organically. Less checkbox-like, and more with an ongoing awareness that God's plans seldom travel in a straight line (at least from our perspective).

What about Moses? He had the great call and purpose of freeing the people of Israel. However, a good chunk of his life looked very much *not* aligned to that goal. How would we look at a person in Moses' position, whittling away time in a faraway land while the people of Israel languished in slavery? Was that out of alignment? Do we just blame it on the fact that Moses didn't follow God's plan, so he got banished for *decades*? I sure am glad I obey God perfectly. All the time.

Or David, anointed by God, but residing in pastures. Where was the alignment? Where were the action steps? He didn't even kill Saul when he had the chance! That's like minus-one action step to ruling the kingdom.

And then there's Jesus, who specifically knew at age twelve what the Father had called him to do. However, up until the age of thirty, his day-to-day jobs and activities did not *look* aligned to the call or mission of God. What a failure.

*"His purposes will ripen fast,*
*Unfolding every hour.*

2. Cowper, "God Moves," in Howard, *Songs of Faith and Praise,* hymn #26.

*The bud may have a bitter taste,*
*But sweet will be the flower."*

## Who's Flying This Plane?

David says in Psalm 23:3, "He guides me along right paths, bringing honor to his name." I'm no farm kid, but I'm pretty sure the farmer gets to decide the right paths, which is a bummer if you've already got the straight-and-narrow completely sorted.

For each transition in our life, Elizabeth and I have tried to listen to God, we've tried to discern his path, and we've been mostly sure (about eighty-three percent) we were heading in the right direction. However, in each case, we did *not* have any idea what the step *after* that step would be. But we pretty much knew what we needed to do to obey today.

~~~~~~~~~~

Have you ever noticed that pilots are dumb? I mean, really, who gets from Chicago to Korea by flying north?! It's like they've never looked at a map. Oh, that's right, they didn't look at a map, the fools added a dimension and looked at the GLOBE. The flight paths of giant airliners look really dumb if you're stuck in two dimensions. But wow, add that third dimension and everyone starts shouting, "O Captain, My Captain!"

I imagine God's kind of like that too. Sometimes, I want to get to Asia and God says, "Um, you know, that's great, let's fly over Santa Claus." And I'm like, "Yeah, that's stupid, I need to go *straight* west and then a bit south." And God says, "You have no idea what you're talking about. Would you like kimchi or chicken fingers?"

God deals in dimensions we know nothing about, and I believe he will sometimes lead us along paths that look wrong, that look out of alignment, that—get this—require faith. If God leads you off target or out of alignment, will you follow him?

There are more parameters, more dimensions, more curvatures of the planet, than we will ever know. If God's plans really are more wonderful than we could imagine, why do we strive so hard to imagine and define them? Can we rest in a loving Father? Can we continue to move forward in obedience, even if we don't know where that obedience will lead?

## Bonhoeffer (Because, Why Not?)

The dude had guts, and I think an uncanny ability to see from a height that helped him understand things. So, after his life deviated from his own plans in a big way (think Nazis and prisons) he was able to write:

> "I'm firmly convinced—however strange it may seem—that my life has followed a straight and unbroken course, at any rate in its outward conduct. It has been an uninterrupted enrichment of experience, for which I can only be thankful. If I were to end my life here in these conditions, that would have a meaning that I think I could understand; on the other hand, everything might be a thorough preparation for a new start and a new task when peace comes."[3]

In other words, he knew his life looked out of whack, it looked grossly misaligned and greatly off-kilter, but he pulled out that pesky thing called faith, got comfortable with some intellectual dissonance and the tension of unknowing, and believed that God had it under control, no matter what.

How could he say these things? Because he knew his God.

> *"Blind unbelief is sure to err*
> *And scan his work in vain.*
> *God is his own interpreter,*
> *And he will make it plain."*[4]

The longer I serve abroad, the less I desire to do great things for God and the more I desire to just be with him. I feel less ambition and more peace. Less like I'm racing the buzzer, and more like I'm being pursued by a lover.

This doesn't mean that I'll work less, caught up in some heavenly romance. It means that I'll work closer: closer to the One my soul desires, closer to the One the world needs, closer to the heart of God.

And frankly, I don't care how straight or how twisted the path is: if it leads farther up and farther in, I'm so there.

---

3. Metaxas, *Bonhoeffer*, 463–64.
4. Cowper, "God Moves," in Howard, *Songs of Faith and Praise*, hymn #26.

# Did God Really Say That?

BY *ELIZABETH*

HOW DO WE KNOW God has really spoken to us? How do we know it wasn't just our imagination, but that it was really him? I once told the story of hearing the words "Forgive you" from God. Later, someone asked how I knew that message was from God. She said that she had thought she'd heard from God in the past, but then it turned out not to be from God—a very painful experience for her. My heart hurt so badly for her. And it's such an important question that I wanted to devote an entire chapter to unpacking the answer.

Before answering the question, however, I want to clarify what I'm *not* talking about: I'm not talking about making decisions. Different people have different ways of interpreting circumstances for decision-making, and it's far too easy to seek God about a decision, think you've heard from him, and then doubt it when trials come. When things go wrong, it's easy to look back and think you didn't hear from God right. Situations may turn tricky and uncomfortable entirely apart from your actions. They might get complicated because of miscommunication or even someone *else's* actions or sins. So that's not what I'm talking about here.

I also don't think it's wise to look back and think, "Oh, I heard from God wrong" or "I misinterpreted him." It only brings pain, and who's to say it was wrong anyway? We don't know the purposes he has for us in each season of life. So I guess I just approach decision-making with the trust that even if I make the "wrong" decision, he is there to pick up the pieces and guide me along further. I think it helps if we are not fatalistic in this regard.

What I *am* talking about are the kinds of stories I've told before, stories of God whispering something to my heart, a heart that needs healing. So how do we know when God is speaking to us? This is how I personally discern these kinds of inaudible messages from God:

1.) *Unexpectedness.* God often gets my attention with an answer I couldn't have come up with on my own, in that time and place. In the story I reference above, I was in really low place. I was thinking God had given up on me because I had given up on myself, and so the unexpected nature of the answer told me it was from him and not my own mind. Another time God's voice surprised me was when he told me to believe he loves me. I was in a place of unbelief when the clear message that came to me was "Believe." So when an answer catches me off guard like that, it feels like it's from him rather than from my own imagination.

2.) *Scripture.* Does the message I just received line up with the truth of the Bible? If it does, I know it's God, and that I just needed a bigger, more intimate experience of him to really receive the truth *emotionally* instead of simply reading the text intellectually. In this case, the truth of Jesus' constant forgiveness of us as we are walking with him is backed up by Scripture (1 John 1:7), so I know I can believe it. Another time, God's message was about following Jesus alone and not being distracted by other things. When these truths are in the Bible, I trust these experiences to be from God, because they are verified in his word.

3.) *Fruit.* Does this truth bring me lasting peace or joy or love? If it does, if it quiets my spirit and brings me closer to God, then I trust it is from him. I believe Jesus' sacrifice is for all time, for all my sins. So to reference the forgiveness story again, it's not that I have to earn his forgiveness by asking for it each time I sin. Rather, repentance is for *us.* It brings us back to God, back to the truth of his holiness and sacrifice for us. Repentance is for us to *feel* the forgiveness that is already accomplished. And so when that conversation with God helped me to continue walking in forgiveness of myself and others, and my anger dissipated, then I knew it was from him, because kindness and forgiveness are his will for us (again going back to Scripture in that).

The other story I mentioned, when God told me to believe he loves me as much as he loves my husband, I was able to start walking in peace. I didn't have to strive for anyone to pay attention to me anymore, because I knew viscerally—and not just cerebrally—that God loves me. I didn't fight with my husband over those things anymore, and I continue walking in that internal and external peace to this day. That, to me, is the fruit of the Spirit at work in my life and marriage, and so I trust the message was truly from him, because I began to walk in freedom, a freedom that was long-lasting.

So that's pretty much my grid for trusting that God has spoken to me:

1.) *Unexpectedness*

2.) *Scriptural alignment*

3.) *Fruitfulness in my life*

I don't know if you're going through these kinds of trials, or whether you're in the middle of decision-making. Regardless, I want to acknowledge the fear of hearing "wrong" and the fear that God won't speak to us at all. I've had those fears too, and they sometimes cause me to avoid speaking to God about my problems. It's scary to ask him to talk to us and feel like we're not getting an answer.

I pray that all of us, regardless of the situation or struggle we are currently going through which is causing us to seek God, will hear from him, that we will know we've heard from him, and that his voice will bring that much-desired peace, joy, and love into our lives.

"May the grace of the Lord Jesus Christ, and the love of God, and the fellowship of the Holy Spirit be with you all" (2 Cor 13:14 NIV).

# Navigating the Night: Three Things to Do When You Have No Idea What to Do

### BY JONATHAN

I USED TO WANT precise answers to all the questions, and I used to think I could actually obtain precise answers to all the questions. But I'm learning that the straight-and-narrow sometimes isn't, and that God might in fact be OK with that. Sometimes, in our efforts to make so many things absolute and perfectly perfunctory, we skid sideways off the bigger, realer absolutes.

What does God want me to do ten years from now? I have no idea. I have a slight idea of what God wants me to do a year from now, but even that's pretty hypothetical. And I don't think I'm alone in this. Sure, we act like we know this road, but I think we're all just trying to figure out what to do with the rest of our lives.

I tested this theory with a group of about four hundred expats. I had everyone over thirty stand up and I said, "Think back to when you were eighteen years old, finishing up high school, maybe preparing for some travel or a gap year. Now, let me ask you a question, 'Are you where you thought you'd be, doing the thing you thought you'd be doing? If so, please sit down.'"

Two people sat down. The rest of us had no idea we'd be here doing the things we're doing. But walking in the dark can be scary, especially when everyone *looks* like they know exactly where they're going and what they're doing. We're walking in the dark pretending we see. And so is everyone else.

If you find yourself in the dark today, not sure of what to do or where to go, I'd like to give you three pinpoints of light. Three true stars by which to navigate the night.

On whatever continent you find yourself, across whichever sea, whatever generation you claim, and whatever country claims you, may these three reminders illuminate your today.

## 1. Adore Him

Maybe you started off adoring him, but it wore off. Maybe you started off really valuing him and loving him with everything, but maybe that was a long time ago. Maybe you started trading.

In the historical Psalm 106:20, the psalmist writes of God's people, "They traded their glorious God for a statue of a grass-eating bull." It's one of the saddest verses in the whole of Scripture. They traded God for a statue of a bull, and sometimes we do too.

We must stop the trade and begin to see the bull for what it is. But rather than pointing out the bull's obvious cheapness, let's point out our God's obvious and immense value. He is amazing. Pause and ponder this:

The smartest surgeons use their hands to fix bodies.
God uses his hands to make bodies.

The most brilliant psychologists understand the brain.
God wires it, connecting neurons and synapses,
washing it all in neurotransmitters.

Skilled poets use words to create feelings.
God uses words to create constellations.

Master artists paint with a thousand colors,
but have you ever seen the sun on fire,
sinking into the ocean?

This is our God. Adore him. Never ever exchange him for a cow.

## 2. Love People

We follow a guy who loved people really well. When he was popular and when he was persecuted, he saw what people needed and he cared. And he still does.

Jesus wasn't afraid to violate all sorts of cultural norms and/or rules to love people. He did not always act like a normal, proper, culturally appropriate, religious Jew. Often, he offended the religious people to love the hurting people.

Some of you have traveled halfway around the world to love people, but you're finding it really hard to love the people you live with. You want to change the world? Start by loving the folks closest to you.

If you love the people of your host country more than you love the people you live with, you're a hypocrite. If you love the people you're serving more than you love the people you left, you're a hypocrite.

If you traveled abroad to love on cute little nationals, but you can't stand your family or the messy toddlers (or teenagers) in church, you're a hypocrite.

Yes, love all the people in the world. Start with the person in front of you.

## A Prelude to Love

To love someone with your heart, you have to be OK spending some time down in there, and frankly, many people aren't. The heart is where we store our pain, and if there's a lot of pain buried in there, it's going to be scary. It's going to hurt. But, if you really want to love people, you're going to need to get down into your heart and see what's there.

If it's pain, so be it. Take that pain to Jesus and let him heal you in the deep places, because the more whole and healed your heart is, the more you'll be able to go down in there and really love people.[1]

## 3. Walk Boldly

Here's what's so cool about following Jesus and being an adopted kid of God: If you are a child of the King, YOU ARE A CHILD OF THE KING! You are loved and adored by the highest. So walk boldly.

If you put a tennis ball 100 meters away from you (about one football field, for our American readers), the ball would be covering up about 3,000 galaxies. And since scientists believe the universe is pretty uniform,

---

1. If you're looking for a safe place to start this journey, check out *Emotionally Healthy Spirituality*, by Peter Scazzero or *Finding Spiritual White Space*, by Bonnie Gray.

if you put that tennis ball 100 meters away from you in any direction (including underneath you), behind it would be another 3,000 galaxies. For reference, nearly all the stars you see in the night sky are in *one* galaxy, the Milky Way.

And assuming all those galaxies have roughly the same number of stars as the Milky Way, then behind that tennis ball, 100 meters away from you, there are six hundred trillion stars.

One tennis ball covers up that much stuff, and the One who spoke it into existence knows you and loves you, so walk boldly. But boldness without humbleness is just jerkiness. Boldness by itself can be really annoying. In Cambodia, some folks drive boldly in their big cars. They're not afraid, because they have power and they know it. In America, we say "Lights on for safety." In Cambodia, they say, "Lights on 'cause we're more important and you need to get out of my way *now!*"

Boldness must sleep with humbleness to give birth to Christlikeness. And if you can figure out how to walk boldly *and* humbly, you will change the world.

Be bold because you know who God is.

Be humble because God knows who you are.

Walk boldly because you know Jesus.

Walk humbly because Jesus knows you.

## Conclusion

I don't like the dark. I never have. I like to know exactly where I'm going, when I'm going to get there, and how many McDonald's there are along the way. But life doesn't seem to work like that, so when I find myself unsure and blind, I remember these three flashes of truth.

I might not know where I'll be a year or ten from now, but I'm pretty sure I've got enough light for now. I can navigate the night when I remember these three burning callings:

Adore Him

Love People

Walk Boldly

There's not much to this, really, but when you're walking in the dark, a little light goes a long ways.

~~~~~~~~~~

You know how I deal with all the "bold" drivers in Cambodia? I sing to them, with thanks to Woody Guthrie. . .

*That lane is your lane, this lane is my lane,*
*Does it really matter if you have the right-of-way*
*You have a big car, I'm so much less than,*
*You flashed your lights first, please go head.*

*You drive a Lexus, I drive a Honda,*
*You have rank, so "Dosvedanya!"*
*You're more important, Jesus still loves you,*
*So I'll just move now, and let you through.*

*That lane is your lane, this lane is my lane,*
*Does it really matter, I might just go insane.*
*You have a big car I need my therapist,*
*You flashed your lights first, I feel so miffed.*

*You drive a Lexus, I drive a Honda,*
*You have rank, so "Dosvedanya!"*
*You're more important, Jesus still loves you,*
*So I'll just move now, and let you through.*

# What If I Fall Apart on the Mission Field?

## BY *ELIZABETH*

THEY SAY THAT LIVING overseas will bring out all our bad stuff. They say it like it's a warning, like it's supposed to scare us out of going. Like only a superhuman could go and survive.

And what if they're right? What if moving overseas *does* bring out all our dark stuff, putting it on display for all to see? What if all the inner turmoil we kept so neatly concealed in our passport countries—or didn't even know existed—starts falling out of our hearts, falling out of our mouths? What if it spills out into daily life, interfering with all the good works we're supposed to be doing?

But—what if that's not such a bad thing? I mean, what if it doesn't end there, with you at the end of yourself? What if all the stuff that surfaces is *supposed* to surface? What if the only way to know what's inside your heart is for it to come out? And what if the junk that needs to come out wouldn't actually come out in your home country?

So maybe those multiple breakdowns have a purpose. Maybe knowing your weaknesses means you know God more intimately. Maybe you are *exactly* where he wants you to be, right at this moment. Maybe living overseas means becoming the person that God created you to be.

You followed him across oceans and continents, across countries and cultures. You prepared for this for years, dreamed of it for longer. And all for what? Just to fall apart on arrival?

No, I don't believe that. You followed him this far for a purpose, because you love him, and because he loves you. And now that you are where he wants you to be, he's not going to leave you alone and without help. If God brought you to this place, don't you think he will use cross-cultural living to shape you into the person he wants you to be?

When all our darkness reveals itself, God is right there beside us, waiting, ready to bring ever greater healing to our hearts. Through all this nasty falling-apartness, I believe God wants to heal the broken pieces of our lives. And living overseas might mean that we're in just the right place to accept those healing changes.

So maybe they're right. Maybe living overseas *will* draw out all our bad stuff. Maybe we won't be able to hide it anymore. But I no longer think that's something to be afraid of—life with God is not something to fear.

So today, if you find yourself in that broken place, at the bottom of a mountain of messes in your life, have faith in the One who called you. Trust him to put you back together again. Because falling apart is not the end of the story, but it just might be the beginning of a new one.

# Demon and Divine

## BY *JONATHAN*

WE MOVED TO CAMBODIA about two years ago, and it's been good. But it's also been very hard. I've had my days of doubt, fear, and deep discouragement. I've looked around at the poverty, abuse, and corruption, and I've despaired. I've heard that raspy, wicked voice taunt, "What can you do? Why are you even here? What about your kids, think of what you're doing to them? You are completely ill-equipped for this. Did God really call you here?"

But on this mountain climb called Mission, there is a phrase that has been a strong foothold to me. When I've despaired, it's grounded me, and when I've been near to giving up, it has given me rest and peace.

It's what Jesus said when he came face to face with the Father of Lies, Enemy Number One, Satan: "I will worship the Lord my God. I will serve only him."[1]

In Matthew 4, Satan attacks Jesus, desperate to win. At this point, Jesus has not eaten for forty days. He hasn't talked with friends for forty days. He's lonely, tired, exhausted, hungry, and Satan himself shows up, on the prowl, to attack.

Satan won't shut up. He keeps talking and stalking, "You want food, right? Nice, fresh-baked bread? How long has it been, Jesus? Eat." "How about you prove God cares for you? I don't think he does. Jump." "OK,

---

1. Jesus says in Matthew 4:10, "For the Scriptures say, 'You must worship the Lord your God; serve only him.'" When Jesus said this, he was in effect saying, "That's what I'm doing right now, I'm honoring the word and obeying my Father. I will worship the Lord my God. I will serve only him." When we respond to the ancient command (originally from Deut 6:13) in this way, we make a serious statement of intent, impacting both heaven and hell.

everyone wants stuff, power, and control. You want some? I'll give it all to you. Bow."

Jesus answers Satan and gives us a key. When I've despaired, this key has given me hope. When I've been tempted, this key has given me a way out. When I've needed more strength for the climb, this key has provided it.

Over the last two years, when I could pray little else, I've stuttered, "I will worship the Lord my God. I will serve only him." I've prayed it silently and I've prayed it out loud. When I've been discouraged, I've begged, "God, help me worship you. Help me serve only you." When I've been tempted, I've declared it, as a reminder to evil and myself: I'm with Jesus.

We sometimes imagine the tempting of Jesus as if it were a nice chat between buddies. Satan tempts Jesus and Jesus cooly brushes it off with a simple, "Oh, Satan, you silly, the Scriptures say. . ." But these two were mortal enemies, the Prince of Evil versus the Prince of Peace. These temptations were real, and Jesus felt them.

So, when Jesus answers this last temptation, he was saying so much more than "no." He was emphatically saying, "I will not listen to you, Satan. I will worship only One, and you're not him. I will not follow you, or obey you, or bow down to you." He was making a dramatic gesture toward the Father and shouting, *"I'm with him!"*

Anytime you wrestle with evil or temptation, you have to know Satan's smarter than you. You do not have this under control. He's stronger, has more charm, more experience. He has more time, more resources.

You can't outlast him, outsmart him, or outcast him, but you can resist him, and you must. How? With this resolution: there is only one God, and I'm serving him. Let this be your stake in the ground, your line in the sand. In stating and restating this truth, you disarm and deflate Satan, reminding him that he loses because Jesus wins.

What was Satan's response to this declaration? He left. What was God's response? He ministered to Jesus through his servants, angels.

Put another way, *Satan responds by leaving and God responds by coming,* and that's a pretty good trade, I think.

Yes, there is temptation and despair, discouragement and evil, but there is still hope, and his name is Jesus. And I've decided that with everything in me, until my last breath, I will worship the Lord my God. I will serve only him.

I hope you'll join me.

# Darkness and Doubt

### BY ELIZABETH

*But as for me, I almost lost my footing. My feet were slipping, and*
*I was almost gone (Ps 73:2).*

A FEW YEARS AGO, I almost lost my footing. My feet were slipping. My faith was almost gone. Most likely triggered by Jonathan's prolonged illnesses, and some circumstances within our families of origin, I had begun to question everything:

- Does God really exist? Did he really create this world I live in?

- Are heaven and hell real?

- Did Jesus really come to earth?

- Is sin really sin?

- Is the Bible even true?

I did my questioning in secret, behind closed doors, and in front of a computer screen. I would read blogs. Blogs I now refer to as Professional Doubter Blogs, or PDBs. They were written by others with the same questions, by people who were losing (or had already lost) their faith.

Psalm 14:1 tells us that the fool has said in his heart, "there is no God," so maybe the community of doubters wasn't the healthiest place for me to do my doubting. But doubt I did, and in their company. I read their doubter blogs, and never did I scrutinize. I told no one.

It was a very dark time.

One day, the darkness started to fade. I'm not exactly sure how it happened, but I know where it happened: I was at church. We sang about

345

the resurrection. We sang about how Jesus saves. We sang about our sins and his power to remove them completely.

We sang about the wonder of creation. I'm in constant awe of this universe, on both the large scale of the stars and the small scale of the atom (and everything in between). Songs about the beauty of nature, and God's power to create it, speak very loudly to me.

Those songs stirred memories deep inside me. Memories of the life I've lived over the past two decades, a full life, walking with God. Memories of truth etched into my soul—my need for God, my need for forgiveness, my need to worship an almighty Creator. I wasn't ready to give up on Someone who had sustained me through so much, who had changed me in ways I was rather grateful for, and whose story has captivated me my whole life long.

I wanted to walk in light again.

I still didn't have the answers to some of my most irksome questions (annoyingly, I still don't), but I stopped worrying about not having all the answers, because what I really wanted was his renewed presence in my life, regardless of my doubts. (Don't misunderstand me, I still want answers, I'm just more willing to wait for them.)

So I came back to God. I believed, once again, that it was he who had created everything, right down to the very laws of physics, and that it is he who has saved us from the mess we've made of his creation. After I returned to God, those doubter blogs didn't hold my attention for much longer.

Worship of the Living God is what restored my faith. Perhaps my way back to God was too simplistic, but it was enough for me. I had found my Lord again.

I discovered he was all I needed.

# When Your Exotic Overseas Life Feels Ordinary

### BY ELIZABETH

SOMETIMES I CAN'T THINK of what to write at the A Life Overseas website. I have so many things to say in general (and I do so, on my personal blog), but when I sit at the computer and ask myself, "How can I help Christian expats and missionaries through my writing?," I come up with nothing. Every time.

It makes me feel useless for the community. My life just feels so ordinary. I'm in the thick of raising children and educating them. At this point I don't have a lot of cross-cultural advice to give, because I'm not doing a whole lot of cross-cultural living or cross-cultural ministering. What I am doing a whole lot of is homeschooling and homemaking.

Then some friends left (some permanently, and some for home assignment), and I felt quite desolate, and I realized I have no desire to make new friends. Every relationship is so temporary, and I'm not in the mood to connect deeply with new people. They might just leave in a few years. But then I thought to myself, "That's not the kind of helpful, encouraging attitude I should be offering the readers at A Life Overseas."

On top of that, I'm not sure I've gained enough wisdom or experience from which to speak. I've only lived here seven years, and that doesn't seem like very much in comparison to friends who've lived here ten or fifteen years (or more). I'm not sure I have enough perspective yet. After all, I wouldn't listen to marriage advice from someone with a five-year-old marriage.

So I figured I might as well just be honest with you: I don't feel like I have anything to offer the expat community during this time in my life. But I thought I might resurrect the following post from my own website. Four and a half years later, it still captures how I feel about my life: Ordinary.[1]

## Ordinary

Learning a new language, interacting with an unfamiliar culture and its customs, living near an orphanage, living near a house of girls rescued from human trafficking—all these things can make my life seem overly exotic to someone living in America.

And while it's true that living cross-culturally has been known to eat away at my mental and emotional margin, most of my life is extraordinarily . . . ordinary. I wash dishes. I fold laundry. I brush my teeth. I often combine those last two.

I cook. I grocery shop. I get to the end of some days and ask myself just *what* am I going to feed these people tonight? I fetch the Band-Aids. I scrub the bathroom. I take care of sick people. I make sure that my children study and that they play. I make sure that they put away their own laundry and that they brush their own teeth (though not necessarily at the same time).

I get irritable for all the ordinary reasons: being tired, being hungry, being hot. And during certain times of the month, I freak out. Even if I'm not tired, hungry, or hot. I like to spend time with my husband. I like to spend time with my friends. I like to spend time by myself. (Translation: I like to check Facebook.)

These are not extraordinary things. These are the very ordinary things of my life, and I feel very ordinary doing them. In fact, I did all these things back in America, including the one-handed-laundry-sort.

And maybe, just maybe, you do all these ordinary things too.

---

1. If you are also an ordinary wife and mother like myself, you might want to check out my other book, *Hats*.

# A Letter for the One Who's Waiting

*BY ELIZABETH*

You in the waiting,
Yes, you
And yes, me too—
For we are all waiting for something—
Dear sister,
Beloved one,
You in the waiting,
This much I know:
There are no shortcuts to healing.
There are no shortcuts to wholeness.
For we can't know God as healer without first being wounded.
And we can't know God as guide without first being lost.
We can't know him as counselor without first being confused.
And we can't know him as comforter without first sustaining pain.
We can't know him as intimate companion without first feeling
abandoned.
And we can't find our identity in Christ alone without first losing it
elsewhere.

You in the waiting,
Dear One,
This much I know:
There is no way around the ache of the human soul.
There is no detour through the pain.
When we walk through the valley—
And we will all walk through the valley—
None of us gets to skirt around the edges.

We are completely baptized in sorrow,
Fully immersed in its grief.
For there are no shortcuts to healing,
No shortcuts to joy.
There is only Jesus.
If anything, he is the short cut:
He is, after all, our way home
Even if that way be long and broken.

So you in the waiting,
Keep waiting.
Keep seeking,
And keep asking,
Even in the silence—
For there may be silence—
And even in the darkness—
For there may be darkness—
But don't you give up hope.
Hold on to hope.
Hold on to the name of our Jesus.
This waiting, it takes time.
It takes space.
And, I wish I didn't have to say this, but—
It takes hard work too:
The hard work of shedding the lies we believe about God,
The hard work of shedding the lies we believe about ourselves,
The hard work of being honest with him about the injuries,
And the hard, Spirit-assisted work of letting go of our entangling sins.

So you in the waiting,
Yes you—
And yes, me too—
For we are all waiting for something—
Dearest sister,
Beloved One,
You in the waiting,
This much I know:
There are no shortcuts to healing,
But in Jesus there is healing.

And there are no shortcuts to wholeness,
But in Jesus there is wholeness.
So we hold on to him,
We hold on to hope,
And together, we wait.

# Something No One Told Me Might Happen

BY *ELIZABETH*

ABOUT EIGHT YEARS AGO I said "yes" to the adventure of living over-seas. I didn't know all that might entail, but I knew I loved the God who had asked me to move, and I was determined to follow him. I didn't, however, know exactly what to expect.

I heard a little bit of what to expect at our pre-field training. There, someone warned me that stepping on a plane wouldn't turn me into a dif-ferent person, or magically make me a superhero Christian. No, I would be the same person as always, possessing the same old faults.

And that's true—I didn't turn into a different person. In fact, step-ping off that plane and entering an unfamiliar culture had the additional effect of revealing my faults, of laying bare my sin problems and defects in character.

But something else happened, too. Something surprising and un-expected, something no one told me might happen: I discovered gifts I'd never had before. They were new and previously unknown gifts. But they were never meant for me—they were meant to be poured out for others. More importantly, they were meant to be poured out for him.

One of these new gifts was the ability to write words that not only told my own story but also seemed to express other people's feelings and experiences. I'd only started writing as a way to process my confusing new life, but somehow it resonated with people. This felt strange at first because I'm a math and science girl, and words have never been my do-main. Yet somehow in the midst of culture shock, I found a voice.

Another one of these gifts was a newfound compassion that helped me connect more fully with people. God first started planting seeds of compassion in my heart while preparing me to move overseas, but after moving here and witnessing the pain and suffering of poverty and human trafficking, those seeds took deeper root. The truth is, I still need God to teach me about love, and the crushed and broken places of my heart are where he does that best.

The other gift was a passion to encourage women that drives all I do, whether it's in the form of blogging, private notes, or face-to-face interactions. After about a year overseas I felt God whisper a new word to me: *encourage*. The next Sunday in church, a woman I'd never met unexpectedly prayed that I would grow in my encouragement of others. This word, spoken by God and confirmed by his people, guides me to this day.

The place where these three gifts intersect has become a brand new calling on my life. It's a calling that fills me with purpose, a calling that adds joy to the greater gift that is my relationship with him. It's a calling to listen to what he is saying and doing, both in me and in those around me. It's a calling to love the person in front of me, and to give people the gift of *really seeing them*. God sees me, after all, and he is the only One who can help me see others.

I've watched the same thing happen to my husband. God has moved in his life and directed him to a place of ministry he never expected yet is clearly gifted in—and I've never seen him so alive. Watching God shift my husband's ministry emphasis and draw out the skills and longings of his heart has been, well, just plain *fun*.

What a creative God we serve, who can take our small lives and do new and exciting things with them. Receiving his gifts is a privilege. Watching his leading unfold in our lives is an honor. Discovering new gifts overseas is not about the arrogance of using "my gifts." Rather, it's about the delight of working in the gifts he has given me, for his glory and *never mine*. It's about declaring, "Look at what the Lord has done!"

It's about cooperating with him in what he's already doing in our hearts and in the world at large. It's about learning to dance, step by awkward step, with the One and Only. It's about standing in awe of Almighty God, Maker of heaven and earth, who chooses to interface with our world, who generously gives us the gift of himself, and who invites us to take part in his story.

# For the Times When You Ask, "What Good is That?"

BY *ELIZABETH*

THE FEEDING OF THE five thousand is such a familiar story to me, it seems like I've always known it. Jesus sees a huge crowd of people coming to look for him and asks Philip, "Where can we buy bread to feed all these people" (John 6:5 NLT)? When Philip only answers that they don't have enough money to purchase food for everyone, Andrew points out a young boy with five barley loaves and two fish. "But what good is that with this huge crowd?" Andrew asks (John 6:9 NLT).

But what good is that?

What good is that?

This is something I repeatedly say to God.

"I offer you this, God. My life, my heart, my all."

And then I turn around and faithlessly say, "But what good is that, with seven billion people on this planet? It's nothing, not good for anything. You'll never do anything important or valuable with that," I tell him.

But Jesus is never in a quandary about how to use his created resources. When he spoke to Philip, "He already knew what he was going to do" (John 6:6 NLT). He already knew he was going to provide for the people. He already knew he was going to use a small sack lunch to feed the hungry crowd. He already knew he was going to perform a miracle and blow their minds yet again.

*He already knew.*

He knew he didn't need much from the boy, only a little bit. He knew only a meager offering was required, because God himself would multiply it, and after he multiplied it, and everyone had eaten as much as they wanted, Jesus instructed them to "gather the leftovers so nothing is wasted" (John 6:12 NLT).

*So nothing is wasted.*

First he takes next to nothing from one of his followers. Then he multiplies it, filling empty bellies. And then—oh then—he scoops up the leftover bits of his miracle-working, and *he wastes none of it*. Not a single scrap.

So when I mourn over my offering to God, grieving that it's not enough, perhaps I should dry my eyes. Perhaps I should remember instead.

*Remember that he is the One who gave me my loaves and fishes*
*in the first place.*
*Remember that when I offer my daily bread back to him, he will use*
*it as he sees fit.*
*Remember that he is the One who will multiply my small sacrifices*
*for his own glory.*
*Remember that he is the One who uses even the leftovers of his miracles.*
*Remember that he is the One who will never waste my worship.*

So when I ask him still one more time, "What good is that, God?," perhaps I would be better served simply to still my mouth, quiet my questions, wait, and keep watch for him to use even the crumbs of my life for himself.

Which is all I really want anyway.

# If Your Year Has Been a Flop

### BY *ELIZABETH*

FOR THE PAST SEVERAL years I've chosen a word for the year. Each word is meant to serve as a rudder for the year, a way to focus my attention and direct my inner life. Sometimes I very specifically sense God's leading in the word; such was the case of "listen" in 2011 and "encourage" in 2013. Both of those words started with quiet whispers from God that were continually confirmed throughout the year. Words—and years— like that feel very successful.

But other times I've chosen words that simply seemed to fit my spiritual needs at the time. In 2015, I chose the word "peace," mainly for the warm fuzzy feeling it gave me. I just wanted a little bit of rest. Some peace and quiet. But throughout that year, God peeled back the layers of my illusory peace and revealed relationships in my life that were not actually at peace. My year felt like a failure until right at the end, when relational reconciliation emerged as an eleventh-hour gift from the Father.

*Maybe that year wasn't such a flop after all,* I thought. It gave me the confidence to choose a word again. So in 2016, I chose the word "steady." I wanted to have steadier emotions no matter the amount of stress I was under, and regardless of which day of the month I was on. I thought this was a great goal. I wanted to be like Caroline (Ma) Ingalls—wise, calm, and gentle in all circumstances.

Basically, I wanted to be perfect.

And it was a complete flop. Right from the very beginning of the year, my emotions were more volatile than ever, and my emotional stability was rather, um, nonexistent. I wanted to cheat and switch words halfway through the year, but instead I chose to ignore the fact that I had ever chosen a word. I went about the second half of my year attempting to survive over-scheduled weeks and power-outaged days, emotional instability and all.

I so skillfully forgot about my dreams of steadiness that when I began processing that year at the beginning of December, I couldn't initially remember what my word had been. I racked my brain a while and then remembered: steady. That's what it had been. I had wanted to be emotionally steady. A rock, a foundation, a cornerstone for my family. Always cheerful, happy, and helpful. I'd wanted to be, you know, *perfect*.

But I was, disappointingly, more unsteady than ever.

At least, on the surface I was more unsteady than ever.

When I paused to look deeper, I was surprised to see aspects of my life that *had* stabilized:

My belief in the Bible as God's word.

My participation in truly life-giving community.

My commitment to homeschooling as the right choice for our family.

I didn't ever manage to perfect myself as I had hoped. I'm still an emotional train wreck. (Though perhaps emotional perfection was too unrealistic an aspiration?) I tried and failed to tread water at the surface of my life, but throughout the year God was working to give the deeper structures of my life more strength and support. Looking back now, I learned—and am continuing to learn—so many things this year, but chief among them is this: when we fail to measure up, God is sufficient. And when we waver, he still stands firm.

I don't know if this past year was a massive failure or a grand success for you. Perhaps it was a bit of both. Or maybe your year was somewhere in between those two extremes. No matter what your year held, what I want all of us to remember is that Jesus Christ is sufficient. He is the foundation upon which our faith rests. He is the Person in whom we live and move and have our being.

So will I to continue to choose a word every year? I don't know. What I do know is that whatever the future, the Christ, the Son of the Living God, will be in it.

# What an Open Sewer Taught Me about Resurrection

BY *ELIZABETH*

A RIVER RUNS THROUGH my city, and on the main riverfront there's a tree. Actually, there are many trees along the riverfront, and they're mostly palm trees. Palm trees grow everywhere in the tropics, and while they are stunningly beautiful, palm trees don't grow very large.

But there's a tree on the riverfront that dwarfs all the palm trees. It's the biggest and greenest tree around, and it's planted on the banks of the river right where raw sewage is discharged. My city's waste rushes thick, black, and odorous right into the river where the tourists walk by.

The first time I noticed this, I was struck by the sight. How could two such unlikely things come together like this? An enormous, thriving tree and an ugly, smelly, polluting flow of refuse? I couldn't stop looking at it. I couldn't stop gazing and pondering: a tree full of life next to a stream of death.

This riverside tree became, to me, a symbol for resurrection, for the ability and tendency of God to take garbage, to take death, and to make new life out of it, to make beauty out of it.

Life comes from death. We know this is true. It's what manure is for crops: fertilizer for the ground, a reusing of old, leftover nutrients to help the new seed burst forth into life and into new sustaining power. A tree as big as the one I saw needs an extensive root system to support it. But its root system can only grow that large if it can reach down and grab enough dead things, that it may turn those dead things into life.

Life comes from death. It has always been this way. This is why the fishing waters off the coast of Ecuador have historically been some of the richest in the world. Equatorial trade winds consistently blow the surface

358

waters away from the land, toward those of us here in Asia. This continual skimming off of the top layer forces detritus, or *dead things*, up from the bottom of the South American ocean floor, thus providing a constant source of nutrient-sustaining life.

Life comes from death, and it gives us hope.

God meets us in the wreckage of our lives. That's where he sees our lost dreams and scattered hopes and where we see our dire need. It's where God picks up the broken pieces of the world we attempted to build for ourselves and rebuilds them into something better.

God does his best work in death. Remember: Jesus was dead until the resurrection. The best news *ever* is God bringing life out of death. What he did for Jesus, he will do for you too, for God is in the business of making dead things alive again.

The deadest thing in your life, that thing you're most ashamed of, your biggest mistakes and your biggest sins, the addictive behaviors you can't shake, the depression and fear that keep you immobilized, the place you most need grace, the deadest, dirtiest, messiest, muckiest thing in your life, *that* is where God is going to do his best work in you. The part of your life you're afraid to reveal to anybody, that's the thing he most wants to redeem. That's the place he's going to grow new life in you.

That's resurrection. Just like a plant takes manure and transforms it into harvest, just like the ocean takes fish corpses and transforms them into a brand new catch, just like the God of the universe takes a cursed Roman cross and transforms it into a message of grace and hope, that same God will take the dirt and mud of your life and transform it into something good and fresh and new. I dare you to believe it.

# COMMUNICATING WELL

# How to Communicate so People Will Care

## BY JONATHAN

NEWSLETTERS. PRAYER UPDATES. ITINERATIONS. Reports. Furloughs. Presentations.

Are you stressed out yet?

For most of us, living and serving abroad means communicating *back* to senders—a lot—but this isn't what we went to school for, and besides that, communicating in person or in print is scary. It's exposing. It's like learning a new culture and language; sometimes when we mess up it's funny, sometimes not so much.

We're all too familiar with the dangers:

- Communicate too much and we'll annoy people or people will say we're not protecting the privacy of the nationals.

- Don't communicate enough and we'll get dropped; people or churches will stop supporting us, because "out of sight, out of mind."

- Talk about the right stuff in the right way. One missionary recently told me that you have to appear miserable enough that people will still support you while not appearing so miserable they want you to come home.

To be sure, communicating with senders (via newsletter or a live missions report) is a unique form of communication, blending a bit of travelogue with a side of sales pitch, and then adding a large spoonful of sermon. It's like a Christmas letter got married to a church bulletin and had an Amway.

## Extreme Sports, Convents, and Space Missions

For some of you, communicating is like an extreme sport: full of excitement and danger and the very real risk of serious bodily harm. And you think it's fun.

For others, communicating (in print or person) makes you feel like you're wearing the appropriate attire for a European beach when you'd much rather be wearing the appropriate attire for a convent. Communicating, for you, seems dangerous, and dangerous, for you, is *never* fun.

Writing or speaking can feel like launching a space probe into the cosmos hoping it just might land on a tiny comet and provide even a smidgen of feedback. And when you get one positive e-mail or comment back, you're all like, "Whooohooo! Mission Accomplished!"

## So, You Want People to Care? Try This. . .

Speak from the heart.
Or be funny.
Or both.
But never neither.
That's it. Communicate like this, and you'll change the world. Or at least your newsletter.

## Why This Matters—The Bride of Christ

It's our great privilege to speak back into the lives of those who send us. They sacrifice too, and not just money: many of our senders have given up relationships and friendships, children and grandchildren. Simply put, they are worth our time.

Additionally, communicating from the field is an amazing opportunity to minister to the Bride of Christ. We can help them see God's passion for his glory as the Kingdom spreads globally. We can enlarge their vision of God and his mission, reminding them that national politics is a small bit of what's going on in the world. We can remind them that the church is alive and well and the Spirit of God is moving in the hearts of people. Of course, none of that happens if we're snooty.

Even a church missions presentation can be ministry, if done with care and thought. A report could be part of what Walter Brueggemann calls "prophetic imagination,"[1] helping folks see an alternative reality, where the Kingdom is advancing and there's more to life than the daily grind.

Please be careful not to love the church only where you serve. Love the church where you came from too. She is no less Christ's Bride.

## Why This Matters—They're Volunteers

The folks reading your newsletters or listening to your missions talks are volunteers; they don't have to pay attention to you or your words. They have chosen to listen to you (except maybe the six-year-old boy in the third row who's been threatened with no McDonald's unless he sits still and pays attention).

They are giving you one of the greatest gifts ever: time. Value their gift, and give something back. Make them glad they came. Be wise and "make learning a joy" (Prov 15:2).

Remember, you're speaking to volunteers. They don't have to pay attention to you, but if you speak from your heart or you're funny or both, they will.

## It's Not Just Data—Speak from the Heart

Very few people get excited about data. We're all tired of data. So, stand in front of a church and give them facts and percentages, sure, for maybe five seconds. And then give them your heart. They can get facts from Google, but they can only get your heart if you give it to them.

Want an easy way to do this? Tell them the why and the who, not just the what and the where. People will care a whole lot more about what you're doing when they see the heart behind it. *Show them that heart.*

*Why* are you going?

*Why* do you live there?

*Why* are you doing what you're doing?

*Who's* behind the newsletter?

*Who's* the project for?

*Who* is God transforming?

---

1. Brueggemann, *Prophetic Imagination.*

What are your newsletters and presentations full of? Are they full of what you're doing and where you're doing it? That stuff's important, but it's pretty sterile. If the majority of your communication is full of details and factoids, please stop. You're boring people, and missions should be anything but boring.

Take a step back and ask yourself how to incorporate more of the why and the who. Put some heart in it.

You're talking about people, right? So don't reduce them to a stat or a large group photo of fifty people no one in your audience knows. There's enough dehumanizing going on in the world already. Go ahead, show the group photo, but then tell a story about *one* person in the group who was impacted.

Why did Cecil the lion get so much attention?[2] It's because he wasn't just a stat, just another lion poached. He had a name and a family. He had a story. If we can give a lion in Africa a name and a story, can't we do the same for people? God does.

So speak from the heart about people, not tasks, about hearts, not projects.

Ask for God's help. Ask him to help you see people as he sees them, because once you connect with the heart of God on the matter, it's all over. You'll never be the same, and neither will your audience.


## How to Be Funny

Sometimes our theology erases our joy. Does yours? I realize that humor and joy are not synonyms, but really, do we actually believe the folks who look completely miserable while they grunt through gritted teeth, "I know I'm not happy, but at least I have the joy of the Lord"? Is there a laughter and peace that comes from God that is actually—really and truly—fun? We take ourselves way too seriously.

God is still in control.

God is still good.

So when was the last time you laughed? Like, really belly laughed? Life is filled with heartache and pain. I am not immune to that, and I've spent a good bit of my time at A Life Overseas writing about outlawed grief, and bleeding grief, and feeling worthless.

It's just that people are really funny creatures.

2. Melvin, "U. S. Dentist Wanted."

We should pray more for the joy of the Lord in our teams and churches and families. There is a time to mourn, for sure, but there is also a time to laugh and dance. Make sure you stay balanced. And remember, there's nothing holier about sadness, just like there's nothing juvenile or immature or sinful about enjoying life so much that you LOL.

Remember, Jesus got in trouble for having too much fun. Be like him.

I guess what I'm trying to say is, if you want to be funny in your communications, learn to laugh, and laugh long and laugh hard. Wrap up your kids in tickle fights and joke about the crazy stuff. Look at other drivers on the road and make up stories about their lives; create a running commentary. Practice various accents. In our family, one person's good at Russian, two are great at British, another imitates Jim Carrey's Grinch scarily well, and the last one's four.

But please, if you don't think you're funny, don't worry. This is not supposed to make you even sadder and even less funny. If funny's not your thing, it's not the end of the world, just make sure you communicate from your heart. No humor required.

## CONCLUSION

Speak from the heart.
    Or be funny.
    Or both.
    But never neither.
    Try it out. See if it changes anything.
    And then add me to your newsletter list.

# Facebook Lies and Other Truths:
# On Learning How to Curate Stories

## BY JONATHAN

HAVE YOU EVER CREATED a fake boyfriend? Yeah, me neither. One woman did, though, and while she's no Chewbacca Lady, I still think she's pretty awesome. Apparently, "It only took one week and five easily stageable posts for Smothers to convince her followers that she had found love."[1]

Facebook, er, Instagram, lies. (And for the purists, Facebook owns Instagram, so the title of this chapter still fits.)

Ms. Smothers succeeded in convincing her followers that something amazing had happened: she had found love! But it was all a ruse.

I'm really glad you've never created a fake significant other, but have you ever created a fake missions point? You know, tweaked a ministry photo of *someone else's* ministry and gently hinted that it was yours? Piggybacked on someone else's success without explicitly giving credit? Ever *not* posted your vacation pictures because they look a bit too exotic for the home team? Ever tweaked your ministry numbers just slightly because you know the people counting?

Using social media to deceive is pretty easy, especially when everything gets washed through thousands of miles of suboceanic internet cables. Using social media to salve our souls (or attempt to) is also pretty simple: Have you ever shared something because you were lonely and you needed some smiley faces and thumbs up and likey hearts? I have.

The accumulated consequences of these behaviors are enormous, both to us individually and to the future of cross-cultural missions. How we use social media really, really matters.

1. Hatch, "Woman Creates Fake Boyfriend," para. 3.

We all know that our online lives differ significantly from our send-ers'. Our supporters and friends probably won't *lose* money by showing a picture of a vacation. We might. On the other hand, our friends won't *make* money by showing a picture of a destitute child or a baptism. We might.

And that's disgusting and gross. It's also true.

Our use of social media, like all communication, can construct or destruct. Our words can be sweetly hospitable or bitterly mean. I want to figure out how to bless the socks off of people with my online presence. I want people to meet Jesus and his power when they browse my Instagram feed or Facebook page. I want them to leave in awe of a God who takes little people, connects them to his heart, and then changes the world.

To do that, I have to own my role as a curator/creator. And so do you.

## Missionaries as Curators

Facebook and other social media allow us to show a curated life, and that's not a bad thing. As it turns out, most of us actually like curated things, like National Geographic and the BBC. To curate simply means to "select, organize, and present, typically using professional or expert knowledge."[2] We really should do that.

Curating is communicating; it's you and me choosing what to communicate to the world outside of our heads.

The alternative of "just being real and showing everything" is a non-option. It's not that people don't care about our *entire* lives, it's that people aren't God. Simply put, no one has that kind of capacity. So, again, we must curate, select, and present.

Now, the key is to remember that the thing *is* curated. The one photo in a National Geographic stands in the place of thousands that didn't make it. The story on the front page of the Huffington Post hides hundreds of others. What we share is what people see. How we spin stuff is typically how it stays spun.

You see, the power to curate is the power to blind. It's also the power to create, raise awareness, instill courage, raise up prayers, disciple, challenge, and bless the world.

---

2. English Oxford Living Dictionaries, "Curate."

## The Power We Wield

*How we talk about missions impacts the next generation of cross-cultural missionaries.* It impacts their expectations and their hopes, and perhaps whether or not they even show up.

Those arriving on the field in two or ten or twenty years won't learn about cross-cultural missions from a book. They'll learn from Facebook, Instagram, Snapchat (Lord, have mercy!), and whatever's next. Will they think it's all safaris and hugging kids with darker skin? Will they think it's all boat rides and baptisms, with a swig of bubble tea to end the day?

Will they think it's all loss and dirt and manual labor? All grief and regret, and after a certain number of years, you just come home weird?

*How we talk about missions impacts how our senders see missions.* Is missions something we do (as in "we, the elite missionary force") or is it something WE do (as in, "we the global Church reaching the people of the globe")?

*How we talk about missions impacts how our senders see the next missionaries.* Do missionaries rest? If we never let our supporters see us resting and having fun, they will go on thinking that the *next* missionary they send can go twenty years without a vacation. That is not a gift I want to leave for the next missionary!

We influence these discussions. A lot.

## Going Deeper—The Curator's Id

Social media can be a dangerous place. We take our fleshy souls and string them up on an http:// and hope for the best. Maybe we hope for love and acceptance, or affirmation. Or maybe we're afraid that if we *don't* post, we'll be forgotten, abandoned, and ignored. The fear is real.

Because the curator's task—our task—is so crucial, we must seek to understand what lies underneath our social media selves:

- FEAR: *Am I afraid of losing support. Am I deeply afraid of being labeled as lazy or ineffective or unworthy? Am I afraid that people will withdraw their love or money?* Fear is such a terrible motivation for everything (except maybe teeth-brushing). If what you post/ don't post on social media is driven by fear, name it, call it out, and talk with God and your close friends about what to do with it. And maybe read some Brené Brown.

- ATTENTION: *I need to be awesome. I need people to think I'm doing amazing things and visiting amazing places because, you guessed it, I'm amazing.* You wouldn't really say that, but does your Instagram account? I'm one hundred percent sure the Pharisees would have been on social media, and they would have looked good—like, perfect, white-washed good. They had their street corners of boasting/prayer. Is social media yours?

- AFFIRMATION: *Am I okay? Am I doing enough? Am I enough? Will my kids be okay? Have I ruined my family?* Are you sharing your life in order to be affirmed by your friends and senders? hopefully, there are people in real life who *do* affirm God's work in you. People who know you deeply and love you unconditionally. Write their names on a list, then talk with them regularly.

## Facebook, Fracking, and Viral Posts

Social media is like fracking. We inject tons and tons into this thing in hopes that we'll get something usable bubbling to the surface. *And we do.* But then we come to find out that we've just destabilized a whole region and earthquakes are now common in Oklahoma!

Facebook "like" buttons and happy emojis offer illusions of care and affirmation; they're nice, but they cannot fill the void. They are empty carcasses, incapable of answering the deeper longings.

It took one viral blog post for this to really hit home for me. It felt really great, sure, and I got a lot of attention. But pretty quickly, "real people world" crashed my internet party with the messiness of kids and ministry and marriage. And you know what I found? Real joy, *lasting joy*, is found in real places with real people. Not online.

It's a ruse. A golden pot at the end of a rainbow on the moon.

## A Word on Vulnerability

Curating your story openly and with vulnerability does not mean you share everything. Transparency doesn't mean everyone sees everything. Jesus himself didn't let it all hang out for everyone. He had layers of subscribers and followers and disciples and friends. And then he had John.

Vulnerability gets hijacked when we use it to meet our own needs, and that's not healthy for us or anyone else. Brené Brown, renowned vulnerability and shame researcher, goes so far as to state in her book, *Daring Greatly*, "*Using* vulnerability is not the same thing as *being* vulnerable; it's the opposite—it's armor."[3]

Are you using your online vulnerability in an attempt to get your own needs met? Is it your armor? One easy way to find out is to quit the internet. Go dark for two weeks and see what it feels like? If you feel like the wind got knocked out of your sails, like you lost all your friends, like a failure, you might need to recalibrate.

I tried this last January, and I was really nervous. I wondered if I'd die. I didn't. In fact, I'm planning to do it again because it was entirely refreshing. It reminded me of the outernet, which is actually way bigger and more entertaining anyway.

## Logging Off

So, I guess what I'm trying to say is, curate an online life, but live a real one. Connect with your neighbors and your teammates and your friends and let them see you. Not the Facebook you, not the Insta-filtered you, but the real you.

Yeah, Facebook lies. So find some friends who won't. Friends. In. Real. Life. Of course, "in real life" doesn't necessarily mean they're physically present; these could be people with whom you spend time connecting, personally—and privately—via e-mail or private message or Skype. We all need people who are close enough and trustworthy enough to hold our stories.

The world doesn't need any more fake boyfriends or fake missionaries. Let's learn how to curate our stories well, and with integrity. Perhaps we could start by praying this prayer:

Serenity Prayer for Social Media

*God, please grant me the serenity to shield the things I cannot share*
*The courage to share the things I should*
*And the wisdom to know the difference.*

---

3. Brown, *Daring Greatly*, 161.

# A Letter to Christians Living in America from a Christian Living Abroad

### BY *JONATHAN*

I HEAR YOU.

Some of you are angry and disenfranchised. I'm on Twitter. I know.

You see the Church and politicians wedded at the hip, and you throw up.

You feel like the American church has sold her soul and is rejoicing about the bargain.

You're embarrassed, like a cool kid with an uncool mother, and now you're asking to be dropped off a couple of blocks away from school.

You're not quite sure what to do. Do you fight and rant and protest? Do you take the Benedict option? Do you just disappear out the back door?

~~~~~~~~~~

Can I just encourage you to pause long enough to remember? To consider the extent of context and history?

Remember: the Church existed *before* America.

Remember: the Church will endure long *after* America.

Remember: the Church is older than Western civilization.

This is old news, of course, but it's worthy of remembrance. Because we forget.

It sounds like some people believe that losing the culture war is equivalent to losing all of Christendom. It's not just hyperbole; people act like this, defending every inch of ground with all their might.

373

But we must remember: the Church is global, and she is not dying. She is not getting into bed with politicians of opportunity. She is strong and she is bold and she remains defiant and glorious in the face of oppression and injustice all around the globe.

So remind yourself. Read the old stuff. Sing the old hymns. Rediscover the old Church, full of embraced mystery and deep sacrament.

And then read the new stuff. Sing the new hymns. Discover the young and vibrant Bride of Christ, expanding and exploding all over the world.

The Church has been around a long time, and she will remain, and the very gates of hell shall not prevail against her.

And the American church? She may seem warty and haggard to you now, but she is young. She is learning. Above all, she is his. She is loved. A washed Bride. And he is jealous for her affection.

Remind her.

Love her.

Pray for her.

Lift up your head, and see the glory of the global Church. She is beautiful.

Lift up your head, and look at the One she's been pointing to all this time: Jesus. He is regal and he is King, and he's coming back.

His promises are true.

He is faithful, and he is not blind or deaf or mistaken. He sees things as they are and for what they are, and he continues to love and to pursue.

Whatever corner of planet Earth you call home, these truths resound and these truths remain:

> "For unto us a child is born, unto us a son is given: and the government shall be upon his shoulder: and his name shall be called Wonderful, Counsellor, The mighty God, The everlasting Father, The Prince of Peace." (Isa 9:6 KJV)

> "I'm here to announce a great and joyful event that is meant for everybody, worldwide: A Savior has just been born in David's town, a Savior who is Messiah and Master." (Luke 2:10–11 MSG)

# When the Lights Go Out

BY *ELIZABETH*

I WANT TO DO all the things, all the very good things there are to do in this world. So I overcommit myself. I don't say "no." I say "yes" instead, and spread myself too thin. Then my soul suffers. My work suffers. My sanity suffers. My family life suffers. My spiritual life suffers.

I suffer in silence, thinking I'm all alone. I'm the only one *failing at everything*. I'm the only one who can't pull it together. I'm the only one who can't catch my breath, who can't catch up on work, who can't catch up on school, who can't catch up with friends, who can't catch up with the God I say I love so very much.

And I, insecure missionary blogger that I am, am afraid to tell people.

To top all that off, the heat in Southeast Asia sometimes crushes me. One hot season we experienced record highs here, and we got a lot of power cuts. I echo Ramona Quimby in *Ramona the Brave* who shouted out "Guts! Guts guts guts!"[1] when she wanted to say bad words. Instead, I yelled "Cuts! Cuts cuts cuts!" and very nearly lost my mind.

After one particularly grueling, twelve-hour, all-night power outage, something inside me broke, flat out broke. I lost my hope. I began to question everything. Why are we here? Why can't we live in America? Why exactly do I serve this God of mine? And *where the heck is he* when I can barely sleep or even breathe in this heat?

I was struggling under the weight of all the expectations I had for myself: be a good mom, wife, home educator, missionary, team leader's wife, friend, writer, editor, Christ-follower. And I couldn't do *any* of it.

1. Cleary, *Ramona the Brave*, loc. 895 of 1199.

If there's one thing that overnight power outage taught me, it's this: I am not nearly as good a person as I thought I was. Cuts cuts cuts: bad words all around.

Finally, *finally*, I asked for prayers. I asked my closest friends and family in the States. I asked my teammates. I asked a few women in my organization. Then I confided my struggles to some other homeschool moms in my city.

I was met on so many levels by people who understood. I went from being alone to being supported. I went from drowning in my despair of cross-cultural servitude to feeling supernaturally upheld.

The next time the power went out in the middle of the night, I didn't curse this land or this life or this electrical grid. I didn't panic. I stayed calm and waited. I sang a worship song (which shocked even myself). I retained my sanity and my faith—something that could *only* have happened because people were praying for me.

The next day I remember waking up and thinking, "Seriously? *Seriously?* Is that really all I had to do? Ask for prayer? Why did I keep my struggles to myself for so long? Why did I think I had to hide? What kind of appearance did I think I needed to keep up anyway? Why did I think I couldn't ask?" Help came fast when I asked.

I spun my hopelessness wheels for too long, but I've learned again that I *can* ask. I can ask for prayer sooner rather than later—and so can you.

So today, if you're spinning your hopelessness wheels, if you're afraid to confide in someone or ask for prayer or even for practical help, can I encourage you to ask? Just ask. The God of the universe is here to help. The body of Christ is here to help. Help is right here waiting, even when the lights go out and we find ourselves in the dark.

All we have to do is ask.

# RETURNING WELL

# Leaving (and Arriving) Well

BY *JONATHAN*

YOU'RE PROBABLY GOING TO leave the field. Someday, somehow, the vast majority of us will say goodbye, pack up, cry tears of joy or sorrow or both, and depart. How will that work out for you?

Well, frankly, I have no idea, but I do know that there are some things you can do to prepare to leave and some things you can do to prepare to arrive. And while a cross-cultural move is stressful no matter which direction you're going, knowing some of what to expect and how to prepare really can help.

The first part of this chapter deals with leaving well, while the second part deals with the oft-overlooked importance of arriving well.

In arriving well, we'll look at:

- Embracing your inner tourist
- Making movie magic
- Identifying your needs, and
- Grieving

We'll wrap up with an arrival benediction, which is a prayer for you, the transitioner, from the bottom of my heart.

## Preparing to Leave Well—How Do I Debrief All of This?

Maybe it was nine months or maybe it was nineteen years. In any case, debriefing is your friend.

For starters, find someone to talk with. A safe person who will value your thoughts and feelings about the whole range of your experience.

They don't have to understand missions or life on the field; they just have to be willing to listen, empathize, and listen. (And yes, I said that on purpose.)

Try making two lists: one of what you've gained and one of what you've lost. And remember, this isn't algebra; you're not trying to balance an equation, and the sides don't have to balance each other out. In fact, they won't.

Some folks more easily list what they've gained. If that's you, it's important for you to wrestle with identifying and grappling with losses. For some, the losses are the prime (or only) thing. If that's you, it's important to wrestle with the truth that there is some good in all of it, even if the only good is God.

There is tremendous power in making room for the paradoxical truths that there was good and there was bad and there *is* God.

## Preparing to Leave Well—Am I a Failure?

Maybe some things failed. Maybe things really did hit the fan. But there is a world of difference between stepping back and saying, "Wow, that thing failed," or even, "I failed to accomplish that goal," and "I AM A FAILURE!" If you find yourself lurching toward the "I am a failure" side of things, heads up, 'cause that'll destroy you.

You'll need to deal with that sense of *being* a failure; if you don't put that to rest right here and now, it will certainly come back. It will blind you to whatever God is calling you to next. Please don't let it.

## Preparing to Leave Well—What Should I Read?

Well, for starters, here are two articles from A Life Overseas writers:

- "Leaving Happy or Leaving Well?" by Jerry Jones
   "Everyone wants to leave happy but not everyone wants to leave well. In fact, some people are so committed to leaving happy that they absolutely refuse to leave well."[1]

- "Transition—Building a RAFT," by Marilyn Gardner

---

1. Jones, "Leaving Happy or Leaving Well?," para. 7.

This one is my go-to when I'm meeting with a client who's preparing to transition. Do yourself a favor and read Marilyn's thoughts about building a RAFT.[2]

If you're willing to invest in a book or two, these are highly recommended:

- *Returning Well: Your Guide to Thriving Back "Home" After Serving Cross-culturally,* by Melissa Chaplin.

  Perry Bradford, President of Barnabas International, says this about *Returning Well:* "Thousands transition back to their home cultures each year without any formal debrief to assist them. *Returning Well* will guide the reader into an in-depth look at their transition and lead them to discover how to manage the re-entry process with spiritual and emotional health."

- *Looming Transitions: Starting and Finishing Well in Cross-cultural Service,* by Amy Young.

  Amy writes for A Life Overseas and Velvet Ashes, and this contribution of hers is excellent. Also check out the companion book, *Twenty-two Activities for Families in Transition.*

## Preparing to Arrive Well—Embrace Your Inner Tourist

Many of us want to hit the ground running. We've got a bazillion things to do and people to see and contracts and license renewals and logistics and ieoafioefoaeifnaeoifneoiafjeio. . .

But you know, much less has to be done immediately than you think. Really. Instead, what I'd like for you to do, for a time, is just pretend to be a tourist. Let jet lag have its day, and then be a tourist. Maybe forgo the tourist pants and camera straps, but if you want to go all in, go for it.

A tourist is one who "is travelling or visiting a place for pleasure."[3] Let yourself enjoy your new place, even if it's your old place; it *is* your new place now. Go to the parks and museums and restaurants. Go where tourists go, and go with tourist eyes. The place has changed, and so has your vision.

---

2. Gardner, "Transition."
3. English Oxford Living Dictionaries, "Tourist."

Enjoy the place. Enjoy the people. Give your soul time to breathe. I always ask clients to list out the stuff that absolutely *has* to be done in the first two weeks. Ask yourself, "Will I die if this doesn't happen *right away*?"

Remember, God's where you're at. You didn't leave him on the field. The Creator's not stranded in customs. Ask him to show himself in this new-to-you part of his creation, and then give yourself time and space to hear his reply.

## Preparing to Arrive Well—Make Movie Magic

Some people will care about your stories. Some won't. Some will act like they care and then their eyes will glaze over like a warm Krispy Kreme donut.

Which is where the movie magic comes in.

*I want you to create a movie poster.* Come up with a three-sentence snapshot of your experience (whether it was six months or six years). I want you to have something that's quick and that you can say without having to use a lot of computing power.

This "movie poster" is for the well-meaning folks who pass you in the church lobby and say, "How was your trip?" I want you to have something to say to them besides, "YOU MEAN MY LIFE? YOU MEAN HOW WAS THE LAST DECADE OF MY LIFE?"

For those folks, give them the movie poster. Maybe it'll intrigue them and maybe at some point they'll want to hear more of the story. But if they don't, whatever.

*Then, I want you to create a movie trailer.* Create a two- or three-minute synopsis of some of the important points. Tell some of the story, but don't reveal it all. Keep in mind that a movie trailer isn't designed to tell the whole story, but to help people decide whether or not they want to invest in the full-length feature film.

Some will watch the trailer, they'll hear your three-minute story, and be satisfied. They'll say, "Wow, that looks cool. I'm never going to see that." And of course, some will say, "Hmm, that actually looks really interesting. When is it showing?"

*And then create the feature film.* The movie. This is your story, shared with the folks who really want to hear it. These are your people.

Not everyone will want to see your movie, and that's okay. Not everyone will *like* your movie. That's okay too. You weren't making it for them anyway.

## Preparing to Arrive Well—Grieve Again (and Again and Again)

Grieving big losses is measured more in years than months. So when you've been back for five weeks and hit a speed bump, please don't be mad at yourself and don't you dare think, "I should be over this by now!" Um, just no. Even if you move back to the same town where you grew up, you've changed and the town's changed and this isn't Kansas anymore.

Big losses take more like two years to grieve, not two months.

## Preparing to Arrive Well—Identify Your Needs

This was originally written about cross-cultural living, but it applies here too: "In an ideal world, what is it that I really need to make it? To thrive? To be okay? To survive where God's called me? What is it that I really need?"[4]

Can I mitigate it, or do I need to sacrifice it? These concepts continue to ring off the walls of my counseling room, and I think transitioners need them too.

## An Arrival Benediction

Here's my prayer for you, a prayer for the middle spaces:

*May you arrive more whole than when you departed, though the intervening time may have been splintering and hard.*
*May you arrive with more hope than when you left, though you've been in hopeless situations more often than you thought possible.*

*Perhaps you'll arrive empty, but may those you've left behind (there and here), fill you with the love of the Father, aged and distilled through time and perhaps darkness.*

---

4. Trotter, "One Question We Must Ask," lines 4–5.

*May you arrive with peace, knowing in your gut that he is good, that he is faithful, and that he isn't finished with you (or with them).*

*May you find rest, safe in the arms of love, behind the Captain of the Lord of Hosts, your healer.*

*And may you hear him ask you the same question he asked a confused and lonely and traveling Hagar, "Where have you come from?" and "Where are you going?" At the end of the day, may you proclaim along with Hagar, "You are the God who sees me."*

*And after your arrival,*
*May you keep your eyes fixed on the horizon,*
*Awaiting the day of all days,*
*When the sky will split,*
*The darkness flee, and*
*He will, finally and irrevocably,*
*Arrive.*

# When a Country is Etched Into Your Soul

## BY *Elizabeth*

WHEN I'M IN CAMBODIA, I assume that I think like an American and that I act like one too—because in many ways I do. But then I return to America and discover I've forgotten some key facts about the way Americans live in America.[1] Things like:

- Americans don't throw their toilet paper in the trash can. (Oops.)

- Americans pump their own gas. (You expect me to do what?!)

- Americans give and receive objects with one hand, not two. (Still working on that one.)

- Americans inherently know how to use shower curtains. (Unlike my children.)

- Americans don't point with their middle fingers. (Also unlike my children.)

- Americans don't get offended if you motion them to "come here" with your palms and fingers pointed up. (I, however, now am offended by palms-up gestures. Even in movies.)

- On the other hand, Americans may very well be offended if you ask them their age. (Oops again.)

- Americans in America don't worry over torn or ripped dollar bills and will use them even if they're not in pristine condition. (Which is one less thing to worry about at the ATM.)

- Americans (in suburbia) don't lock doors and windows obsessively like I do.

1. This was originally written during our 2nd Stateside Service.

- Americans don't worry about shoes in the house. (Is it because of the vacuum cleaners?)

Much more deeply than these surface-level customs, though, there's no getting around the fact that Cambodia has been etched into my soul. I've encountered God so fiercely, so intimately, and so many times in Cambodia that it's been written into my heart.

In prayer, in Bible study, in worship, and in fellowship with other believers, Cambodia has marked me. It has been for me Bethel, the house of God, a gateway to heaven. It has been for me Beer-lahai-roi, the well of the Living One who sees me.[2]

It's where I've found purpose and calling in writing and encouraging fellow sojourners. It's where I've fallen deeper in love with God and with his church. How can I not love Cambodia?

Sometimes I love God so much *in Cambodia* that I forget he's also in America. My first home assignment was really spiritually dry. Almost like a desert, in fact. It made me want to hurry back to Cambodia. It also made me nervous about returning to the States a second time.

And sure enough, one morning early in this current visit, I was out on my parents' deck, discouraged and feeling sorry for myself. *God, where are you? Why are you so hard to find in America?*

In the midst of my pity party, Jonathan walked out. He listened to me complain about my circumstances. Then he told me, "Remember, if you can find God in Cambodia, then you can find him here."

Ouch! Exhortation received, dear husband. And thankfully, I'm here to say it's true. This time, I'm finding him here. I'm seeing him and I'm hearing him. He's not silent. He's not far away. He's present, and he's good.

I miss my raggedy red couch in Cambodia, it's true. I miss my palm trees and my early morning meetings with God, drinking my cheap coffee in a room thick with heat, street noise, and river dust.

I relish the comforts of first-world living—the plush carpets and the comfy furniture—and I delight in the joy of meeting old friends, but I miss the pressure cooker of God's love and the fellowship of like minds that I've found overseas.

I also know that in two months' time, I'll slide right back into my old, familiar routines. I'll rise on the wings of the dawn and fly straight back to Bethel, back to Beer-lahai-roi. For the present, however, I'll continue to meet God wherever and however he shows up.

2. Gen 16:14.

# Here's My heart, O Take and Seal It

## BY ELIZABETH

I WANT TO FINISH the Christian life well, to continue to press in to God, listen to him, and influence others to do the same. But what if don't? What if I fizzle out, forsake my first love, fail to follow him to my dying breath? I'm not talking about losing my salvation; *I know my salvation is secure.* What I am talking about is slacking in my obedience, and not consistently seeking him till the end of my days. (I know I'm not very old, but I still think about these things.)

This dread of mine is echoed in the songs of old. I hear it in James Waddel Alexander's "O Sacred Head, Now Wounded": "What language shall I borrow to thank Thee, dearest friend, for this Thy dying sorrow, Thy pity without end? O make me Thine forever, and should I fainting be, Lord let me never, never outlive my love to Thee."[1]

I sense it in Robert Robinson's "Come Thou Fount": "Let Thy goodness, like a fetter, bind my wandering heart to Thee. Prone to wander, Lord, I feel it, prone to leave the God I love; here's my heart, O take and seal it, seal it for Thy courts above."[2] If you know this song, you know the first verse soars with a longing and love for God, but the fear of our own depravity overtakes this later verse.

So among the great hymn writers at least, the fear of not ending well is in good company. If I want more proof that this fear is indeed valid, I need look no further than the Old Testament kings, who tended to start well and then finish poorly.

A classic example of this is Solomon, whose early wisdom led him to ask God not for riches, but for more wisdom. God granted his request

1. Alexander, "O Sacred Head, Now Wounded."
2. Robinson, "Come Thou Fount."

for "an understanding heart to govern God's people well and to know the difference between right and wrong" (1 Kgs 3:9, my paraphrase). Even so, in his later years, his heart was led astray, and he embraced the idol worship of his thousand wives and concubines (1 Kgs 3, 4, 11).

Likewise, Uzziah initially did what was pleasing in the Lord's sight, and he depended upon God for his military success. But when he became powerful, pride overtook him. His pride led him to dishonor God by entering the Temple and burning incense on the incense altar. Only the priests were allowed to do that, so as punishment, God struck Uzziah with leprosy. He then lived in isolation until his death (2 Chr 26).

Other kings were the same. Asa banished temple prostitution and demolished idols in Judah. It is even said his heart remained completely faithful to the Lord throughout his life (1 Kgs 15). His full trust in God's power, however, wavered in his final years as king. He no longer trusted the Lord to save him from the king of Israel, and he looked to the king of Aram for protection instead. Later when he developed a serious foot disease, he did not look to the Lord for help at all, but only to doctors (2 Chr 16).

These stories haunt me. I do not want to relive these men's lives. I do not want to have it said of me that in the beginning chapters of my life, I "did what was pleasing in the Lord's sight," only to falter in my later years, to stop trusting in the one true God, and to neglect my worship of him.

## How Can I End Well?

Perhaps clues to this mysterious question are found in the stories themselves. Several years ago at an organizational meeting, one of the breakout sessions took us to the story of King Joash. Joash is recorded as having done "what was pleasing in the Lord's sight throughout the lifetime of Jehoidah the priest" (2 Chr 24:2 NLT).

As long as Joash's godly influencer was alive, Joash listened to him and managed to obey God. This is good news, sort of, because after Jehoidah's death, the other leaders of Judah persuaded Joash to abandon worship at the temple, and to worship idols instead. This is really bad news. And when Joash was confronted by Jehoidah's son for his idolatry, Joash had him stoned to death rather instead of repenting (2 Chr 24).

When Jehoidah died, Joash's obedience died with him. Joash could be influenced for good or evil, depending on who was speaking into his life. The story of King Uzziah also gives this telltale warning. Scripture says he "sought God during the days of Zechariah, who taught him to fear God" (2 Chr 26:5 NLT). Again, as long as Uzziah listened to a godly man, he followed God. But when Zechariah was no longer available to influence him, Uzziah drifted from faithfulness.

So what does it take to end well? Well, if these stories are any indication, ending well means surrounding myself with faithful Christians and allowing them to speak truth into my life. Ending well means I'm not done listening to other believers and submitting myself to their collective wisdom, *until I die*. I must never stop inviting wise counsel or stop listening to godly leaders. And I must choose my influencers carefully.

Proverbs 13:20 tells us to walk with the wise and become wise. When Joash and Uzziah walked with the wise, they made wise decisions. They obeyed God more closely. I want to walk with the wise. I want to stay faithful. I want to make God-honoring decisions all the way to the end. And I don't want to leave a trail of brokenness in my wake. So I must stay in touch with God every day, keeping in step with the Spirit, even into my eighties and nineties. I must listen to the wisdom of believers I trust, and I must never presume I can walk this path alone.

God, help me walk with the wise, and become wise.

# The Far Side of Somewhere

BY *ELIZABETH*

[NOTE: THIS WAS WRITTEN in preparation for my second home assignment.]

I remember my first home service. All those awkward experiences like drinking water from the tap and flushing the toilet with potable water again. Or feeling naked and exposed with no metal security bars on the windows. Or handing payment to cashiers with two hands (like I do in Cambodia) and then being embarrassed, because *normal people don't do that here.*

What was up with the laundry smelling nice all the time? (Come to think of it, what was up with everything smelling nice all the time?) Could a load of laundry really take a mere two hours to complete, all the way from wash to wear, without having to hang on the line for two or three days in rainy season and *still* be damp—and smelling of fire and whatever dish the neighbors last cooked over said fire?

I wanted someone to explain to me why Americans felt the need to store hot water *in a tank*. Seemed like such a waste of energy when you could use a tankless water heater instead, thereby providing a never-ending source of hot water for yourself. (Running out of hot water in the winter is a big problem for me.)

Today I'm facing another home service. I'll temporarily close down life here and leave my Cambodia home. I'll board a plane and begin the process of temporarily reentering my American home. I need to go. It's time. After a second two-year stint in this country, culture fatigue has hit me hard. I'm worn out from the collective sin patterns of this culture, and I need a break. I love Cambodia, but I sometimes need a break from Cambodia.

Still, there's nothing like preparing to go on home service for bringing on an identity crisis. *Who am I, and where do I belong?* I live in this city and traverse its Asian streets, all without quite belonging to them. Yet I don't quite belong to the immaculately clean American streets I'll soon be walking, either. Belonging is a slippery feeling for a global nomad. It can be everywhere, and it can be nowhere, all at the same time.

Nevertheless, when I walk in the door of my parents' house tomorrow, I know I will once more experience the words of Bernard Cook, words that hung on the walls of every one of my childhood homes: "We need to have people who mean something to us; people to whom we can turn, knowing that being with them is coming home."[1] Growing up in a military family, I always knew home was with my family. Home is with the people I love. And as a Christian, I know home is with God himself.

I love these words from Christine Hoover's book *From Good to Grace*: "With Christ as my city, I can traipse all over the globe and never once not be at home. Because I dwell in his grace."[2] Christine knows a bit about this unmoored feeling of mine. She and her husband didn't cross country borders when they moved to Virginia to church plant, but in leaving their home state of Texas to follow God's leading, they certainly crossed the kind of deep cultural divide that make you wonder where in the world you belong.

I want Christ to be my city. I want to dwell in him. The best part about finding home and belonging in him is that he goes with me wherever I go. Psalm 139 is a gift to us global nomads in this regard. In verses 7 through 10 (NIV), the Psalmist asks:

> "Where can I go from your Spirit? Where can I flee from your presence? If I go up to the heavens, you are there; if I make my bed in the depths, you are there. If I rise on the wings of the dawn, if I settle on the far side of the sea, even there your hand will guide me, your right hand will hold me fast."

When I moved to Cambodia nearly four years ago, I traveled west across the ocean on a morning flight, literally rising on the wings of the dawn. And when I stepped off the plane in Phnom Penh, I found that not only had God flown the skies with me, but that he was already here in this place—for I cannot flee from his presence. Even on the far side of

---

1. Cooke, *Formation of Faith*, 24.
2. Hoover, *From Good to Grace*, 132.

the sea, he holds me fast. And no matter how deep the depths of my life, I know he is with me.

From now on, wherever I go and no matter which side of the sea I settle on, I will always be on the far side of somewhere I love. There is just no getting around that. But how precious of God to include David's words in his word. David could not have known about jet propulsion when he penned Psalm 139, but thousands of years later, his words are a balm to the global nomad's soul. For we rise on the wings of the dawn, and we settle on the far side of the sea, and because God lives in us, we can find home in every place he has made.

# To the Returning Missionary

*BY ELIZABETH*

YOU HAVE WALKED WITH God in this place a long time, and he has walked with you. He has been beside you and *in*side you this whole time. The same Spirit remains in you and with you in your new place.

This place has changed you, and you have changed this place. Do not be distressed if you don't understand everything that has happened or is happening. Remember that the stories God writes are always long. They unfold over generations, not days or weeks or even months.

You have been here long enough to understand some of what God is writing for both yourself and the people you've served, but some things may not make sense yet. Do not fret, and do not fear. The Father will show it all to you one day. Until that day, remember that you leave with our love, even as you live within God's love.

Many years ago you came to this place as a foreigner, and the place you're going now may also seem foreign to you. Everyone and everything has changed, including you.

So in the days and months and years to come, when you feel misunderstood, remember that no one understands your foreignness like Jesus, the One who came to the most foreign land to show his beloved creatures truth and light. He will understand your sorrows like no other.

You have seen so much change in your years here. Change in the people around you, change in yourself, change in the people you're returning to. And you are tired. So tired. No one can work and live as long as you have and not be tired. Remember that Christ is your rest. (And on your journey, also remember to sleep.)

Circumstances change, and communities change, and in the end, he is all we have to hold onto. So don't lose hope: he is our hope. Hold onto him, and remember that his love never fails. It will never fail you.

Though organizations may fail you, though supporters may fail you, though cultural acquisition may fail you, though years of experience may fail you, though people you love and invested in may fail you, though you may even feel you've failed yourself, still one thing will not fail you: the love of the great Three-in-One will never fail.

And one day, this squeezing in your heart and this aching in your bones from all these years and all these travels and all the years and travels to come, it will all be undone. Everything will be made new. Remember this.

# Seven Tips for Goers and Stayers

## BY *ELIZABETH*

As a MILITARY KID I grew up hearing about these things called "Hail and Farewells." I didn't really know what they were; I didn't even know it was three separate words. I thought of it more as "hailenfarewell" and was at a complete loss as to what it was.

But when I contemplate the yearly season of expatriate goodbyes, I can't get the phrase out of my mind. So naturally I went to my mom, Mary Hunzinger, and asked her to tell me everything she remembered about Hail and Farewells. Her answers blew me away with their spiritual applications.

Let's have a look, shall we?

1. *"Hail and Farewells were an integral part of military life. Whether we were stationed at a military installation or a university in the States, or were stationed abroad, we all took part in these monthly events."*

    Hellos and goodbyes happen at regular intervals, and they touch the entire community. Nobody gets to skip out on the good-byes (or hellos), and nobody is immune to the transience—either the leaver or the stayer.

2. *"It always involved food, whether it was at someone's home and everyone brought food, or at a restaurant and we purchased our meal."*

    Okay, so we need food. It's perhaps kind of obvious, but this answer stood out to me. As humans we celebrate—and mourn—with food.

3. *"They were usually more dressy events, except those that were barbeques, etc. There was always a gift, usually a memento that represented your unit and also some kind of plaque that commemorated*

*your time there. Oftentimes others would gift you with items that*
*spoke personally to the officer leaving."*

Whether we're leaving or whether we're staying, we honor our
friends with something special. Whether it's a physical gift repre-
senting our relationship or our country of service (for the gift-givers
among us), a special event (for the quality-timers among us), or
something else, we don't let them fade away without that special
honor.

4. *"The commanding officer would do the introductions of new people,*
   *and we would find out where they came from and a little about them*
   *and their family. Then the farewells were saved for last with the usual*
   *good things said about people. Those that worked closest with the de-*
   *parting officer would also have an opportunity to share about them."*

   We honor the newcomers by trying to find out a little about
   them. And we honor the leavers by sharing our cherished memories
   about them.

5. *"Something I always saw in the groups we were in was the total will-*
   *ingness to accept and 'get behind' a new commanding officer. Often-*
   *times the departing commander was beloved and the idea of someone*
   *else coming in and taking over could be hard in a way, but your dad*
   *and I and others were intentional about welcoming and following new*
   *commanders just as we followed the departing one."*

   This gets to the heart of welcoming new people, whether they're
   in leadership over us or not. Being new is hard, and the least we
   can do is welcome new people even as we say a painful goodbye to
   beloved friends. Whether we're the leaver or the stayer, no one can
   replace our friends, but our hearts can expand to love more people.

6. *"We were usually notified about 6 months in advance of our new duty*
   *station, and something strange and wonderful always happened after*
   *we found out where and when. Usually it was met with, 'Uh, okay,'*
   *but that time in between notification and actually leaving, our minds*
   *turned it into something good that we were actually looking forward*
   *to, and we were very ready to leave."*

   If circumstances allow (and I know they don't always allow), we
   plan time between the decision to leave and the actual leaving. That
   time gives us the space to say goodbye well to people and places, to
   mentally and physically prepare ourselves for the next step, and to
   physically and mentally prepare our friends and co-workers for our

departure. We realize that nothing can completely prepare us for our next stage, but a little time to reflect and say goodbye is helpful.

7. *"It was sad to say goodbye, but many times we figured we'd meet up again."*

To a certain extent, expatriate life also allows us to meet up again. (And I'm always thankful when that happens!) But even if we never see each other again on earth, as Christians we know we will meet again in heaven, and (at least for me) that reminder does cheer the aching heart.

This time of year is painful. I will not deny that. April and May are months of many tears for me. I've often written about these heart-rending goodbyes. Each year I feel the feelings afresh, and sometimes I fear they will break me. But I do want us, as the body of Christ, to carry on in a way that honors both our earthly fellowship and our faith in a mysterious God. With that in mind I offer you my Expat Manifesto:

> We acknowledge that we will always have Hail and Farewells. We will bid farewell to our people. We will honor them with our tears, with our laughter, with our food, with our stories, with our hugs, and with our time. And we will bid farewell to seasons, whether satisfying or sad. We will welcome new people. We will honor them with our open (though sometimes wounded) hearts and remember that they may one day be our old people.

We will remember that in Christ goodbye is never forever, but only for a time. And with Christ as our anchor, we will embrace each new season, whether dreaded or longed for. *We will Hail, and we will Farewell: This is how we carry on.*

# To the Ones Who Think They Failed

BY *JONATHAN*

SO, YOU FAILED TO save the world.

You failed to complete the task of global evangelism.

You failed to see massive geopolitical change in your region.

You failed. Or at least you feel like it.

Good-hearted people in your organization (maybe) and your churches (hopefully) tell you you're not a failure. But you still feel like one because you came home before you planned to. Maybe it was for health reasons, maybe for burnout reasons, or maybe you don't need reasons. You were done, so you finished. You came "home."

But now you're finding home's not home anymore. You knew for sure you didn't fit in there, but now you're very much afraid you don't fit in here anymore. You failed there, and now you feel like you're failing here. You want to believe that some good came of it, or will come of it, or something.

For now, though, you mourn. And you should, because you lost something. You lost dreams, maybe, and years. You lost relationships. Some of those relationships you wanted to lose; others, you didn't. And still, other relationships you thought you'd regain, you haven't yet.

So mourn. Mourn well. Jesus is near to those who mourn. Feel the loss. Welcome it, even. It is a bitter pill that you should swallow as often as needed.

You're still part of the team. You're not a washed-up, has-been, burnt-out, broken-down, used-up person. You are a child of God who is dearly loved and cherished, and you are still needed. The church still needs you. The Father still wants you. Jesus still loves you. And the Holy Spirit is still near to you.

The church still needs your voice. You've seen things that many folks "back home" haven't. Your voice is different, weird maybe, but it's so needed in the church that sent you. Don't let them forget the global nature of the Kingdom of God. The church still needs you.

The foreign mission field needs you. You can counsel, caution, and console in a way few people can. Those still serving abroad need you. Be a voice for them. Be a voice to them.

May you find God to be the great Restorer, the One who heals.
The Great I AM at both departure and destination.
The King who knows you're always en route.

May you find peace. May you realize that God's love for you was never conditioned on your performance. Ever.

He loved you then. He loves you now.
He asks you to love him.
He asks you to obey him.
Today.

So whether you're here or there, whether you feel like a wonderful success or an abject failure, may you remember his love.

May you believe his love, shining most eloquently through his Son, and may that belief lead to obedience here, there, and everywhere.

And in the middle of it all, may you hear the Father calling you.
Home.

# A Blessing for the Road Ahead

Thank you for allowing us to walk with you down this little stretch of road. We'd love to hear from you, so keep in touch. In the meantime, we pray for you an ancient prayer:

*In times of trouble, may the LORD answer your cry.*
*May the name of the God of Jacob keep you safe from all harm.*
*May he send you help from his sanctuary*
*and strengthen you from Jerusalem.*
*May he remember all your gifts*
*and look favorably on your burnt offerings.*

*Interlude*

*May he grant your heart's desires*
*and make all your plans succeed.*
*May we shout for joy when we hear of your victory*
*and raise a victory banner in the name of our God.*
*May the LORD answer all your prayers.*
*Now I know that the LORD rescues his anointed king.*
*he will answer him from his holy heaven*
*and rescue him by his great power.*
*Some nations boast of their chariots and horses,*
*but we boast in the name of the LORD our God.*
*Those nations will fall down and collapse,*
*but we will rise up and stand firm.*
*Give victory to our king, O LORD!*
*Answer our cry for help.*
*(Ps 20:1–9 NLT)*

# About Us

Elizabeth is the editor-in-chief for the missions website, A Life Overseas (alifeoverseas.com). She also writes regularly at trotters41.com and Velvet Ashes (velvetashes.com).

After a military childhood, a teenage Elizabeth crash-landed onto American civilian life. When she married her high school sweetheart, her life plan was to be a chemical engineer while he practiced law. Instead, they both fell headlong into youth ministry and spent the next ten years serving the local church. When her husband later decided he wanted to move overseas, Elizabeth didn't want to join him. Now, after seven years of life in Cambodia, she can't imagine doing anything else. Elizabeth loves math, science, and all things Jane Austen. Days find her homeschooling her four children, while nights find her eating hummus by the spoonful.

~~~~~~~~~~

Jonathan writes for A Life Overseas, but spends most of his time providing pastoral counseling at a local counseling center in Phnom Penh, Cambodia. He also serves as one of the pastors at an international church. He has written for the IMB (International Mission Board), Velvet Ashes, Huffington Post, and Gottman Institute.

Before moving to the field, he served as a youth pastor in the Midwest for ten years and as an inner-city ER/trauma nurse for three years. He is also a pilot and a licensed attorney. He enjoys walking with people towards Jesus and eating imported Twizzlers.

Connect with Jonathan and Elizabeth here:
Website: www.trotters41.com
Twitter: @trotters41
Instagram: trotters41
Facebook: /trotters41
E-mail: trotters41@gmail.com

# Bibliography

Alexander, James. "O Sacred Head, Now Wounded." In *Songs of Faith and Praise,* edited by Alton H. Howard, hymn #318. West Monroe, LA: Howard, 1994.

Allender and Longman, *The Cry of the Soul.* Colorado Springs, CO: NavPress, 1994.

Bell, Aubrey. *In Portugal.* London: Lane, 1912.

Belmonte, Kevin. *A Year with G.K. Chesterton.* Nashville: Thomas Nelson, 2012.

Benson, Kyle. "Couples that Talk about Sex have Better Sex." https://www.gottman.com/blog/couples-talk-sex-better-sex/.

Bianchi, Tracey. "Ladies Who Lunch—with Men." https://www.christianitytoday.com/women-leaders/2016/june/ladies-who-lunch-with-men.html.

Bonhoeffer, Dietrich. *Psalms: The Prayer Book of the Bible.* Reprint. Minneapolis: Augsberg Fortress, 1970.

Bowman, Chis. "God Can Heal Our Broken Potatoes." http://www.alifeoverseas.com/god-can-heal-our-broken-potatoes/.

Brown, Brené. *Daring Greatly: How the Courage to Be Vulnerable Transforms the Way We Live, Love, Parent, and Lead.* New York: Avery, 2015.

Brueggemann, Walter. *The Prophetic Imagination.* 2nd ed. Minneapolis: Augsburg Fortress, 2001.

Bruner, Kay. *As Soon as I Fell.* Cedar Hill, TX: CreateSpace, 2014.

Bushong, Lois. *Belonging Everywhere and Nowhere.* Indianapolis: Mango Tree Intercultural Services, 2013.

Calvin, John. *Institutes of the Christian Religion.* Translated by Henry Beveridge. Grand Rapids: Eerdmans, 1986.

Chapman, Gary. *The 5 Love Languages: The Secret to Love that Lasts.* Chicago: Northfield, 2015.

Cleary, Beverly. *Ramona the Brave.* New York: HarperCollins e-books, 2008.

Cloud, Henry. *Necessary Endings.* New York: HarperCollins, 2010.

Cooke, Bernard. *Formation of Faith.* Chicago: Loyola University Press, 1965.

Cordeiro, Wayne. *Leading on Empty: Refilling Your Tank and Renewing Your Passion.* Bloomington, IN: Bethany, 2009.

Cowper, William. "God Moves In a Mysterious Way." In *Songs of Faith and Praise,* edited by Alton H. Howard, hymn #26. West Monroe, LA: Howard, 1994.

Crabb, Larry. *Inside Out.* Colorado Springs, CO: Navpress, 1988.

Crossman, Tanya. *Misunderstood.* London: Summertime, 2016.

DeYoung, Kevin. *Crazy Busy: A (Mercifully) Short Book About a (Really) Big Problem.* Wheaton, IL: Crossway, 2013.

Donne, John. "Holy Sonnets: Death, Be Not Proud by John Donne." https://www. poetryfoundation.org/poems/44107/holy-sonnets-death-be-not-proud.

Emmons, Shirlee, and Wilbur Watkins Lewis. *Researching the Song: A Lexicon.* Oxford: Oxford University Press, 2006.

English Oxford Living Dictionaries. "Curate." https://en.oxforddictionaries.com/ definition/curate.

———. "Tourist." https://en.oxforddictionaries.com/definition/tourist.

Faithful, George. "Recovering the Theology of the Negro Spirituals." https:// theologyjournal.files.wordpress.com/2009/01/final_george2.pdf.

Feldman, H., et al. "Impotence and its Medical and Psychosocial Correlates." *Journal of Urology* 151 (1994) 54–61.

Gardner, Marilyn. "Learning to Grieve Well." https:// communicatingacrossboundariesblog.com/2013/05/07/learning-to-grieve-well/.

———. "Some Thoughts from Adult TCKs to Those Who Raise Them." https:// communicatingacrossboundariesblog.com/2014/05/22/some-thoughts-from- adult-tcks-to-those-who-raise-them/.

———. "Transition – Building a RAFT." https://communicatingacrossboundariesblog. com/2014/06/12/transition-building-a-raft/.

Godfrey, W. Robert. "Why I Love the Psalms." https://www.ligonier.org/blog/why-i- love-psalms/.

Gottman, John. *Why Marriages Succeed or Fail: And How You Can Make Yours Last.* New York: Simon and Schuster, 1994.

Gray, Bonnie. *Finding Spiritual White Space: Awakening Your Soul to Rest.* Grand Rapids: Revell, 2014.

Hatch, Jenavieve. "Woman Creates Fake Boyfriend on Instagram, Successfully Dupes Everyone." https://www.huffingtonpost.com/entry/woman- creates-fake-boyfriend-on-instagram-successfully-dupes-everyone_ us_56b379fbe4b04f9b57d89c07.

Hiebert, Paul. *Anthropological Insights for Missionaries.* Grand Rapids: Baker, 2006.

Hoover, Christine. *From Good to Grace: Letting Go of the Goodness Gospel.* Grand Rapids: Baker, 2015.

Howard, Alton H., ed. *Songs of Faith and Praise.* West Monroe, LA: Howard, 1994.

"Interstate Highway Standards." Wikipedia. https://en.wikipedia.org/w/index. php?title=Interstate_Highway_standards&oldid=872428521.

Ireton, Kimberlee. *The Circle of Seasons: Finding God in the Church Year.* Downers Grove, IL: InterVarsity, 2008.

Jones, Jerry. "Leaving Happy or Leaving Well?" http://www.alifeoverseas.com/leaving- happy-or-leaving-well/.

Jones, Karin. "What Sleeping with Married Men Taught Me about Infidelity." https:// www.nytimes.com/2018/04/06/style/modern-love-sleeping-with-married-men- infidelity.html.

Jones, Rachel Pieh. "Marriage is the Beautiful Hard." https://velvetashes.com/marriage- is-the-beautiful-hard/

———. "Why I Will Not Say 'I Never Made a Sacrifice.'" http://www.alifeoverseas.com/ why-i-will-not-say-i-never-made-a-sacrifice/.

Kroll, Woodrow. "The Psalms: Woodrow Kroll." http://wkministries.com/the-psalms/.

Lautsbaugh, Lindsey. "Let's Not Say that Anymore (Pretty Please?)." http://www. thisisloveactually.com/lets-not-say-that-anymore-pretty-please/.

Lewis, C. S. *The Lion, the Witch, and the Wardrobe*. New York: HarperCollins, 2000.

Luther, Martin. "A Mighty Fortress Is Our God." In *Songs of Faith and Praise*, edited by Alton H. Howard, hymn #10. West Monroe, LA: Howard, 1994.

Manning, Brennan. *Reflections for Ragamuffins*. New York: HarperCollins, 1998.

McCarthy, Barry. *Sex Made Simple: Clinical Strategies for Sexual Issues in Therapy*. Eau Claire, WI: PESI, 2015.

Melvin, Don. "U. S. Dentist Wanted for Killing Cecil the Lion." https://www.cnn.com/2015/07/28/africa/zimbabwe-lion-killed/.

Metaxas, Eric. *Bonhoeffer*. Nashville: Thomas Nelson, 2012.

Moore, Beth. *Beloved Disciple*. Nashville: Broadman & Holman, 2003.

Nouwen, Henri. *The Return of the Prodigal Son*. New York: Doubleday, 1992.

———. *Show Me the Way*. New York: Crossroad, 1992.

Patterson, Kerry, Ron McMillan, and Al Switzer. *Crucial Conversations*. New York: McGraw-Hill, 2012.

Percival, Brian, dir. *Downton Abbey*. Season 1, episode 1. "Episode One." Aired September 26, 2010, on ITV.

Peterson, Eugene. *A Long Obedience in the Same Direction: Discipleship in an Instant Society*. Downers Grove, IL: InterVarsity, 1980.

Popova, Maria. "Mars and the Mind of Man: Carl Sagan, Ray Bradbury and Arthur C. Clarke in Cosmic Conversation, 1971." https://www.brainpickings.org/2012/08/20/mars-and-the-mind-of-man-sagan-bradbury-clarke-caltech-1971/.

Robinson, Robert. "Come Thou Fount." In *Songs of Faith and Praise,* edited by Alton H. Howard, hymn #226. West Monroe, LA: Howard, 1994.

Rosenau, Douglas. *A Celebration of Sex: A Guide to Enjoying God's Gift of Sexual Intimacy*. Nashville: Thomas Nelson, 2002.

Sanford, Timothy. *I Have to Be Perfect, and Other Parsonage Heresies*. Colorado Springs: Llama, 1998.

Sargent, Joseph, dir. *Skylark*. Kansas City: Hallmark Hall of Fame Production, 1993. DVD.

"Saudade." Wikipedia. https://en.wikipedia.org/w/index.php?title=Saudade&oldid=870432937.

Scazzero, Peter. *The Emotionally Healthy Church*. Grand Rapids: Zondervan, 2015.

———. *Emotionally Healthy Spirituality: It's Impossible to be Spiritually Mature, While Remaining Emotionally Immature*. Nashville: Thomas Nelson, 2006.

Setton, Dolly. "Neutrinos: Ghosts of the Universe." http://discovermagazine.com/2014/sept/9-ghosts-of-the-universe.

Speare, Elizabeth George. *The Witch of Blackbird Pond*. New York: Houghton Mifflin Harcourt, 1958.

Swenson, Richard. *Margin: Restoring Emotional, Physical, Financial, and Time Reserves to Overloaded Lives*. Colorado Springs: NavPress, 2004.

Thomas, Gary. *Sacred Pathways*. Grand Rapids: Zondervan, 1996.

Trotter, Elizabeth. *Hats: Reflections on Life as a Wife, Mother, Homeschool Teacher, Missionary, and More*. Self-published, CreateSpace, 2018.

———. "Paul, the Mysogynist?" https://trotters41.com/2014/07/31/paul-the-mysogynist/.

Trotter, Jonathan. "On Making Love." https://trotters41.com/2017/11/25/on-making-love/.

————. "The One Question We Must Ask." https://www.alifeoverseas.com/the-one-question-we-must-ask/.

Vedantam, Shankar. "Guys, We Have a Problem: How American Masculinity Creates Lonely Men." https://www.npr.org/2018/03/19/594719471/guys-we-have-a-problem-how-american-masculinity-creates-lonely-men.

Wright, Joe, dir. *Pride & Prejudice*. 2005. New York City, NY: Focus Features, 2006. DVD.

Wright, N. T. *The Case for the Psalms*. New York: HarperOne, 2013.

Young, Amy. *Looming Transitions: Starting and Finishing Well in Cross-cultural Service*. Self-published, Amazon Digital Services, 2015.

Young, Amy. *Looming Transitions: Twenty-two Activities for Families in Transition*. Self-published, Amazon Digital Services, 2016.

Young, William. *The Shack*. Los Angeles: Windblown Media, 2008.

Made in the USA
San Bernardino,
CA